D1366740

AN OVERVIEW OF
ADULT EDUCATION RESEARCH

EDMUND deS. BRUNNER

DAVID S. WILDER

CORINNE KIRCHNER

JOHN S. NEWBERRY, JR.

ADULT EDUCATION ASSOCIATION of the U.S.A.
1225 — 19th Street, N.W., Washington, D.C. 20036

ACKNOWLEDGMENTS

The Adult Education Association and the authors are grateful to the Fund for Adult Education for the support of this project, to the professors of adult education for their unstinting cooperation in the discovery of sources, and to the project's advisors, Professors Wilbur C. Hallenbeck and Coolie Verner, who contributed much to whatever merit it has but are not responsible for any of its faults.

First Printing 1959
Second Printing 1965
Third Printing 1967

Library of Congress Catalog Card Number 59-13763.

CONTENTS

PREFACE

I
AN OVERVIEW OF ADULT EDUCATION RESEARCH   1

II
ADULT LEARNING 8

III
MOTIVATION TO LEARN 27

IV
ATTITUDES 48

V
ADULT INTERESTS AND EDUCATION 62

VI
PARTICIPANTS AND PARTICIPATION
IN ADULT EDUCATION 89

VII
ORGANIZATION AND ADMINISTRATION
OF ADULT EDUCATION 119

VIII
PROGRAMS AND PROGRAM PLANNING 125

IX
METHODS AND TECHNIQUES
IN ADULT EDUCATION 142

X
THE USE OF DISCUSSION 163

XI
LEADERS AND LEADERSHIP:
LAY AND PROFESSIONAL 177

XII
GROUP RESEARCH AND ADULT EDUCATION . . . 191

XIII
THE COMMUNITY AND ITS INSTITUTIONS
IN ADULT EDUCATION 211

XIV
PROBLEMS OF EVALUATION RESEARCH 243
INDEX 275

PREFACE

In July 1957 the Fund for Adult Education made a grant to the Bureau of Applied Social Research, Columbia University, to undertake an inventory of research in nonvocational adult education. The major objective of the project is to discover whether such research has produced any generalizations on which policy could be based, and which could be offered for the guidance of those preparing to be professional adult education workers on either a full- or part-time basis. A second objective is to suggest both specific problems and broad areas which need the attention of research workers in order to strengthen the conduct of nonvocational adult education. Implicit in the pursuit of these objectives is some degree of appraisal of what has been done and some search for the beginnings of theory attested by research.

The limitation of this project to nonvocational adult education eliminates from consideration a large sector of the field, and one in which an appreciable amount of research has been carried on. Most of that research, however, has understandably been relatively narrow in scope, dealing largely with the methods and techniques of teaching the skills and knowledge content of specific occupations. The motivations of persons enrolled in adult vocational education appear also to be different from the motivations of participants in nonvocational, or better, the liberal aspects of adult education. These and other differences rationalize a separation of the vocational from the liberal in this project, but inclusion of adult vocational education research was beyond the resources of this project. However, research dealing with, or applying to, both liberal and vocational adult education has been utilized.

Liberal adult education itself is a huge field. It encompasses most of the areas of knowledge. It is largely conducted on a voluntary basis with none of the compulsions of formalized education in school or college. It lacks the economic incentive of vocational education. Its participants have many motives but their consistent pursuit of learning, through whatever avenues and agencies of adult education they have chosen, is largely determined by personal values and satisfactions. Adult educators therefore face problems in gaining and holding their constituents unlike those of other educational workers. From this has sprung a basic tenet in adult education philosophy: that the participant must be offered what he wants.

From this situation also has come the need for research differing sharply in character from that which services the public school or other formalized educational enterprises. For nonvocational adult education, with few exceptions, has no entrance requirement save interest, no homogeneous groupings, no grades and no grading, no graduation, no diplomas or degrees. It is available from no single recognized and accredited agency like the school but rather from hundreds of agencies and institutions which differ widely in character, support, and objectives.

Outline of report. In approaching the objective of this project it would have been possible to explore the research done by the institutions representing the chief areas of adult education, or to seek out research done in the major subject matter fields, such as the arts or discussion of public affairs.

A different approach was, however, decided upon, since many problems in liberal adult education are common to most, if not all, of the institutions engaged in adult education, and comparably to many areas of interest. After a general introductory chapter, a major part of this report is devoted to matters pertaining to the educatee, such as learning, interests, participation and motivation. The next major section is devoted to matters pertaining to the educator. Here organization, program building, methods and techniques, and the role of groups in adult education are discussed. Finally, a brief section is given to concerns about education as such, chiefly in terms of evaluation. Suggestions with respect to needed research, instead of being brought together in one chapter, are, it is believed more logically, included in each chapter.

Procedures. The titles considered for this study of adult education research were gathered from many sources. Professors of adult education furnished lists of Doctor of Philosophy, Doctor of Education and Master's dissertations and theses, as did professors of extension education in those colleges of agriculture which offer graduate programs for rural adult educators. Several made available their own research bibliographies. Their assistance is gratefully acknowledged. The annual annotated reviews of research published in *Adult Education* were examined, as were the two reviews of research in adult education published in the June 1950 and June 1953 issues of *The Review of Educational Research.* The annual summaries of research in agricultural and home economics extension, published for over a decade by the United States Department of Agriculture were reviewed, since an increasing amount of this considerable volume of research is either devoted to the nonvocational aspects of that program or has general application. It is the belief of the authors that not many titles emanating from the field of adult education escaped them, unless they also escaped the editors of the source publications named.

Beyond that, studies in social psychology, psychology, sociology or anthropology dealing with or having clear implications for adult education were sought. Here, admittedly, the coverage was less complete, though use was made of bibliographies, especially such as were given in the studies examined.

No complete count was made of the total number of books, monographs, bulletins, articles and unpublished theses examined, but it is known that over 3,000 titles from adult education sources were considered. Between 4,000 and 5,000 titles all told were scrutinized for possible usefulness. Over 600 of these titles are cited in this report. With few exceptions, all of these titles were the products of American scholars. A comparable examination of untranslated European sources was beyond the resources of the project.

Criteria for selection. Obviously, not all of these titles were read. Those which were obviously vocational in character were eliminated, unless the table of contents showed some attention to general adult education problems. Next, all purely descriptive studies dealing with specific programs or communities were dropped because, interesting and valuable as many were and necessary as descriptive studies are in any new discipline, they could not contribute to the objective of finding valid generalizations applicable to the broad field of adult education. The place and contribution of such studies are discussed in Chapter I.

These eliminations reduced the total list by half or more. The remaining studies were examined, abstracted and their findings on each topic recorded and compared. Through this process generalizations or findings began to emerge which, though limited in scope, were sufficiently well-developed methodologically to suggest tenable and researchable hypotheses. This report is based upon the studies in this group.

It has not been the practice to describe and list every such study bearing on each point. This would have meant wearisome repetition.

Rather, as the findings and generalizations are recorded, the study or sometimes several studies that best illustrate and validate the point being made, are used. The authors' judgment as to the rigorousness and validity of the research methods used influenced this final selection. Inevitably a measure of subjective judgment entered into selection on this basis. It is not to be supposed that a different team of workers would emerge with an identical list or agree at every point with such critiques as are offered. It is, however, believed that there would be very substantial agreement with respect to the generalizations made on the basis of the data.

Gaps in the data. The reader will discover that a number of topics considered in the literature of adult education are not present in this report. The explanation of such omissions is very simple: either no studies meeting the canons of adequate research happened to be found in these areas or the findings of what research was discovered were too contradictory to permit of valid generalizations.

One gap of a different character must be noted. No bibliography accompanies this report. At this stage of the development of adult education, none should be presented without careful annotation. To prepare and annotate such a bibliography covering over 2000 titles would not only double the length of this report, but was beyond the resources of the project.

Responsibilities of authors. The first three authors named on the title page were in constant association in the offices of the Bureau of Applied Social Research throughout the study. They shared in the reading and abstracting of the studies selected for possible mentioning in the report. They conferred on the selection of the research studies used and on the manuscripts each prepared. Final drafts were written after this process of criticism as indicated in footnotes at the beginning of some of the chapters. Those carrying no footnotes were prepared by the senior author.

Dr. Newberry was unable to share in this process. He was chosen for this project because he was remarkably well qualified to prepare the two chapters for which he was responsible due to his participation in research underway at Florida State University where he worked with one of the advisors to this project, Professor Coolie Verner.

Edmund deS. Brunner

THE ADULT EDUCATION ASSOCIATION

The Adult Education Association of the U.S.A. is a nonprofit organization founded in May 1951, and its general purpose is "to further the concept of education as a process continuing throughout life." In addition to publishing studies and materials describing techniques and methods of adult education, it encourages research and investigation in all aspects of the field. The application of these findings to program planning and development is one of the Association's chief concerns. In AN OVERVIEW OF ADULT EDUCATION RESEARCH is found for the first time a careful analysis of much of the pertinent research relating to adult education. AEA's publication of this book represents a sincere attempt to provide a much needed service to its members as well as to related fields.

AN OVERVIEW OF ADULT EDUCATION RESEARCH

This report, as the Preface explains, is a survey of nonvocational adult education research. An adequate understanding of the report requires a general discussion of the status of that research and its development, especially since the mid-1920s, when the modern adult education movement may be said to have begun with the organization of the first national body to make adult education its sole concern. Many of the early research studies were paid for by money made available through this organization. The body of research herein examined also needs to be viewed in relation to the development of the movement itself. For the purposes of this report research is considered to be the use of scientific, standardized procedures in the search for knowledge.

Adult education is considered to include all educational activities in which adults engage that are part time or leisure time activities, usually of a noncredit nature. Thus enrollees in the graduate schools of our universities working for advanced degrees or others for whom education is a full time activity are excluded from consideration, but participants in extension courses conducted by these same universities on or off their campuses could be considered as in adult education. Some of the research examined in this report is concerned with both credit and noncredit students.

Organized adult education has existed in the United States for well over a century. Its roots in western culture extend over a far longer period,[1] in the United States to Benjàmin Franklin's Junto, which was founded in 1744 and led to the American Philosophical Society. From its very beginnings adult education was concerned both with liberal or nonvocational education and with vocational education, though initially it was largely the former. In sheer bulk of numbers involved, it is probable that in the last half century the vocational aspect commanded the greater amount of support. This was a reflection of the developments in American culture. However, many agencies have made and now make no differentiation between them, supplying offerings in both to their constituencies. Often the same class is participated in by some with a vocational motivation and by others with nonvocational interests. Moreover, some topics explored by researchers also have implications for the whole field. Research in adult learning, discussed in the next chapter, is an illustration of this.

HANDICAPS TO RESEARCH IN ADULT EDUCATION

Any examination of research in adult education reveals a rather chaotic situation. A few pertinent areas, such as adult learning, have been explored far more thoroughly than others. Some have received almost no research attention. Where any considerable body of effective research is available, other than in the field of methods, typically it has been conducted, not by adult educators, but by social scientists who had available a considerable body of theory, generalizations and methodologies developed by their disciplines, which could be applied to the problems of adult education. Thus the movement has benefited much from the work of psychologists, and to a considerable but lesser extent, from that of social psychologists and sociologists.

Pressure of large enrollments. The reasons for this are not far to seek. In the first place the participants in adult education have increased at a tremendous rate in the last third of a century. It is all but impossible to estimate the number of adults actually participating in educational activities. A quarter of a century ago Morse Cartwright, director of the American Association of Adult Education, attempted estimates for 1924 and 1934,[2] though he regarded such estimates as "hazardous." His survey indicated 14,881,500 participants in 1924 and 22,311,000 in 1934. Essert raises the figure to over 29,000,000 for 1950.[3]

[1]C. Hartley Grattan, *In Quest of Knowledge: A Historical Perspective on Adult Education,* New York: Association Press, 1955.
[2]Morse A. Cartwright, *Ten Years of Adult Education,* New York: The Macmillan Company, 1935.
[3]Paul Essert, *Creative Leadership of Adult Education,* New York: Prentice-Hall, 1951.

Knowles claims almost 50,000,00 by 1955, but, like the others, admits a wide margin of error.[4]

The categories used in making these estimates are in themselves informative. They include the Cooperative Agricultural and Home Economics Extension Services, public school programs, college and university extension, private correspondence schools, armed forces educational programs, library adult education, radio and television educational programs, and "all others." This last category covers many others, a number of which at one time or another were dignified by organized sections in the American Association of Adult Education. Included are alumni education, Americanization classes, forums and lyceums, parent education, education for prisoners, in-service training by corporations, workers' education, vocational rehabilitation, adult vocational guidance and education, classes given by art and other museums, adult religious education, courses in settlement houses and comparable institutions and so on. A compilation in 1946 listed more than 400 organizations which conducted adult education "representing the major areas of activity in which men are endeavoring to improve the society in which they live."[5]

It is obvious that in an area as diffuse as this no firm estimate of the number of individual participants is possible. Among other difficulties, there is no way of determining duplications. The records of some agencies are themselves simply estimates. The mere projection of past estimates, which some have attempted, is even more hazardous than the original estimates. On the other hand, there is no question but that the present number of participants in adult education in the United States runs into many millions and is growing. This is shown by dependable data in specific situations, a few examples of which will illustrate the trend.

In 1924 only nine high schools in a nationwide representative sample of 140 village-centered agricultural communities offered any adult education, and almost all of it was vocational. In 1936, 42 of these schools had adult education offerings, over one-fifth of them nonvocational. By mid-century, according to another study, better than three-fourths of the school districts with populations under 10,000 conducted courses for adults, many nonvocational. Urban proportions were higher.[6]

[4]Malcolm Knowles, "Adult Education in the United States," in *Adult Education*, vol. V, no. 2, Winter 1955.

[5]Charles R. Read and Samuel Marble, *Guide to Public Affairs Organizations*, Washington: Public Affairs Press, 1946.

[6]J. H. Kolb and Edmund deS. Brunner, *A Study of Rural Society*, Boston: Houghton-Mifflin, 1952, pp. 346-48.

Another sample illustration among many is taken from a report of the Adult Education Division of the Florida State Board of Education. For public schools alone in the decade from 1947-48 to 1956-57, the number of teachers in adult education rose from less than 100 to nearly 1,500, classes increased from around 100 to 2,200, and participants increased from about 1,500 to more than 60,000. These figures include only nonvocational programs.

Newness of profession. The implications of this situation for research are clear. Adult education is a new profession. Its practitioners are all but overwhelmed by the demands upon them resulting from the millions of clients. A vast majority of the actual teachers of adults are part-time workers giving only a few hours a week. Many are volunteers. Adult education is in its infancy as a discipline and with relatively few universities and graduate students in the field, the labor force available for needed research has been totally inadequate.

Moreover, many of those occupying or preparing to occupy positions of leadership in the field are not primarily research-minded. Under the pressure of large enrollments, if for no other reason, adult educators have become very practical-minded. They also tend, when engaging in graduate work, to be significantly older than the general run of graduate students. Typically they come from jobs and expect to return to them. If they embark on research at all most want it to apply to their own situation. Whereas it is hard to keep some doctoral candidates in sociology from trying to rival Booth's 17-volume social survey of the city of London, it is hard to drive an adult education major to see any part of the forest except his own pet tree if he goes in for research at all. It is more than likely that he will want the practitioner's degree—Doctor of Education.

Imbued as adult educators are with the philosophy of giving clients what they feel they need, it is perhaps difficult to require graduate students to consider the needs of the field as an educational discipline, when the pressure of local problems connected with their jobs is so great. As a result, too few practicing adult educators have acquired the competence to do sound research even of a type that would contribute to a more effective operation of their own programs.

Profusion of agencies involved. Another handicap to the development of adult education is the large number of agencies engaged in it. There is great diffusion of responsibility, for adult education has never developed, and probably in our type of culture never can develop, a single institutional pattern comparable to the pre-adult, university, or cooperative extension pattern of education. There is, therefore, a diffusion of professional effort. Many agencies conduct no research at all, and most of what is done is a peripheral activity of an administrative or service type, directed by persons whose primary obligation lies in the area of operations.

Furthermore, especially on the local level, most agencies have sought to cover as many broad areas of adult education as possible, rather than being content to specialize on a few. Years ago the New York City Adult Education Council analyzed almost 10,000 offerings distributed among eight broad subject matter categories by types of agencies responsible for the offerings and found little difference among them on a percentage basis. Thus one-third of the courses made available by business concerns were almost equally divided between human relations and the arts. Private agencies offered them the same proportion, and even exceeded by a couple of percentage points the vocational courses offered by business concerns.

More remarkable was the fact that the proportion of courses in philosophy and religion was practically identical for all organization groups.[7] Thus to a diffusion of adult education among many agencies is added a diffusion of subject matter among all agencies. This still further reduces the possibilities for definitive research by the agencies concerned. To make this situation concrete it may be useful simply to note the large amount of research with respect to elementary and high school education and administration and the miniscule quantity of adult education research in school systems, despite the fact that schools are one of the primary agencies of adult education.

Lack of funds. Another reason for the paucity of adult education research has been lack of financial support. Among all the agencies concerned, only the Agricultural and Home Economics Extension Service—the joint rural adult education enterprise of the United States Department of Agriculture and the state colleges of agriculture—has devoted appreciable amounts to research. This, of course, is tax money. The public schools, though also tax-supported, have not followed this policy, largely because with them adult education is a new and often a minor activity. Many school boards have been lukewarm in their support of adult education, and what funds were available have, understandably, gone into operating the educational program. This comment on the use of available funds has thus far applied with even greater force to the voluntary agencies of adult education.

Emphasis on descriptive studies. This is not to say that there has been no research in adult education. The need for it is recognized

[7]New York Adult Education Council, *A Picture of Adult Education in the New York Metropolitan Area as Shown by a Study of the Files at the New York Adult Education Council*, New York: The Council, 1934.

and some efforts have been made to meet it. The several thousand titles examined for the present study are evidence of a research interest. However, an examination of the works listed in adult education research bibliographies reveals an exceedingly liberal definition of what constitutes research. Works which seem to be merely statements of philosophy based on the author's personal experience and his inevitably limited knowledge of the experience of others, are freely included. So are descriptive or narrative accounts of specific projects, programs or agencies. While these may be suggestive to practitioners, and some even imply possible hypotheses for exploration, they hardly meet the accepted canons of social science or educational research. This the writers themselves sometimes admit.[8,9] Professor Abbott Kaplan, for instance, in writing the annual review of research for the Summer 1957 number of *Adult Education,* states that many of the titles he lists can qualify as research only by a very loose or general definition of that term. The nature of the objective of the present study made it essential to adopt more rigorous criteria of research.

A majority of the titles examined fall into two main categories:

1. Descriptive studies which record, sometimes with satisfactory detail and analysis, the experiences, successes and mistakes of a single program or of the total effort in a single community or area.

2. Studies of local situations used for building programs appropriate to the people and locality studied.

Though neither of these types of studies was considered in the present report, this is not to decry the value of such work. Description is the first step in the development of research in any discipline. It lays the foundation for later effective and definitive research by suggesting hypotheses and lines of inquiry. Only when these are followed up do useful generalizations emerge, and the search for such usable generalizations was the major objective of this study of existing research. As Carl C. Taylor wrote in reviewing a recent history of rural sociological research:

> Indeed it is more than possible that opportunities for these early studies would not have opened if the building of research method-

[8]American Educational Research Association, *Adult Education,* June 1950 and June 1953 issues of the *Review of Educational Research,* National Education Association, Washington.

[9]An illustration may be pertinent here in explanation of the statement. The senior author of this report was surprised to find two books of his listed a number of times in the publications noted in footnote 8. Neither of them was a research study. One, for instance, was a purposely simplified account of the organization, program and principles of operation of the Cooperative Agricultural and Home Economics Extension Service of the United States Department of Agriculture and the several state colleges of agriculture, prepared in part for the use of trainees and visitors from other countries interested in extension work among rural people.

ology or social theory, instead of interest in situations, had been insisted upon.

Description, as accurate and precise as possible, is truly the first step in analysis. The early descriptive studies, therefore, played a real part in the growth of rural sociology as a science.[10]

To illustrate this point, Jesse Reid's *It Happened in Taos* is an inspiring report of an adult education project in a county in New Mexico, which, among other things, was notable for the high degree of cooperation achieved by federal and state agencies in the service of the people. Some of the procedures could probably be applied to other counties in the Southwest, but to generalize even on so successful an experiment and apply comparable procedures to a county in "exurbia" would invite failure. The scientific use of such descriptive studies and service or action surveys awaits a patient ordering of the results into categories of comparable situations, since it is obvious that the successful enterprises were tailored to conditions existing in each locality. This is a service which in many disciplines has been performed by the early textbook writers.

The present report, therefore, offers a picture of research in liberal, nonvocational adult education at an early stage in the development of a new discipline within the total universe of education. It reflects even in the varying length of its chapters the wide differences in the amount and quality of research in the various divisions of the field and in the applicability to them of research and theory derived from the social science disciplines. It shows that a large part of the research interest of adult educators themselves has been devoted to patterns of organization and teaching techniques—as indeed is natural, since methods of instruction and their success or failure are at the point of primary contact between the participant in an adult education experience and the adult educator. In this respect, the pattern conforms to that of research in elementary and high school education. In common also with childhood education, adult education has profited much from the research in the learning process, to which this discussion now turns.

[10]*Adult Education*, vol. III, no. 3, Spring 1958, p. 188.

ADULT LEARNING

Perhaps no area of research pertinent to adult education has been more influential than the studies on the psychology of the adult, particularly those dealing with adult intelligence and capacity to learn. The pioneer and fundamental research in this area is E. L. Thorndike's famous *Adult Learning*,[1] a study too well-known to require extended summary. Suffice it to say, this elaborate and well-designed study completely disproved the folk proverb, "You can't teach an old dog new tricks," so far as human beings are concerned. It showed that adults can learn, but at a slowly declining rate of about one per cent a year from ages 45 to 70 years. In view of subsequent research, it is important to emphasize that the focus of Thorndike's study was on the *rate* of learning.[2]

Adults can learn. The Thorndike study was published at an opportune time. The American Association for Adult Education had just been formed as a result of the quickened interest in the role of adults in a democracy facing the unprecedented problems of the post-World War I situation. Thorndike's findings gave a tremendous impetus to this movement and its morale. They were a final answer to school

---

[1] E. L. Thorndike, *Adult Learning*, New York: Macmillan, 1928.

[2] Significant also in this connection is Ruger's study of Sir Francis Galton's data on some of the physiological changes accompanying age. Henry A. Ruger and Brenda Stoessiger, "On the Growth of Certain Characteristics in Man (Males)", *Annals of Eugenics*, vol. II, parts I and II, 1926.

boards and other agencies doubtful of the wisdom of appropriating funds for adult education. The social significance of the study was therefore second only to its importance as a foundation upon which to build adult education programs.

Among the practical implications of this work, Thorndike pointed out that adults learn less than they might partly because they underestimate their power to learn and partly because of self-limitations resulting from the narrowness of their interests and from the related attitudes and values which they hold. The first point is also made by Welford, who found that in some cases even before reaching age 40, adults lacked confidence in their ability to do things outside of the familiar or routine. It has also been noted that in test situations highly anxious individuals learned less rapidly than others.[3] Sorenson adds as a result of his studies[4] that the lower scores achieved on new learning by adults are often chargeable to the disuse of their powers to learn rather than the lack of them. Among other data the learning performance of students returning to college after a long absence from such academic activity points in this direction, until an adjustment to the requirements of the classroom situation is made.[5]

This would seem to indicate that in building an educational program for adults, developing adequate motivation is an aspect to consider, a problem dealt with in a later chapter. The same point is also made by a recent interpretive review of the scores of studies of teaching methods broadly defined, done over the last 30 years by the research unit of the Extension Service of the United States Department of Agriculture. The authors state unequivocally that motivation largely determines the rate of learning. Desire to learn must be aroused by teaching methods applicable to any given situation and the satisfactions that flow from learning and action based on

[3]A. T. Welford, *Skill and Age: An Experimental Approach*, London and New York, Oxford University Press, 1951, and G. Mandler and S. B. Sarason, "A Study of Anxiety and Learning," *Journal of Abnormal and Social Psychology*, 1943, 50, 370-96.

[4]Herbert Sorenson, *Adult Abilities*, St. Paul: University of Minnesota Press, 1938. Cf. also, his "Adult Ages as a Factor in Learning," *Journal of Educational Psychology*, 1930, 21, 251-55.

[5]One interesting study which, however, used scores on five comprehensive tests rather than a measurement of learning, arrived at somewhat different conclusion. The Armed Forces gave these tests to 6000 men. The highest scores were made by the 221 men who had been out of school 25 or more years. The lowest scores were made by those out of school only three years. The tests also showed that the scores increased with the amount of education of the subjects, but no complete tabulation was reported comparing men of equal educational experience by years out of school. The older men, however, had had less schooling. Harry C. Eckhoff, "General Educational Development Tests in Adult Education," *Adult Education Bulletin*, June 1949, pp. 144-49.

that learning.[6] Further confirmation of this point emerges from a study by F. L. Auch, who experimented with age groups ranging from 12-17 years to 60-82, using both meaningful and nonsense or false items. The oldest group did less than one-half as well on learning the nonsense or false items as the meaningful.[7] It is possible that this result might be due to the older people's finding that learning became more difficult as the items became increasingly divorced from experience or reality. It is likely that there was actual or subconscious resistance to learning nonfunctional and useless items. If this latter interpretation is correct, it suggests a warning that future research, especially that dealing with the aged, should eschew techniques that impress the subjects as meaningless.

Another contribution of Thorndike's study was to call attention to adult learning as a highly important but heretofore neglected area for psychological research. Others entered the field and from the 1930s on studies began to appear. They confirmed Thorndike's basic finding but also refined and extended it. These studies have been given a unified treatment by McGeoch.[8]

The power to learn. The intelligence test given to the armed forces personnel in World War I, the famous Army Alpha, the results of which began to be critically studied and analyzed in the 1920s, gave a rather pessimistic picture of the mental age of Americans. This test and most of the other standardized instruments require the completion of the tasks set within specified time periods. But achieving results within time limits is a measure of learning performances, in addition to whatever the results show about intelligence. "Intelligence is the power to learn." Performance is a function of many factors such as motivation, physical health, and possible physiological declines in reaction time, hearing and vision. A test with time limits thus confuses the power to learn with the efficiency of performance. The actual intelligence of adults is thus underestimated. Eliminating the speed factor significantly reduces the difference between adults and youth in intelligence test scores.[9]

One of the basic researches on this point has been conducted by

[6]M. C. Wilson and Gladys Gallup, *Extension Teaching Methods,* Washington: U.S. Department of Agriculture, Extension Circular 495, 1955.

[7]F. L. Auch, "The Differential Effects of Age upon Human Learning," *Journal of Genetic Psychology,* 11, 261, 1934.

[8]John A. McGeoch and A. Irion, *The Psychology of Human Learning,* New York: Longman's Green and Co., 1952.

[9]Walter R. and Catherine C. Miles, "Mental Changes with Normal Aging," chapter 5 in Edward J. Stieglitz, *Geriatric Medicine,* Philadelphia: W. B. Saunders Co., 1949, and G. Lawton, "Mental Decline and its Retardation," *Science Monthly,* vol. LVIII, 1944.

Lorge. He divided a large number of W.P.A. workers into three age groups, 20 to 25 years, 27½ to 37½, and 40 and over. To these he gave five intelligence tests, all timed, and the Institute of Educational Research Intelligence Scale CAVD. This last is a test of intellectual power with no time limitations. On the timed tests the scores declined as the age of the group advanced. The average scores of the two older groups were respectively 15 to 25 per cent below those of the youngest. On the CAVD the scores were almost identical, with less than one-tenth of one per cent difference between the low group, those 20 to 25 years old, and the other two which were equal.[10] These data are reproduced in Table 1. Lorge also devised a formula to make the scores on speed tests more comparable with those of power. When this formula was applied to intelligence tests involving the factor of speed, the differences between the young and old greatly lessened and some five-year age span groups above 40 ranked above those who were younger.

Table I

Power vs. Speed and Power

Group	Age Range	Ave. Age (Mos.)	Power CAVD	Army Alpha	Bregman Alpha	Wells Alpha	Otis SA	20'Thorndike HS
			Means					
I	20 to 25	274	405	150	149	158	44	67
II	27.5 to 37.5	384	406	142	149	147	39	60
III	Over 40	605	406	129	132	130	33	53
			Standard Deviations					
I	20 to 25	15	13	33	28	32	13	15
II	27.5 to 37.5	34	13	26	30	30	11	15
III	Over 40	90	13	32	31	31	12	17

Functional illiteracy can be overcome. Army experience in World War II with actual or functional illiterates also offers encouragement to adult educators. Houle, who analyzed the results of the Army's educational program with 225,000 men of this group concludes that almost all people without the basic tools of learning can achieve them if well taught and properly motivated. He points out that several weeks of full-time training sufficed to give almost all army students fifth grade competence.[11]

Indeed, 80 per cent completed the work in half or less of the time

[10]Irving Lorge, "The Influence of the Test Upon the Nature of Mental Decline and the Function of Age," *Journal of Educational Psychology,* vol. 27, February 1936. Cf. also his *Power vs. Speed and Power,* mimeographed.

[11]Cyril Houle and others, *Armed Services and Adult Education,* Washington, D.C.: American Council on Education, 1947, p. 235. Cf also Samuel Goldberg, *Army Training of Illiterates in World War II;* New York Teachers College Bureau of Publications, 1951.

allowed by the Army. A small sample of this large group were followed through their army experience to discharge. One-quarter
achieved the rank of corporal or sergeant and more than two-fifths
became privates first class. Only 13 per cent failed to justify the
educational investment made in them.[12]

Age is not the only factor in learning. These results were confirmed
in a different context in 1949 by Owens, who retested 127 males who
had taken the Army Alpha test in 1919 at Iowa State College as an
entrance requirement. Thirty years later this group had gained both
in total score and in seven of the eight subtests, especially those dealing with vocabulary, disarranged sentences, common sense, analogies
and general information. There was a nonsignificant loss in arithmetic.[13]

Welford's study, noted above, also indicated that older people put
more effort into learning tasks than younger subjects and were more
accurate, though slower. In arithmetic, however, this finding is con-
tradicted by an investigation sponsored by The National Institute of
Health, in which 413 subjects, 16 to 90 years of age, added single
columns of 2 to 25 digits. The elderly were slower and less accurate
and their accuracy decreased with the length of the problem.[14] The
authors suggest that the aged individual may have "slowed performance for compensatory purposes."

This type of test at best must be artificial since it takes no account
of interests or experience and other factors. When this is done there
are different results. For instance, professional persons progressively
increased vocabulary through ages 60 to 70 years, while persons for
whom language was not a major factor in daily living showed an
opposite trend.[15] Further, capacity for comprehension, reasoning and
judgment appears to be maintained at a relatively constant level as
long as mental work and intellectual interests are continued.[16]

Other studies indicate that the vocabulary level of adults remains

[12]Eli Ginzberg and Douglas Bray, *The Uneducated*, New York: Columbia University Press,
1953.

[13]William A. Owens, Jr., "Age and Mental Abilities," *Genetic Psychology Monographs,*
XLVIII, 1953.

[14]James E. Birren and others, "The Relation of Problem Length in Simple Addition to
Time Required. Probability of Success and Age," *Journal of Gerontology,* vol. 9, no. 2, April
1954.

[15]C. Fox, "Vocabulary Ability in Later Maturity," *Journal of Educational Psychology,* vol.
38, 1947.

[16]W. R. Miles and C. C. Miles, "Principal Mental Changes with Normal Aging," in E. G.
Stieglitz, *op. cit.* Cf. also Ross McFarland, "Psychological Aspects of Aging," *Bulletin,* New
York Academy of Medicine, January 1956, which concludes that functional age is more impor-
tant than chronological.

stable in the later years,[17] and that there may even be some increase with age.[18]

Lorge sums up the findings of research in this area effectively when he says,

> Whenever learning ability is measured in terms of power ability—
> i.e. learning without stringent time limits, the evidence is clear that
> the learning ability does not change significantly from age 20 to 60
> years.[19]

Bromley adds that when "general intelligence is held constant, there are no sex differences in learning power."[20]

A further conclusion seems warranted, namely, that though learning power of adults as defined by Lorge is relatively constant through the years, it will vary according to the amount of education, the experience and the social background and circumstances of the individual. Some of the evidence for this generalization is noted in other connections elsewhere in this report. Suffice it to say here that both educational status and social status influence the response of adults to educational programs.

The United States Department of Agriculture, for instance, found that although two-thirds of a sample of nearly 1,700 farmers in three Middle Western states received farmers' bulletins, only two-thirds of these put the information they contained into use, and the proportions both receiving and utilizing bulletins increased rapidly with education.[21]

The processes of learning. The literature of research on adult learning shows that as yet little attention has been given to the processes of learning despite frequent emphasis on the need for such research. Welford indicates that there are six stages in the learning process:[22]

1. Perception and comprehension of the material to be learned.

2. Some form of short term storage of the material for long enough to enable longer term retention processes to take place.

3. Retention by means of some more or less enduring biochemical or structural change.

[17]T. Weisenburg, *Adult Intelligence*, New York: Commonwealth Fund, 1936.

[18]Sol Garfield, "Age, Vocabulary and Mental Impairment," *Journal of Consulting Psychology*, October 1952.

[19]Irving Lorge in *Education for Later Maturity*, New York: Wm. Morrow and Co., 1955, Chapter 3.

[20]Dennis B. Bromley, "Some Experimental Tests of the Effect of Age on Creative Intellectual Output," *Journal of Gerontology*, vol. 11, no. 1, January 1956.

[21]M. C. Wilson, *The Distribution of Bulletins and Their Use by Farmers*, Washington: United States Department of Agriculture, Extension Circular 78, 1928.

[22]A. T. Welford, "Psychological Aspects of Learning," Chapter 4 in W. Hosen, (ed.) *Modern Trends in Gerontology*, London: Butterworth, 1956.

4. Recognition of a further situation demanding the re-use of the particular material learned rather than any other item of knowledge.

5. The recall of the material retained.

6. Its use, with adaptations if necessary, in the new situation.

Welford argues that measurement of the results of learning is possible only at stage six but that the breakdown of the process at any point in stages one to five would affect seriously the results of measurements applied at the final stage.

There are, of course, assumptions, both scientific and philosophical, implicit in this categorization of learning stages and it is important to recognize that the learning process is a complicated one. But stages there certainly are in the learning process susceptible of research attention.

Lewin takes a different approach, consonant with his interest in education as a tool for producing change, which many adult educators share. He says: "Within what we call learning we have to distinguish at least the following types of changes:

1. Learning as a change in cognitive structure (knowledge).

2. Learning as a change in motivation (i.e., learning to like and dislike.)

3. Learning as a change in group belongingness or ideaology. (This is an important aspect of growing into a culture.)

4. Learning in the meaning of voluntary control of the body musculature." (This is an important aspect of acquiring skills such as speech and self-control.) [23]

Learning and retention. Lewin's work, with its high interest in the practical outcomes of learning, involving first a change of opinion—for example, with respect to the suitability of certain foods—and then action, as in preparing and serving them, raises an interesting question as to the part played by adult education in changing opinions. Related to this is the further question of the retention of learned information and its effect on opinions.

Consideration of these related questions is not usually included in discussions of adult learning. Social psychologists and sociologists, who are largely responsible for research of this type, do not use the concept *learning.* They speak rather of the retention or recall of information or of opinions presented. Retention is, however, related to learning in that what is not retained in the memory is not truly learned. It seems appropriate, therefore, at this point to relate research on this point to that on adult learning before proceeding to

[23]Kurt Lewin, "Field Theory and Learning," in *41st Yearbook of the National Society for the Study of Education,* Chicago: University of Chicago Press, 1942.

discuss the social and physiological factors which influence learning, since these appear also to influence the retention and use of information designed to produce changes in opinion and behavior.

Learning and opinion change. On the basis of 35 studies over a period of 20 years, Beal and Bohlen arrive at a somewhat different formulation than those suggested above with respect to the process by which individuals adopt both new ideas and new practices.[24] The findings therefore have applicability to both vocational and nonvocational adult education, though they were based more largely on research with respect to the adoption of new agricultural practices. As these authors see it, the process involves five stages:

1. Awareness or learning about the idea or practice.
2. Interest, being concerned enough to seek further information.
3. Evaluation, weighing the merits of the idea or practice.
4. Trial, seeing how it works in practice.
5. Adoption.

It was also demonstrated that individuals differ greatly in the readiness with which they accept new ideas and practices. There are, especially in terms of practices, innovators who come to a decision quickly, make an idea their own and act upon it—perhaps two to three per cent of the population concerned. These persons are not necessarily leaders, though in some situations they are. More typically the leader becomes an early adopter after the experience of the innovator indicates that there will be no unfortunate results from so doing. These early adopters constitute around five per cent of a given population. They are the more alert members of the general population and are soon followed, but after a measurable time lag, by the great majority, who habitually look to these leaders as a source of ideas and information. Finally, there is a small residue who never shift their position or adopt the idea or practice.

It is possible to categorize these groups in terms of measurable or definable social, economic, or cultural attributes such as status, community activity, education, formal and informal contacts both within and outside of the community, age and economic status.[25] In one sense all four of these types might be subsumed under Welford's sixth

---

[24]George M. Beal and Joe M. Bohlen, *The Diffusion Process,* Ames: Iowa State College Special Report, no. 18, 1957. This research has been summarized by The Farm Foundation, Chicago, Ill., in the monograph, "Increasing Understanding of Public Problems and Policies," 1956.

[25]Interestingly enough, these results are very similar to those secured by the Bureau of Applied Social Research in a study of the diffusion process among doctors in the use of a new antibiotic drug. J. Coleman, E. Katz and H. Menzel, *Doctors and New Drugs: A Case Study in the Diffusion of an Innovation,* (tentative title), Glencoe, Ill.: The Free Press, forthcoming.

point, in that all are to some degree susceptible of testing by research.

The tests psychologists have devised to measure adult learning and intelligence have for the most part used items of high specificity. Little has been done with reference to learning as related to ideas and attitudes, and what is available in this field raises some disquieting implications and questions for adult educators. It is known that exposure to a single, brief communication can produce opinion effects that last several months, but a cluster of stimuli from a real and relevant event can effect changes in these opinions sharply different from those built up by the previous communication. The impact of events contradicting a prior communication can be cushioned if the latter has been in optimistic terms. However, even valid and reliable communications do not easily overcome skepticism as to their validity if that skepticism has resulted from past experiences. Such findings, if confirmed by later research, have important implications for public affairs adult education.[26]

The credibility of the communicator appears to have an influence on learning, or at least on the acceptance of the message. Hovland and Weiss[27] introduced the same content to different groups as coming from high, low and neutral credibility sources. Tests both directly after the presentation and four weeks later showed that there was no difference in the amount of information learned from the three different sources. The effect on opinions, however, was a different story. Directly after the communication opinions changed in the direction advocated by the presentations but the change was much greater among those who were told that the source to which they listened was one of high credibility. However, after four weeks there was a significant decrease in the extent of agreement with the high credibility source and an increase in agreement with the low.

In a later study Kehman and Hovland concluded that this so-called "sleeper effect" tends to occur when the subject is not reminded of the message source—recalling the connection tends to re-establish the initial effect.[28] A positive and credible communication initially tends

---

[26]S. H. Britt, "Retroactive Inhibition: A Review of the Literature," *Psychological Bulletin,* June 1935; Irving Janis, A. Lumsdaine and A. Gladstone, "Effects of Preparatory Communications on Reactions to a Subsequent News Event," *Public Opinion Quarterly,* Fall, 1951. This study used two groups of high school students. Cf. also *Agrisearch,* vol. 3, nos. 4 and 5, April and May, 1957, which summarize a number of studies in this area.

[27]Carl I. Hovland and Walter Weiss, "The Influence of Credibility on Communication Effectiveness," *Public Opinion Quarterly,* vol. XV.

[28]H. C. Kehman and C. Hovland, "Reinstatement of the Communicator in Delayed Measurement of Opinion," *Journal of Abnormal and Social Psychology,* July 1953; Cf. also, Walter Weiss, "The Sleeper Effect in Opinion Change," *Journal of Abnormal Psychology,* April 1953 and *Agrisearch,* op. cit.

to change opinions in the intended direction significantly more than one from negative sources, but both positive and negative presentations tend to be remembered better than neutral ones. However, both Stouffer[29] and Houle[30] show that among the Armed Forces personnel a negative communication must at least give the impression of fairness to be effective.

It is possible that such results as those just given are at least related to some of the unplumbed processes of learning as given by Welford and Lewin and noted earlier in this chapter. Socio-economic factors may similarly influence learning, as the following discussion suggests.

Effect of socio-economic conditions on learning. Past experiences, social psychologists have shown, often explain unreasonable prejudices. This raises the question as to whether social, socio-psychological and economic factors also influence learning, as, it is clear from Chapter VI, they certainly influence participation. The evidence indicates that they do. Wilkening, for instance, found not only that new ideas are accepted, i.e. learned, more readily if associated with existing values, but also that they could be spread most effectively through local leaders who, in the area he studied, tended to represent from five to fifteen farmers and were important, indeed necessary, communication links in the dissemination of both ideas and scientific information about agriculture and rural life. There was a high correlation between most indices of socio-economic status and the acceptance of innovations in farm technology. While this was less evident in the realm of attitudes and ideas, the correlations were positive. Wilkening indicates that the acceptance of innovations is largely a function of status factors. He also showed that some ideas failed of acceptance, i.e. were not functionally learned, because of feelings of economic deprivation and because they were associated with feelings of social isolation from those who attempted to disseminate them. It was also clear that the stronger the cohesiveness and hence influence of neighborhood and kinship groups, the slower was the acceptance of both new practices and new ideas. This last point has been confirmed by other studies.[31]

From one point of view the acceptance of an idea represents in

[29]Samuel Stouffer and others, *The American Soldier,* vol. III, Princeton: Princeton University Press, 1949.
[30]Houle, *op. cit.*
[31]Eugene A. Wilkening, *The Acceptance of Certain Agricultural Program and Practices in a Piedmont Community,* Ph.D. thesis, University of Chicago, 1949. Also summarized as *The Acceptance of Improved Agricultural Programs in a Piedmont Community,* Raleigh, North Carolina: Agricultural Experiment Station, 1949. Cf. also, James Duncan and Burton Kreitlow, "Selected Cultural Characteristics and the Acceptance of Educational Practices and Program," *Rural Sociology,* December 1954.

effect the formation of an attitude rather than an evidence of something learned. In the research to date the emphasis has been upon attitudes, which are discussed more fully under that heading in Chapter IV.

The purpose of the preceding discussion is to suggest the hypothesis that there is a relation between the acceptance of ideas considered as something that has been learned and the processes by which an attitude is formed or changed. Research workers in learning and in attitude formation have proceeded independently of each other. The authors venture to suggest that it might be fruitful for adult educators to relate them. For this reason, some of the data presented in the section above will also be considered in Chapter IV which discusses attitudes and attitude formation.

Sociologists working in this field, it will be noted, use the operational concept *acceptance* rather than the term learning. Acceptance appears to connote the application of learned behaviors and ideas. It is also interesting to note that the acceptance or learning of both vocational and nonvocational information were affected by the same factors, though not equally. One of these factors was schooling.

Schooling and learning. Psychology has made another contribution to adult education in its demonstration that intelligence, or better, what so-called intelligence tests measure, is not immutably fixed as once supposed. Rather the amount of schooling received is definitely related to intelligence test performance. Among others, Lorge demonstrated this in a 1941 follow-up of boys first tested in 1921 when in the 8th grade. In 1941 those boys who had received additional schooling performed better on the tests than their equally intelligent peers at age 14, who had never gone beyond grade eight.[32] The study by William Owens, Jr., noted earlier in this chapter indirectly offers confirmation of this point.[33]

A more recent study by one of the staff of the Conservation of Human Resources Project of Columbia University has produced a significant evidence on this point. In an effort to check the hypothesis that the reported declines in intellectual ability as age advances might be the result of limited educational experience, a group of about 600 persons were divided by age and educational levels as shown in the grouping on the following page.

When the "t" technique was applied to the differences in test scores between the two pairs of age groups at the same educational level,

[32]Irving Lorge, "Schooling Makes a Difference," *Teachers College Record*, May 1945. Cf. also, John W. Tilton, "A Measurement of Improvement in American Education Over a Twenty-Five Year Period," *School and Society*, January 8, 1949, and D. Tuddenham, "Soldier Intelligence in World Wars I and II," *American Psychologist*, March 1948.
[33]William Owens, Jr., *op. cit.*

Groups	Number
8 years schooling or less, 35-44 years of age	82
8 years schooling or less, 55 and over	228
9 years schooling or more, 35-44 years of age	188
9 years schooling or more, 55 and over	104

it developed that there was no reliable difference among those with eight years of schooling or less, "t" equalling .05. However, as between the two groups with nine or more years of school experience, the difference was significant and favored the older group; "t" equalled 2.35, significant at approximately the .02 level, which indicates that there was only about one chance in 50 of these results occurring by chance. When the scores of the entire 600 persons were treated as a whole a decline with age was noted, but with the better educated separately considered, this trend of the undifferentiated group is completely reversed.

It must be admitted that the grouping is very coarse. Unfortunately the median years of schooling are not given. Had the sample been large enough to permit a finer classification and thus a more accurate matching according to educational level, the superiority of the older subjects at the same educational level might be quite marked and might reach significance even with the lower level groups. Indeed, the author states that this would be the case.[34]

There is one point, however, at which the optimism engendered by such results may have to be tempered if confirmed by later studies, especially with respect to adult education in public affairs and current social issues. Older adults may be more dogmatic or more persistent in their attitudes than those who are younger. In one attitude study those 55 to 65 years of age indicated emphatic agreement or disagreement with statements far more frequently than those who were younger despite provision for several intermediate steps.[35] This confirms an earlier study by Lorge, who compared two groups equated for intelligence on the basis of the CAVD test for the power of learning. One of these groups contained only persons 20-25 years old, the other, those 40 to 70. The older group had more firmly fixed attitudes than the equally intelligent younger adults.[36]

The finding with respect to the influence of schooling on intelli-

[34]John B. Miner, *Adult Intelligence,* New York: Springer Publishing Co., 1957, pp. 88-90.

[35]C. Taylor, *Age Differences in Rigidity as Revealed in Attitude Scale Responses,* Unpublished Ph.D. dissertation, Syracuse University, Syracuse New York, 1955.

[36]Irving Lorge, "Thurstone Attitudes Scale: II, The Reliability and Consistency of Younger and Older Intellectual Peers," *Journal of Social Psychology,* May 1939.

gence test performance furnishes adult educators with an important tool for classifying enrollees and also for appraising the educational level of a community. The "highest grade reached" correlated significantly at about .70 with the Army General Classification Test in World War II.[37] While higher correlations were secured when the AGCT was correlated with several other tests of adult intelligence, the single item of highest grade of schooling reached is the simplest and from a practical point of view, the cheapest datum obtainable. As the correlation of .70 indicates, this measure is not absolute. About three-fourths of those scoring in the top grade on the Army tests were not college *graduates* and a minority had not completed grade school.[38]

Data on school experience available. On the community level the United States Census gives useful information by presenting for cities and for every county separately for urban, farm and rural nonfarm groups, the median numbers of years of schooling, and the number with no school—1 to 4 grades inclusive, usually considered functional illiterates, 5 to 8 grades, some high school, high school graduates, some college, and college graduates. Variations of three to five years in the median educational status among political units and age groups within a state are not unusual. Thus a rough indication of the level of intelligence of an area is available. This is important to adult education agencies with broad programs seeking to achieve a general coverage of the adult population. Especially should it be noted that the educational level of the American people is rising, which means that the research on reading ability of itself and in relation to adult intelligence, now almost 20 years old, may need correction.

Physical conditions affect learning. Research in the field of adult learning and intelligence offers encouragement to adult educators. However it is clear that as age advances, care must be taken to allow for physiological characteristics and changes. Visual and auditory acuity decrease steadily throughout life.[39] The National Health Survey, for instance, shows that clinically normal hearing is enjoyed by 85 per cent of the population 5 to 14 years of age, but by only 12

[37]U.S. Adjutant General's Office, Personnel Research Section, "The Army General Classification Test with Specific Reference to the Construction and Standardization of Forms Ia and Ib," *Journal of Educational Psychology*, Nov. 1947.

[38]Walter V. Bingham, "Inequalities in Adult Capacity from Military Data," *Science*, August 16, 1946.

[39]C. L. Crouch, "The Relation between Illumination and Vision," *Illuminating Engineering*, Nov. 1945. This report reviews the research material on the relationship between visual acuity and age.

per cent of those included in the survey who were 65 and over.[40]

Goldfarb studied the reaction time of 168 subjects of above average intelligence and educational experience from 18 to 65 years of age, almost two-thirds of them men, to discover its relationship to age and also in relation to various tests of intelligence and mental power. He found that the reaction time of men was quicker than that of women and that it increased with age, but also with increasing discrimination on the part of the subject. Variance in the scores increased with both increasing age and discrimination in comparison with mean reaction time. There was a decline with age in motor or mixed speed and power tests but speed of reaction in verbal and power tests did not change significantly with age.[41] Almost all studies of physical factors related to learning have used only measurements of physical power. The significance of this study lies in the fact that while reaction time slowed with increasing years, a psychological factor, discrimination, was also of influence.

Results of studies of hearing acuity are similar to those noted above. Hearing acuity also declines with age. It is worth pointing out, however, that even these results may have in part a nonphysical explanation. Years ago, G. T. Buswell, in comparing 1,000 adults with a sample of high school seniors and sixth graders, found that 74 per cent had a narrower span of recognition than the seniors and 52 per cent than the sixth graders. This is something susceptible of correction by training. Buswell also pointed out the possible skewness in adult reading scores that comes from confusing the ability to read in a familiar field with ability to read in an entirely new one.[42]

The implications of these facts for adult learning have long been known to adult educators and need no elaboration. Improved lighting can compensate measurably for slowly declining visual acuity. Distinctness of speech and the use of adequate volume or amplification by the speaker, together with a not too rapid tempo, can reduce the handicap of loss of hearing acuity except where actual deafness has set in. Judicious repetition can also contribute to this end and even more to comprehension of content on the part of those of average or less than average educational experience.

[40]U.S. Public Health Service, *National Institute of Health Bulletins,* Nos. 3, 5, 6, 7, Washington, 1938. An earlier study showed 77 per cent of those under 20 years of age to possess normal vision, 55 per cent of those 35 to 39, but only six per cent of those 60 or more. S. D. Collins and R. H. Britten, *Public Health Reports,* XXXIX, 1924, and U.S. Public Health reprint no. 979, Government Printing Office, Washington, 1925.

[41]W. Goldfarb, *An Investigation of Reaction Time in Older Adults and its Relationship to Certain Observed Mental Test Patterns,* New York: Teachers College, Columbia University, Bureau of Publications, Contributions to Education, no. 831, 1941.

[42]Guy T. Buswell, *How Adults Read,* Chicago: University of Chicago Press, 1937.

Learning brings results. The studies described thus far may in one sense be characterized as academic. It may be of interest therefore to note the practical results of a study chiefly in the area of methods, which, however, applies to adult learning. As a result of training conferences, out of 460 volunteer adult leaders of Home Economics Extension Service groups, 458 learned new hobbies or more about their hobbies in order to lead successfully the hobby interests of their groups, and 434 learned enough more about community service to render leadership service in what for them were new types of activity. Thus there was not only learning but, in addition, new adult interests were acquired.[43]

Anderson has recently made an extensive review of research findings with respect to adult learning applicable to later maturity. His approach is somewhat broader than that employed thus far in this chapter and some of his points will emerge more appropriately in other chapters of this report, but it is useful in this connection to summarize some of his main conclusions, since several of them introduce sociological factors which are perforce omitted in wholly psychological studies and which have important practical implications for adult education programs and institutions.

1. Principles of good pedagogy apply to adults as well as to school children.

2. Learning is more rapid and efficient when the learner is a participant rather than simply a spectator.

3. When a visible and tangible product appears as a result of a learner's activity, interest is greater and the learning will be longer continued. There is a high interest value in knowledge of the results of learning.

4. Group learning is better, i.e. more effective, than individual learning.

5. The greater the number of sensory channels used in the learning process, the greater is the actual amount of learning.

6. Learning must be used to be retained.[44]

In summary. There would, of course, be individual exceptions to these generalizations, doubtless affected by, among other things, both the intensity of the learner's motivation and the social situation. Nonetheless, in this area of adult education there is an encouraging

[43]L. Crile, A. Sundquist, and G. Maloch, *Relative Effectiveness of Three Combinations of Extension Methods in Wisconsin,* Washington: U.S. Department of Agriculture, Extension Service, 1947.

[44]John E. Anderson, "Teaching and Learning," Chapter 4 in *Education for Later Maturity,* New York: Morrow, 1956.

amount of assured knowledge. Adults can learn and, given their own time, can learn as effectively in later maturity as in earlier adulthood, unless physically handicapped. The processes of learning are now known to be more numerous and complicated than once imagined but already adaptations in techniques and to the environment can improve the outcome of adult education. While the amount of schooling makes a difference in later learning, the educationally disadvantaged can and do learn. Learning is most rapid when motivation is strong and goals are clear, and in all adult educational programs the social situation in both community and group terms influences both participation and outcomes.

Research still needed. Although research in adult learning has probably progressed further and produced more definitive results than in any other area of adult education, there are still unsolved problems to which research must be applied.

One gap in research in this area is perhaps in terms of the learning process. More could be done to procure answers to such questions as *how* adults learn, especially the middle-aged and elderly. Such research would probably have practical applications for teaching methods.[45]

Most measurements of human performance in relation to age have been of three main types:

1. Surveys using tests of performance or of mental abilities.

2. Performance under controlled laboratory conditions.

3. On the vocational side, studies of present practices and age distribution in relation to labor turnover.

None of these appears sufficient in itself. As measured, the extent of the decline in various capacities as age increases varied according to the test used and even by sub-tests with a total instrument.[46] Even validated tests have the limitation of concealing highly differential performances. Conventional tests sample a rather limited number of intellectual processes, for the most part those which are required for scholastic success. They contain, moreover, large elements of social or cultural bias. Nor is there any evidence that scores achieved on conventional problem-solving types of tests are significantly correlated with nontest problem-solving behavior in real-life situations. There is need for research which has as its objective the observation and calibration of problem-solving behavior in nonschool and nontest

[45]F. C. Bartlett, *Schemes of Research Initiated or Considered: Old People,* A Nuffield Foundation Report, London and New York: Oxford University Press, 1947.

[46]D. Wechsler, *Measurement and Appraisal of Adult Intelligence,* Baltimore: Williams and Wilkins, 4th edition, 1958.

situations. There are competent psychologists who maintain that because the variety of intellectual processes is far greater than previously thought, "the further use of conventional tests and test scores in practice and research is likely to be, at best, nonproductive."[47]

Again, laboratory tests are too artificial, laborious and costly to use in studying performance or power over time. There is great need for better measuring instruments and especially for longitudinal studies so that changes in the same group of individuals can be recorded and compared. Thus far studies have dealt with cross-sections of the population of different ages and varying backgrounds. There are even a few who aver that there is yet no unequivocal evidence on the influence of age[48]—a challenge which should be met.

Moreover, a considerable volume of the research in this field, especially that related to older adults, is focused on the institutionalized. The known physical losses as age advances, as Lorge points out, are organized around the concept of mental deterioration.[49]

Conventional tests not only are related to experiences, situations and problems unrealistic from the adult's point of view, as already pointed out, but they give little if any attention to the adult's ability to get along with others, or to the sociological factors to be mentioned later. Again, studies to date have not allowed for the force of habit, which could well retard adult test performance. Habits are a crystallization of experience. What force do they exert in the learning process and how do learning and maturation differ in the aging? Despite the many studies of the mass media, nothing is known of their relative appeal to or usefulness for adult educational purposes to various age groups.

Lorge, in the article mentioned above, also raises such pertinent questions as the following:

"Is the so-called rigidity or inflexibility of the aging process a crystallization or an integration? Is the person who has a diversity of experiences during maturity less crystallized and more flexible? Or is rigidity the attitudinal hardening of the arteries?" To which one might add: Is increasing inflexibility, if in truth a fact, less likely to occur if the number of group or interpersonal contacts of the older adult can be increased? Some of these queries are more

[47]Seymour Sarason and Thomas Gladwin, "Psychological and Cultural Problems in Mental Subnormality: A Review of Research," *Genetic Psychological Monographs*, vol. 57, 1958.

[48]Austin Edwards, "The Myth of Chronological Age," *Journal of Applied Psychology*, October 1950. Cf. also, A. T. Welford, "Extending Employment of Older People," *British Medical Journal*, November 28, 1953.

[49]Irving Lorge, "Research Needs," *Adult Education*, December 1950. This whole article is eminently worth study.

pertinent in terms of the relatively new interest in the growing number of older adults and their problems, but many of them span the total concerns of adult educators in their work with adults.

Little is known also about some of the sociological aspects of adult learning. As another chapter shows, the motivations of participants in adult education are often not only social in character, but rather different from what their instructors or leaders imagine them to be. Does the degree of learning differ according to the educational purity of the participant's motive? Does this vary in later maturity as compared with early middle age? Is learning better accomplished when existing cohesive groups are made the vehicle of instruction or when institutions seek to attract those of like mind and interest? In the latter case, would learning be facilitated by efforts not merely to carry on a class or program, but also consciously to weld the participants into a group? Is learning ability related to, or better, conditioned by the socio-economic status of the participant in adult education to the extent at least that persons of equal ability might be differentially affected by their statuses and life experiences? Would the effects of such differences, if found to exist, be reduced by variations in teaching techniques? These are but samples of unanswered questions.

It has long been known that the educational status of adults, which, as previously noted, is the best single index of what is measured as intelligence by conventional tests, is greatly affected by a considerable variety of social factors, even on a regional basis. For instance, the Armed Services rejection rate for functional illiteracy and mental deficiency was from two to six times as high in the Southeast and Southwest as in the other six regions.[50] It is possible that such differences and comparable differences in learning as measured by the usual tests may indicate not variations in intellectual power, but rather differences in the conceptions the people have with respect to the function of education, and in their conceptions of the relationships between schooling and later adjustment to the society in which they live.[51] Such factors greatly need exploration.

Research is also needed with respect to changes in motivations and values, with respect to learning and all leisure-time activities, which occur as adults grow older. Perhaps another way of putting this is to call for research as to the most effective ways by which people can

[50]Sarason and Gladwin, *op. cit.*

[51]Ginsburg and Bray, *op. cit.;* Edmund deS. Brunner, "The Educational Status of the American Adult," *Teachers College Record,* February 1943; "The Educational Status of the American Adult" as of 1950, *Teachers College Record,* May 1959. Sloan Wayland and Edmund deS. Brunner, *The Educational Status of the American People,* New York: Teachers College Bureau of Publications, 1958.

be stimulated through education to purposeful participation in the life around them outside their vocational obligations.

Needed too is a great deal of research which will evaluate the effectiveness of adult education in improving the adjustment of various types of programs designed to meet the needs of adults of all ages, all levels of learning ability, and all major types of community experience.

It must not be forgotten that the adult education movement has grown with such rapidity that it has not been compelled to ask many important questions of itself. The time is approaching, if it is not already here, that such questions should be asked. The answers have implications beyond adult learning as such. They involve interests and methods and also the type, quantity and even quality of participation. Most of all they concern motivation. The research shows that most adults have the ability to learn rather than a burning desire to do so. There must be adequate motivation to bring learning ability into play. The discussion now turns to that topic.

CHAPTER III

MOTIVATION TO LEARN*

Research in motivation has been conspicuously lacking in the field of adult education despite the fact that there are specific problems which adult educators face whose only solution may be based on empirical understanding of motivation. It is important therefore to understand why this area has had so little attention even in terms of applying the findings of psychologists.

One reason is clearly the fact that the rapid growth of adult education showed that thousands of people were motivated to participate in its programs and to such a degree that certain institutional and administrative pressures were created which seemed to demand more immediate study.

There has been also the cultural inhibition which still often regards as sacred the "why" of any human action and thus precludes scientific examination; especially is this true where the implication is that such investigation is to be used to influence future behavior. Perhaps this taboo has been strengthened in the field of adult education to the extent that not only the name, but also the bulk of "motivation research" has emanated from the world of advertising and marketing. Especially with the publication of books such as *The Hidden Persuaders*[1] people are likely to feel that they are being directly, and what is worse, economically, exploited by "motivation research." This

---

*This chapter was written by Corinne Kirchner.
[1] Vance Packard, *The Hidden Persuaders*, New York: David McKay, 1957.

cultural factor is consonant with the adult education philosophy that people should be offered what they want.[2]

There is, however, another, more serious inhibition to research in motivation, which may itself be an index of the significance such knowledge might have not only for adult educators but for social scientists in general: this is the theoretical complexity of the problem under investigation. MacIver[3] points out both the logical and methodological problems generic to the study of motivation: insofar as motivation is the casual determinant of human action, the "imputation of motives" is subject to the difficulty of objective study of subjective phenomena, as well as to the fact that "all causal imputation is inferential." But MacIver indicates that motives are expressed in behaviors and these may be studied situationally. This is a call for a sound empirical groundwork of *typical* social behavior under *well-defined* conditions.

Early psychologists such as MacDougall advanced theories which postulated lists of separate instincts in each individual which could account for almost all behavior, and therefore could explain none. Seemingly at the other extreme but basically doing the same thing, with the same limitation, were the early psychoanalysts such as Freud and Adler, who postulated *one* basic instinct, whose workings determined all forms of action and reaction.[4]

Recent writings emphasize a "middle of the road" theory which assumes that all behavior is motivated, but that there can be useful, limited classifications of motives according to the more obvious classes of satisfactions to which they are directed, e.g. visceral, sensory or cognitive.[5] These solutions are not merely a theoretical accession to the "least of three evils," but signify an empirically deprived em-

---

[2]There is an unrecognized conflict within adult education at this point between those who hold the permissive philosophy and those who see adult education as a means of upgrading the understanding of adults about public affairs or of producing social change. A knowledge of what motivates adults to enlarge their understanding through formal educational experiences is more important to those who hold the latter position than to the permissive school. Yet there are numerous instances of adult educators who, sometimes within the same speech or article, take both points of view. It is not likely that well-designed research with respect to motivation in adult education will emerge until this issue is clarified.

[3]R. M. MacIver, "The Imputation of Motives," *American Journal of Sociology*, vol. XVLI, July 1940.

[4]Lazarsfeld considers a basic drive theory, such as Adler's "drive for personal security" useful, especially because it can suggest hypotheses about the mechanisms by which everyday activities are linked to the basic drive (e.g. repression, inferiority complex, etc.); he points out that we need greater knowledge of such mechanisms. P. F. Lazarsfeld, "Progress and Fad in Motivation Research," from *Proceedings of Third Annual Seminar on Social Science for Industry—Motivation*, Stanford Research Institute, 1956.

[5]Gardner Murphy, "Social Motivation," *Handbook of Social Psychology*, G. Lindzey, (ed.), Cambridge, Mass.: Addison-Wesley, Inc., vol. II.

phasis on the intervening variable, between innate drives and social actions, of social and cultural influences. This approach is embodied in the work of social psychologists and seems to offer the most promising frame for empirical research, as well as for meaningful generalizations for adult education. The adult, after all, is best characterized in psychological terms by the ramification of his basic drives through socially learned possibilities, as well as by the restriction of such drives through social controls. Gardner Murphy relates this aspect of the social psychological framework to learning in the following terms, ". . . the adult has not *fewer* but *more* emotional associations with factual material [than do children] although we usually assume that he has less, because the devices of control are more elaborate and better covered in the adult." An example of a major motivational factor in this process, which is "almost universal in a given adult group is fear of not having the right, socially approved feelings, tastes and values."[6]

Motives defined. In the classic and basic statement of the frame of social psychology, Sherif defines the generic term, motives, as "goal-directed behavior."[7] He then divides this into the "unlearned, biogenic motives" which originate in the functioning of organic needs, and the "learned, sociogenic motives" which are acquired in the course of genetic development of the individual, and the goals of which are derived from interpersonal experience. The latter, or learned, motives are of primary concern herein.

Krech and Crutchfield point out the major inadequacies of the search for the basic or ultimate causes of behavior, as exemplified by the biocentric and psychoanalytic schools. They emphasize the need for a distinction between the "genetic" approach, just mentioned, and the more practicable "immediate dynamic approach" to motivational analysis. In other words, the immediate researchable problem for adult educators concerned with motivation is "how the needs and goals of a given individual at a given time in a given situation determine his behavior". This question is different from, though related to, the genetic problem of how the needs, goals and situation have come into being during the course of the individual's development.[8]

In any social situation, especially that of education, motivation and

---

[6]Gardner Murphy, "Individuality in the Learning Process," in *Notes and Essays,* no. 12, Chicago: Center for the Study of Liberal Education for Adults, 1955.

[7]Muzafer Sherif, *An Outline of Social Psychology,* New York: Harpers, 1948.

[8]D. Krech and R. Crutchfield, *Theory and Problems of Social Psychology,* New York: McGraw-Hill, 1948, pp. 33 ff.

learning are concomitant psychological phenomena—but for the purposes of research, these may be independently varied, and the adult educator may seek answers to the crucial questions: How may particular motivations be learned? and, What are the effects of differential motivations upon learning?

Laboratory psychology and motivation. The study of motivation has a substantial history in laboratory psychology. This work has been concerned generally with discovering the effects on learning of varying strengths of motivation in relation to certain objective incentives. In the majority of these studies, school children were given tasks, such as solving arithmetic problems or tracing. The measure of motivation was made on the basis of amount of work done within limited amounts of time. Thus Thurstone calls motivation a "rate concept"[9] and Maller[10] presents a formula for measuring motivation in a manner analogous to a physical force, i.e.

$$\text{Motivation} \atop \text{(Force)} = \frac{\text{Work}}{\text{Distance} \atop \text{(Time)}}$$

It is clear that this type of research is far removed from the actual life situations of voluntary adult education and from the type of "tasks" involved in much of this education, but precisely these conditions have enabled researchists to isolate some generalizations about specific incentives which affect the intensity of motivation. Most relevant here, perhaps, are the findings that telling the subjects they will be given the results of their work increases the amount and rate of work done, as well as its accuracy.[11] Evidence also shows that knowing the purpose of doing the work increases efficiency.[12] It has also been shown that, although output may be less where the work seems to have no aim, fatigue is greater. Similarly, knowledge of the impossibility of accomplishment of the task (solving the puzzle, etc.) decreases the amount of work done.[13] Studies have also shown that recall of unfinished tasks is greater than for those that have been finished—here the sustaining power of an unfulfilled motivation is evidenced.[14]

The time limit has also been studied as an incentive; in this case accuracy of work is used as a criterion of motivation. Myers tested children on the learning of word lists without time limits and then

[9]L. L. Thurstone, "Ability, Motivation and Speed," *Psychometrics*, vol. 2, 1937.
[10]J. B. Maller, *Cooperation and Competition: An Experimental Study in Motivation*, New York: Teachers College Bureau of Publications, 1929.
[11]G. F. Arps, C. C. Ross, W. F. Book, and L. Norvell, cited in Maller, *op. cit.*
[12]William Wright, in Maller, *op. cit.*
[13]*Ibid.*
[14]B. Zeigarnik, cited in Krech and Crutchfield, *op. cit.*

again with a time limit of the minimum time used in the first test. He found that greater accuracy occurred with the use of the time limit.[15] Prescott, having reviewed studies that show that either pleasant or unpleasant affect during learning facilitates learning, hypothesizes that the "knowledge of the time limit heightened affective tension to the point of mild emotion."[16] Of course, it has been found too that there is a "point of diminishing returns" in motivation, so that too great emotion or too intensive incentives may inhibit performance.[17]

Nedzel studied the time incentive for learning by adults in a relatively unstructured situation of museum education.[18] She found that the group allowed "individual saturation" time to view the exhibit did no better, in fact did exactly the same on the average, in a test of their learning, as did the group allowed only 40 seconds of viewing. However, a group allowed only 15 seconds showed no significant learning and complained that they were rushed.

The above findings, as they stand, seem to have strong implications for adult education program planning and policy. They stress particularly the importance of well-defined goals for particular programs; of clear statements about the difficulties and possibilities of achieving these goals, and if total achievement is remote, of planning the program in clear stages which can be successively attained; and lastly, of allowing each individual to have some knowledge of his achievement at appropriate points.

Unanswered questions. However, it is equally apparent that research is called for. Are the laboratory conclusions true with the less mechanical types of goals of nonvocational adult education? Are adults more willing than children to defer knowledge of their own results in view of larger implications of their work? Do the differences in educational backgrounds of adults affect their willingness to work with less clearly defined goals? Prescott points out that all learning is not alike, "therefore we may expect variations in the influence of affect upon different types of learning."[19] Certainly in the extensive scope of adult education such variation must be very significant and should be investigated. The "time limit" as an effective motivating factor for adult learning should be of particular research interest in

[15]G. C. Myers, "Learning Against Time," cited in Prescott, *Emotion and the Educative Process,* Washington: American Council on Education, 1939, p. 174.

[16]Prescott, *op. cit.*

[17]*Ibid.;* cf. also P. T. Young, *Motivation of Behavior,* New York: Wiley, 1936.

[18]L. Nedzel, *The Motivation and Education of the General Public Through Museum Experiences,* Ed. D. dissertation, University of Chicago, 1952.

[19]Prescott, *op. cit.*

view of the consensus of clinicians and others[20] that the adult psychological make-up can be characterized largely by an increasing awareness of time limitations in the broad sense as related to life experience.

Lorge's paradigm for the study of incentives for learning in adult education offers many items under the categories of what "people want to gain," "want to be," "want to do," and "want to save." If this formulation were found to be truly useful for research, it might serve to define the types of learning in specified areas of adult education according to their effective incentives.[21]

Motivation and level of aspiration. Research in social psychology has approached the problem of motivation largely by means of the concept of "level of aspiration." The major premise for this concept is that an individual raises or lowers his goals within certain frames of reference which are relevant to these goals. Perhaps the most interesting of these studies are those which consider the effect of social groups in determining an individual's level of aspiration.

The psychological rationale for the operation of social frames of reference is that goals are picked in terms of the preservation of one's self-image and are modified to the extent of his ego-involvement in any particular decision. Studies show[22] that level of aspiration does not begin to operate before some ego formation has been achieved, i.e. "until the child has formed some conception of his 'self,' has developed a sense of 'pride' which he feels must be maintained." Since adult ego formation is highly advanced and complex, the setting of levels of aspiration would seem to be clearly significant for adult choices of goals.

A study by Chapman and Volkmann sought to determine the effects of certain social determinants, or "anchoring points," on the level of aspiration of students in Extension and regular Experimental Psychology courses.[23] The students were divided into four groups, one a control group. The first experiment presented the subjects with a test of literary ability. Before taking the test, all of them were asked

[20]See pp. 53 ff.

[21]Irving Lorge, "Effective Methods in Adult Education," *Report of the Southern Regional Workshop for Agricultural Extension Specialists,* Raleigh, N.C.: North Carolina State College, June 1947. Examples of Lorge's lists of incentives are: People want to gain: health, time, money, popularity, etc. They want to be: good parents, sociable, hospitable, up-to-date, etc. They want to do: express their personalities, satisfy their curiosity, appreciate beauty, etc. They want to save: time, money, work, worry, etc.

[22]Sherif, *op. cit.,* p. 260.

[23]D. W. Chapman and J. Volkmann, "A Social Determinant of the Level of Aspiration," in *Readings in Social Psychology,* T. M. Newcomb and E. L. Hartley, (eds.), New York: Henry Holt and Co., 1947.

to estimate the score they would make—the control was told nothing more, but one experimental group was told that W.P.A. workers had averaged 37.2 on the test; another was told that literary critics had averaged 37.2; and the last, that psychology students averaged 37.2. The results showed that the mean level of aspiration was lowered in relation to the score of a superior group, raised with reference to the inferior group, and approached the stated average of the psychology student group. However, with no experience on the test, none of the students indicated levels of aspiration as high as the average scores suggested by the experimenter.

In the second experiment, the students first took a test, were then grouped according to their scores, and were told these scores. The three groups were then again given the "average scores" of, respectively, a superior, inferior, and similar group. In this case, levels of aspiration did *not* vary with the reference group but were based on the subject's knowledge of his own previous performance. The authors suggest that "the subject's own labor takes on ego-value, even if not comparatively good." Furthermore, one's previous scores form a more objective basis for judgment of future work.

The authors point out that in a given life situation, several anchoring points operate at once and more research would be necessary to determine how the effects of anchoring points combine, and what these combined effects are, on levels of aspiration.

Here again the findings suggest that further research would be desirable in specific adult education situations. Does the concept of level of aspiration explain the disturbing fact that in our society, where education is generally highly valued, those who "need" education most often participate the least? To what extent do those who have not had experience with adult education, and tend to associate it with people "superior" to them, set their levels of aspiration low so as to avoid participation? On the other hand, to what extent may adults with more formal education perhaps associate informal adult programs with those "inferior" to them, and thus decline to participate? The concept of levels of aspiration is particularly relevant for an understanding of differential motivation within noncredit adult courses where prerequisite levels of knowledge are generally not specified and there results a great and apparent diversity of educational experience among the students.

The above experiments also give two more clues for further study in adult education situations:

1. When the students had an objective measure of their own performance, the group comparisons did not significantly affect their

choice of goals. In other words, a self-evaluation device was more effective than comparison with other groups or other students. If measurement is to be used in adult education, self-evaluation is more consonant with the philosophy of adult educators than the other devices used in this experiment.

2. All groups, no matter what their reference group for the task in question, set their aspiration levels relatively low when they themselves had had no experience with the task.

Some objective indicators of adult education motivation. Greenwood's study of participants in adult education classes in Philadelphia evening high schools attempted to make inferences about motivation by means of statistical correlations between certain social characteristics and persistence rates—persistence rates being determined by the ratio of continuous attendance to total class periods.[24] The data were based on questionnaires given to a large and carefully selected sample of 3813 students in four high schools.

Among the findings, it was discovered that Negroes generally had a higher persistence than whites, which was interpreted to show that the former group was more selective in terms of determination or intense motivation than the whites.

An interesting finding concerned the time necessary to get to school and the mode of transportation used: Those who used public conveyance and took a long time to get to school (group 1) had an equally high rate of persistence as those who lived close by (group 2) —the middle time group and those using cars (group 3) had the lowest rate. The first two groups are explained, respectively, by their determination, and by the convenience. Thus extreme distance may be a good indicator of motivation, but questions arise about the motivation of the group living close to the school. More generally, this breakdown suggests that in other studies where persistence *per se* is taken as an indicator for motivation, there should be further analysis in terms of factors such as convenience, which may play a significant part in the results.

With this qualification in mind, some further correlations may be presented. It was found that those who had completed a year of eve-

---

[24]This type of traditional statistical procedure is at best an indirect means of assessing motivation. The correlation of social characteristics with persistence or participation rates can reveal certain patterns which may lend themselves to psychological interpretations or inferences, and/or they can give clues for further research which would, as Lazarsfeld puts it in his discussion of these methods of motivational analysis, "delve more directly into the factors which make people act as they do." Lazarsfeld, *op. cit.*

Walter Greenwood, *A Study of Persistence of Public Evening High School Students,* Ph.D. dissertation, University of Pennsylvania, 1932.

ning school had a higher persistence rate than those who had registered but had dropped out before completing the course at some previous time, or had had *no* previous experience. In a large number of cases the students' employers had encouraged their attendance, but these students had a lower persistence rate than those not thus encouraged. The author speculates that the former were not "wholeheartedly eager" to attend, but were merely influenced by their employers. It was found, further, that stated reasons for attending evening school had significance only in connection with the particular course of study involved. That is, a reason that is effective for high persistence in one course, may in another course, lead to a relatively higher rate of dropouts. Greenwood's finding is based primarily on the differences in reasons for attending vocational and nonvocational courses, and he does not pursue this point, but further research into the differential effectiveness of stated motives for particular courses within nonvocational education should be of great significance for program planning in adult education. This finding also suggests that certain studies that measure the relative significance of different stated motives for whole programs may lose some validity by not distinguishing among specific courses within these programs.

Greenwood also asked his subjects how they had chosen their particular courses. He found that if the influence for choice came from within the school rather than from any other source, the persistence rate was higher. However, he says this may show that the more motivated students sought advice, rather than clearly attest to the effects of good counseling.

No correlation was found between scores on I.Q. tests and persistence or between the teachers' evaluations of the students' ability to do the work and persistence. Although this finding shows that, situationally, motivation and ability can be distinguished and may not be correlated, there still remain some theoretical issues in making the distinction between motivation and ability for all research purposes. Thurstone,[25] using the rate concept of motivation, shows by means of a "psychometric surface" that motivation and ability can be experimentally isolated so that differences in ability can be measured. He assumes that since motivation is measured by the amount of work done in a limited time, then, if there is at least some positive motivation to do the task and time is unlimited, differences in performance will be purely functions of ability. He argues cogently that one may work faster with greater motivation, but greater motivation cannot

[25]Thurstone. *op. cit.*

create ability. But in the larger social situation within which adult education programs exist, motivation may be measured as a subjective phenomenon and then related to ability—in this sense, greater motivation may very well "create" ability. That is, to the extent that ability is rewarded by social prestige, parental or employer approval and the like, the motivation for such reward will lead one to develop certain abilities; where the appropriate incentives do not exist, the absence of motivation may result in the neglect of a potential ability. Some studies discussed in the chapter on learning inferentially bear on this point.

The findings of the Greenwood study have been presented in some detail because of their inherent interest and the methodological care with which the study was conducted. However, it can be seen that the measure of persistence alone has limitations for describing the relative degrees of motivations of the students, especially among the large body of those who meet the minimum criterion of persistence.

An attempt to construct an objective measure of motivation which would distinguish among adult students, all of whom have the same attendance rates, has been made by L. Briggs.[26] He devised a motivational rating scale based on a checklist of student behavior to be filled out by instructors. The subjects for the original construction of the scale were trainees in an Air Force educational program, but the items, such as "Is late to class often," "Asks many questions," etc., may have wide applicability in adult education programs.

Personality and social needs in motivation. The distinction between personality and social needs as bases for motivation is one whose relation either to the theoretical frame of learned and unlearned motives, or to the research distinction between motivation and interests, is not entirely clear. The confusion lies primarily in the definition of "personality." However, the "personality-social needs" distinction does have some acceptance, mainly in the field of counseling. It is generally accepted that personality is "learned" to some extent through social influences, but personality needs are usually considered "basic" for motivation, and social interests are thought to be largely functions of personality needs. MacIver[27] in this connection calls for more psychological study of the relation of motives to types of personality— how are developing interest-complexes or typical motivations dependent on the interplay between personality and environment?

[26]Leslie Briggs, "Development and Appraisal of a Measure of Student Motivation," *Research Bulletin,* San Antonio, Texas: Air Force Personnel and Training Research Center, August 1954.
[27]MacIver, *op. cit.*

When the emphasis of research in adult education shifts from the "personality" needs of any one individual to his "social" needs, it is possible to separate, at least in terms of intensity, one's motivation from his needs. In a study of about 250 men and women, 40-70 years old, interviews elicited each person's activities, his feelings about these activities, and changes in such feelings from ten years before.[28] The aim was to codify the major social roles of the different age groups. Ten such roles were identified (parent, spouse, community member, etc.), and each person was rated for his performance in each role, according to criteria derived from the consensus of opinions of "social philosophers." This is valid if such opinions reflect the dominant cultural values. Ratings of high, medium or low were also made of the motivations of each individual on the basis of energy expenditure and quality of efforts in each social role.

By considering each social role as a "developmental task," this study was able to isolate "teachable moments" when a particular role must be filled within a limited time or presents itself suddenly and with urgency, such as becoming a parent, entering retirement, etc. These are considered crucial areas through which adult education programs can be most meaningfully related to individual motivations. From the point of view of the individual, the study suggested that one is best suited for education in an area of social responsibility when, according to the rating scores, his motivation, i.e. energy expenditure in a social role, is high or average, and his participation in that role is average.

Goal definition important. Kuhlen and Johnson attempted to determine the change of dominant motivations with age by means of a question eliciting subjective statements of goals.[29] The sample consisted of 467 single women, 280 married women and 218 married men, age 20-65, all of whom were teachers. The replies to the question, "What would you most like to be doing ten years from now?" were grouped into categories of: same job, remain in education but different job or promotion, different field of work, retired with no plans, retired with plans, get married and have family, be a housewife, and "no answer." Analysis of the replies by five-year age intervals showed significant changes in goal orientations. The generality of these find-

[28]R. Havighurst and B. Orr, *Adult Education and Adult Needs*, Chicago: Center for the Study of Liberal Education for Adults, 1956. Cf. also, Havighurst, "Social Roles of the Middle-Aged Person—A Method of Identifying the Needs of Adults," in *Notes and Essays*, No. 4, Chicago: the Center, 1953.
[29]R. G. Kuhlen and G. H. Johnson, "Changes in Goals with Adult Increasing Age." *Journal of Consulting Psychology*, vol. 16, 1952.

ings would, of course, have to be established and their direct implications for particular adult education programs investigated, but they do indicate broad age differences in motivations within which any educational program may be meaningful for the individual. It was found that the goal of marriage for single women in the 20s declines by the 30s and the desire for vocational adjustment becomes dominant. Married women who are working show a greater desire to be housewives in the 20s and their vocational goals are secondary compared to those of single women. Married men are clearly vocationally oriented and through their late 40s put an emphasis on vocational advancement; they showed some evidence of vocational restlessness by desiring a different job or a different field in their late 30s and 40s. Plans or thoughts of retirement began for all groups in the 40s.

These findings are consonant with the analysis made by a psychiatrist of case studies of individuals 25-35 years of age.[30] Dr. Billings finds that this period of "mid-life is a transition period in which bodily changes and social role changes necessitate a re-ordering of personality organization. . . . The major focus of reorganization" seems to be the new perception of time as no longer unlimited; there is greater awareness of past, present and future, and actions of the present are more clearly defined as means to a future end.[31] As a result, goals must be modified and made more specific. The implication for adult education seems clear—for personal adjustment, as well as for learning, it is important that goals be well-defined and clearly related to action.

Social situation influences motivation. To the extent that the above findings concern basic and pervasive motivations it follows that all the daily behavior of adults will proceed within the appropriate motivational context. The significant question to ask, therefore, is what factors in motivation or in the social situation of the individual will lead him to satisfy his needs or seek his goals via an educational setting. This was the question underlying the study by Robert Love whose purpose was "to determine the underlying attitudes toward education which might motivate persons to overcome obstacles to obtain adult education at college level."[32]

Love used "motivation research," in this case depth interviews, to analyze the psychological process through which an individual must

[30]E. G. Billings, "The Clinical Importance of some Normal Attitudinal and Ideological Transitions of Mid-Life," *American Journal of Psychiatry*, vol. 105.

[31]For further discussion by psychologists of adult self-image with reference to adult needs in education, cf. Murphy and Kuhlen, *Notes and Essays*, no. 12, *op. cit.*

[32]Robert Love, "The Use of Motivation Research to Determine Interest in Adult College-Level Training," *Educational Record*, 34, July 1953.

go before he decides to enroll in evening or extension courses. The motivations of noncredit students at the College of the City of New York and nonstudents matched by sex, age, major subject interests, etc., were compared. The basic finding to explain the channeling of general motivations into educational activities was that there had to be, before the actual "sequence of enrollment" could begin, two "preconditions": an awareness of education as a positive value for solving problems in a general sense, and an equation of education with happiness and success.[33]

But these in themselves were not sufficient for enrollment; nor was a general feeling of inadequacy even in educational areas sufficient. The individual had to have, first, a current and to himself well-defined problem arising out of a specific situation. Secondly, he also had to be aware of some specific matching course, a perception which would be likely to occur in terms of his motivational set. It was not enough that he rely on a general interest to motivate him to seek the school's advice about a field of study. The third step was the focusing of the individual's attention on certain institutions according to their prestige and general clientele. The final step is enrollment. This first school contact is a decisive one, since the student starts with a sense of inadequacy and if he feels rejected, he may give up for a long time. "If he doesn't feel rejected, he will overcome many barriers such as cost, distance, or travel, which may be great but do not have a deep-seated emotional basis."

This type of study offers many possibilities for further research, both in its method of investigation, which should be applied with regard to programs less formal than those of universities, and in its substantive implications. For example to what extent is the motivating "well-defined" problem necessarily *realistically* defined,[34] so that adult edu-

---

[33]Nedzel hypothesizes that the basic attitude which accounts for the "enduring dichotomy" between the educationally motivated and those not, is that for the former new intellectual and aesthetic development is a pleasure. "The educationally motivated persons are those whom some [social] influence caused identification of excitement and adventure with education, while for the unmotivated education is a bore." Nedzel, *op. cit.*

[34]B. James illustrates the problem of poorly-defined educational needs through his experience with a group of ten people who requested a University Extension course in "Creative Writing." All the members had either taken correspondence courses in composition or were associated with the Rural Writer's Organization. As the course progressed it became clear that the group felt that they "knew how to write"; they really sought to learn gimmicks and slick styles in order to *sell* their writing. Such, of course, was not the University's educational goal, and the group failed. James' use of this case was to point up the fact that individual needs alone should not define educational goals—the existence of a need cannot itself determine *how* it should best be filled—it is the educator's role to "focus group goals." B. James, "Can 'Needs' Define Educational Goals?" *Adult Education*, vol. VII, no. 1, 1957. Cf. also, James and Montross, "Focusing Group Goals," *Adult Education*, vol. VI, 1956.

cation can truly provide satisfaction for the underlying need? Is it possible that a person will formulate a problem to himself in such terms that it leads him to courses not suited to his real need, so that he finds only disappointment which he blames on that program or on education in general? If so, is it not a requirement of education that it help a person not only to solve his existing problems but to clarify them and turn them to realistic channels? Of course, this is also a major function of counseling.

It might also be well to investigate Love's use of the phrase "well-defined problem in a specific situation." To what extent does this mean that only a short-range problem can be effectively motivating; to what extent is it also possible for long-range and generally significant problems to be clearly defined for an individual? Love himself indicates that many men first enrolled at City College for a business course related to a specific vocational problem but later expanded or switched to liberal arts study. Ostensibly, it is the purpose of adult education to bring about this broader view of what is relevant to the individual.

Such a definition of education is at the basis of Wilbur Schramm's suggested classification of motives. Schramm is referring specifically to reading motivations, but his formulation is easily transferred to educational processes in general—he suggests,

> a typology that would extend along a continuum corresponding to the socialization process from 'immediate reward' to 'delayed reward.' [This typology] is grounded in psychological learning theory based on analysis of the process of socialization as a combination of problem-solving and associative (or conditioning) learning in which motivations may be determined in terms of the stages of socialization.[35]

Although Schramm presents examples of reading motives which would fall along this continuum, research in adult education programs should be conducted to provide a solid base on which to construct a sound and useful typology.[36]

The subjective aspects of motivation. The studies discussed at the outset of this chapter were based on objective indicators of motivation; in general, they compared variations of direction and intensity

[35]Wilbur Schramm, "Why Adults Read," *Adult Reading,* 55th Yearbook, Part II, National Society for the Study of Education, 1956.

[36]Examples of reading motivations, progressing from "Immediate" to "delayed reward" are: Compulsive ritualistic reading, regardless of content; Reading for respite; For sense of personal security; For social security; For vicarious experience; . . . As a tool of self-improvement; As a device for scanning the horizon of society; For interpretation. Schramm, *op. cit.*

of motivation in relation to certain incentives. This research derives primarily from the definition of motivation as "goal-directed behavior." Waples *et al.*, however, define motives as "expected satisfactions."[37] It is clear that the difference in definitions is essentially only one of emphasis, but this very shift provides a suitable frame for the concerns and methods of the study of the *subjective* aspects of motivation, some of which have been illustrated in the preceding section.

The prime methodological issue here concerns the validity or value of peoples' statements of motive, both in direct answer to questionnaire or interview and in normal daily action. Substantively, the prime concern is with the meaning for himself of each individual's acts of goal-directed behavior—how does he evaluate his own behavior; how does he assign primary or secondary importance to his own actions and to his own reasons or motives for these actions; how does he compare his own motivations with those of other people? Theoretical issues lie at the basis of all these questions, and even of raising them; certainly the questions indicate that careful theoretical appraisal is necessary during the whole process of studying the subjective aspects of motivation, and especially before adult education can build upon the results of such study.

MacIver points out that one count against the study of motivation is that a person "may not know his own motives—he may announce them because their credence helps him to gain his objectives."[38] But he calls this a "positive" objection because it assumes some way of getting at *real* motives. The rather well-known techniques of psychoanalysis represent one such way. Studies of buying motivations and even of reading motivation have used adaptations of psychoanalytic techniques to analyze decisions to obtain particular products and reading materials.[39] The value placed on these techniques is not necessarily based on the assumption that people will lie or deliberately or unconsciously conceal their true motivations, but rather on the assumption that the average individual is not able to formulate verbally the effective factors for his particular action in the complex "instant of decision."[40]

But it would seem that educational motivation is at least *quantita-*

---

[37]D. Waples, B. Berelson, and F. R. Bradshaw, *What Reading Does to People,* Chicago: The University of Chicago Press, 1942. C. Wright Mills indicates that "motives stand for anticipated situational consequences of questioned conduct—intention *is* awareness of anticipated consequences." Mills, "Situated Actions and Vocabularies of Motive," *American Sociological Review,* 5, December 1940.

[38]MacIver, *op. cit.*

[39]Cf. for example, Lazarsfeld, *op. cit.,* and Waples, *et al., op. cit.*

[40]See Chapter V for a discussion of the concept "instant of decision."

tively different from a buying decision or a choice of reading material, if only in terms of the time period commitment involved in the respective actions.[41] That is, to enter upon an educational venture always, although in varying degrees, requires one's commitment to extended, formalized and often regulated expenditures of time and effort. Therefore, it would seem that the educational decision would be described better as a relatively extended process rather than an instant, and that this process is in essence the individual's formulation for himself, in fairly specific and explicit terms of his expected satisfactions from education.

The above statements must be taken primarily as a hypothesis about the nature of adult educational motivation which requires further testing, although the Love experiment offers some support for it. It has been presented here partly to serve as a temporary rationale for the research in adult education which bases program evaluations and even policy suggestions on students' statements of motives. It must be recognized, however, as Mills points out,[42] that such stated motives are not to be used as an index to personality factors, but for greater understanding of social actions in defined situations.

Motives as seen by participants in adult education. In this light, some of the findings of surveys of stated motives in adult education may be presented. The following are essentially descriptive results and may provide a basis for questions for experimental study of aspects of education as related to the various motives.

Beals surveyed motivations for college alumni education.[43] The students were, in general, out of college 10 to 25 years, and the median age was 41.6 years. The questionnaire answers revealed that more than one motive was operative for each person. The relative frequencies of motives were: 52 per cent, intellectual curiosity, subject interest and desire for mental stimulation; 19 per cent, college sentiment, renew friendships or support college; 16 per cent, relaxation, to get away from business cares, etc.; and 13 per cent, miscellaneous.

[41]Nedzel, *op. cit.*, says "educational activities are distinguished from others by active intellectual participation." This view represents one of the schools of thought mentioned by Birnbaum in his discussion of the "role of cognition vs. the role of emotion and the irrational" in adult education. One of the aims of research into motivation should be to clarify this opposition and some of the issues arising from it concerning teaching methods and the effects of education on values and attitudes, as well as to reveal the distinctive nature of educational motivation, insofar as it is truly distinctive.

Cf. M. Birnbaum, "Mind and Emotion in Adult Education," *Adult Education*, vol. VII, no. 3, Spring 1957.

[42]Mills, *op. cit.*

[43]R. A. Beals, *Aspects of Post-Collegiate Education*, New York: American Association for Adult Education, 1935.

In a different educational context, that of listening groups for the Canadian Farm Radio Forum, an extensive survey revealed the following motivations for joining: 70 per cent, neighborliness, community spirit; 56 per cent, educational advantages; 14 per cent, better understanding of farm problems; 22 per cent, help to strengthen unity of farmers; 11 per cent, to present farmers' point of view to government; and 10 per cent, enjoy discussion,[44] an average of nearly two stated motives per participant.

Flood and Crossland asked adult students in Science and Psychology extension courses in Britain, to check their chief motive and any secondary motives for participation.[45] It was found that the motives were mixed, and varied, though only slightly, by school subject and by age and sex for each course. The chief motive for science study was "to understand the present world" with the implication that science is necessary for this, and the main motive for psychology was "to understand other people." In both cases vocational motives were strong, though more so for science and for men. Practical, nonvocational motives were especially strong for psychology.

Styler,[46] reviewing the above and other British studies of adult student motivations, draws the following conclusions from, as he points out, "the limited research in this field:"

1. In social and political subjects and in natural sciences, the chief motive is interest in the world in which students live.

2. In psychology, Flood and Crossland's conclusions are generally true, but the present interest in social psychology relates the motives of many psychology students with those in the social and political group.

3. In appreciation of music courses, the chief motive is prior interest.

4. The desire for additional education is a very important motive, and may be considered a result of the general advance in educational attainment.

5. Vocational motives appear to be more powerful in the natural sciences than in any other subject.

6. "Personal" motives are much more powerful than are "social" motives, i.e. the desire to improve society.

[44]J. Nicol, A. A. Shea, G. J. P. Simmins, R. A. Sim, (eds.) *Canada's Farm Radio Forum*, Paris: UNESCO, 1954.
[45]W. E. Flood and R. W. Crossland, "Origins of Interest and Motives for Study of Natural Sciences and Psychology Among Adult Students in Voluntary Courses," *British Journal of Educational Psychology*, 18, June 1948.
[46]W. E. Styler, "The Motives of Adult Students," *Adult Education* (London), 23, September 1950. Styler bases his discussion on Flood and Crossland, *op. cit.*; W. E. Williams and A. E. Heath, *Learn and Live*, London: Methuen, 1933; Leeds University, *Tutorial Class Students*, 1949; and Manchester Inquiry, 1947-48.

Perhaps the most comprehensive survey of adult student motivations and their relation to social characteristics was made by Nicholson.[47] He presented a questionnaire containing a checklist of 30 possible reasons for attending adult education classes and eliciting information about the students' sex, age, marital status, veteran status, childhood background (rural-urban), income, previous formal schooling and present type of schooling, to 5,211 students in all types of adult education; the majority were in part-time classes and were taking liberal arts subjects.

Nicholson found, as did the authors just cited, that there were usually several motives with one or more dominant, and that most people had some specific educational motive. The most significant variables were sex and amount of formal schooling: if these were similar for several people, their motives tended to be similar. Vocational motives were dominant at ages 20-40, and for married men, separated or divorced women, and for people planning an occupational change. Intellectual-cultural motives were highest for women, single men, and people with higher previous education.

A study by S. R. Deane related stated principal motivations not only to social characteristics of the students, but also to their persistence in the course and their general life orientations; in terms of these variables, he compared three distinct types of programs—Great Books, college credit, and noncredit evening.[48] Deane found great variations among the programs both in terms of social characteristics and reasons for participation. Those in college credit courses were most interested in the practical aspects of their school work and enjoyed it; they liked competitive activities and sought vocational success and financial security as lifetime goals. By way of contrast, those in the Great Books program, a slightly older age group, sought cultural broadening with no relation to their vocational interests; they felt dislike of competitive activities, and reported greater interest and activity in community affairs as a result of the course. In general, Deane found that the purpose for entering courses correlated with dropout rates, with vocational reasons most effective for continuance and completion.

Some methodological questions. Aside from the fairly specialized applicability of some of the above survey findings, it is clear that even within each educational or social area, methodological questions present themselves. Is it more fruitful for adult educators to ask open-

[47]D. Nicholson, *Why Adults Attend School—An Analysis of Motivating Factors*, University of Missouri Bulletin, vol. 56, no. 30, 1956.

[48]Stephen R. Deane, "Who Seeks Adult Education and Why," *Adult Education*, October 1950.

ended questions about motives or to use checklists or categories of motives in future research? Checklists may suggest and prompt answers that are not necessarily the actual reasons. However, if categories of motives are to be used, what should they be, and how carefully should they be specified in order to be meaningful to the respondents as well as the testers? Meaningful categories or statements of motives may themselves vary with the social characteristics of the respondents, as may the function of the motivation in each specified situation. Solutions to these problems depend on further theoretical and empirical consideration. For purposes of comparability among studies, where such comparison is justified on the basis of some other variable, empirically determined motivations might later be categorized in terms of a theoretical model.

The above studies validate the generalization that several motives per individual almost always play a part in adult educational participation. However, without invalidating this generalization on a certain level of analysis, it should be pointed out that the finding may be a function both of the method of eliciting motivations and of the major concern of the research. Love's study, for example, using depth analysis, found that one specific motivation, within a generally favorable attitudinal frame, was necessary and sufficient for an adult to venture into educational participation.

For the study of differential motivation and its effects among those who *are* students, the concept of mixed motives is probably more useful than the search for a single or basic motive. Is there any relation between the *number* and *scope* of unstructured "reasons" given for participation, and variations in *intensity* of motivation as measured by objective indicators? What changes occur in the number or scope of motives during the progress of a program or with changes in methods of teaching?

Adult student motivation and agency goals. The concept of "goals" referred to in speaking of the "goal-directed behavior" of adult students is clearly theoretically different from what is meant by the "goals" of educational agencies. The latter cannot be conceived to have a subjective aspect; they are rather institutional norms which serve to define the situation in which typical motives operate. Of course, again theoretically, the content of agency norms and of student expectations must be in some minimum agreement in order for the program to continue—but empirical research is necessary to determine what is the minimum, and even what is the maximum, agreement necessary not only to bring about the effects of participation and persistence, but also of learning and increased interest.

The possibilities of this focus of research are more thoroughly discussed in the chapter on Evaluation. One study will be mentioned here which surveyed and compared agency goals and student motivations, but did not relate them to other aspects of participation or program. Sillars presented questionnaires to 40 agencies working with adult education for international understanding, and to a sampling of their students; the agencies were widely diversified as to locale and organizational structure.[49] The agency goals, in decreasing order of frequency, were: increase understanding, 47 per cent; change attitudes, 25 per cent; get action, 18 per cent; arouse interest, 7 per cent; and help critical thinking, 3 per cent. The students' reasons for participation were: desire for information, 37 per cent; general interest, 18 per cent; sense of personal concern, 13 per cent; for socializing, 13 per cent; self-improvement, 4 per cent; attraction of big names, 4 per cent.

In general it would appear that the predominant motive of the students coincides with the major educational aim of the agencies, but where there are secondary differences, questions for further research arise. Sillars summarized the implications of his findings thus: "The problem consists of adjusting agency goals to the educational needs of clients which, in the public affairs field, are rooted in economic, social and psychological relationships to local, national and world communities." These relationships should be explored, and the findings studied in connection with subsequent motivational questions. Is there a problem of dropouts in these programs, and if so, to what extent is it the result of certain unmet latent student motivations? Does a certain amount of discrepancy between student motivations and agency goals work for an actively functioning program, or toward one that is disorganized and losing force? Are some student motivations met as a "by-product" of the program even though agency goals do not explicitly account for them, and vice-versa?

In summary. It is clear that an attempt to understand the intimate connections between motivation and education is crucial for the achievement of adult educational goals. In social psychological terms, for each individual the learning process proceeds selectively in the context of motivational forces. With increasing age and ego development, basic motivational forces are socially defined, channeled and ramified—new motivations are learned. Sociologically, with increasing societal development, this social learning is institutionalized into a complex and pervasive educational system.

Adult education, therefore, must deal with well-developed, subjec-

[49]R. Sillars, "Education for International Understanding: Report of a Survey," *Adult Education Journal*, April 1949.

tively meaningful motivations in relation to complex social influences and social values. Within this broad framework, the studies above have been cited to illustrate some of the mechanisms by which motivation and learning are related, such as levels of aspiration, and some of the social and psychological factors which may best account for differential motivations, such as previous formal education, socio-economic status, and personality configurations. Further research in the field must first draw on much of what already has been done and replicate it in adult educational situations. For example, those incentives that have been isolated as effective for learning by school children should be tested for their effectiveness with varying populations of adults.

What are the effective incentives for learning in adult education situations? How significant are those incentives which are rooted in the educational situation, such as group characteristics, programming features and teaching methods, in relation to those rooted in the general social situations of the learners? It is important to make this classification to the extent that the former set of incentives are more amenable to variation for the purpose of increasing motivation and learning than are the latter. What is the relation of effective incentives to the manifest goals of programs, and how do differing relations correlate with the varying success of programs as a whole?

What are the general situational characteristics of different populations of adults which serve to define for them the meaning and desirability of participation in adult education? Put another way, how do attitudes toward education and educational values, differ with socio-cultural characteristics of groups of adults?

What is the relative flexibility of existing adult motivations, and what factors contribute to differential flexibility of motives? How does participation in adult education programs modify relevant motivations?

The above are summary questions, which, for the purposes of research, would need further specification in terms of the relevant variables to be studied. They are obviously not exhaustive of the relations between motivation and education, but are intended primarily to indicate the broad potential significance of findings which may emerge from careful empirical research into adult educational motivation.

ATTITUDES*

The field of attitude research is today the largest and one of the most significant in socio-psychological inquiry. Its continuing expansion over the last 40 years[1] has been, to a large extent, concurrent with the history of the adult education movement. This parallel is drawn not in order to indicate a neat and direct influence of one field on the other—unfortunately such a relation is all too lacking to date—but to suggest a pervasive and increasing cultural awareness of the significance of the individual's role, subjectively defined, in a mass society facing great social issues.

Throughout the present report attitudes are a major focus of the research discussed. Whether studies concern participation, program planning, leadership or other areas of adult education, the chances are that an instrument which elicits attitudes has been used as a research tool, often a major one. This chapter will not deal with attitudes in terms of specific content with relevance to subject matter areas covered in more detail in other chapters. Rather, it will deal with implications for adult education inherent in the study of attitudes as entities in themselves.

Education, at least potentially a great and practical social force, is

*This chapter was written by Corinne Kirchner and David Wilder.

[1]Muzafer Sherif and Carolyn Sherif, *An Outline of Social Psychology*, (revised edition), New York: Harper and Brothers, 1956, p. 488.

fundamentally "something which happens inside an individual"[2]; the theoretical construct employed to account for and deal with this "something" is the concept of attitudes. The Sherifs discuss attitudes as the "end-products of socialization,"[3] and Allport indicates that, as significant data for study, attitudes are the concrete embodiment of culture.[4] In any given group, therefore, the adult educator faces individuals who have accepted large elements of the cultural milieu but who, because of the richness and diversity of the American culture and because of their varying experiences, will hold differing opinions and attitudes about many issues and ways of behaving which lie outside of the universally accepted, basic elements of the culture. These diversities will be far more apparent in liberal than in vocational adult education activities. In these terms, and especially in relation to the process and institution of education, this discussion therefore focuses on *social* attitudes, i.e. those which are the products of social interaction.

It must be stressed that the discovery and measurement of attitudes is a more difficult and complex matter than the mere recording of the opinions of sample populations by pollsters. Indeed, operationally the recording of opinions is only a first step. Basic to the planning of an adult education program, or for that matter a propaganda campaign, is the need to know how and why reported opinions and attitudes came to be held. The very assumption on which attitude measurement rests, that attitudes are distributed in a population in some uniform way and may be ranked, implies their social nature and also provides a clue for the discussion of the formation of attitudes. This point illustrates the close interplay of methodological considerations and the development of theory, an interaction which is generally acknowledged in scientific study, but which is most keenly felt in those psychological areas where the objects of study can only be inferred, or at best indirectly studied. Just as intelligence is, from this point of view, "what intelligence tests measure," so attitudes and interests may be defined largely in terms of their measurement.

It is important, first, to identify the general nature of the phenomenon under discussion, but this knowledge alone is not adequate for the practical problems in adult education. It is necessary, second, to distinguish attitudes, to whatever extent is feasible and useful, from

[2]Wilbur C. Hallenbeck, "A Sociologist Looks at Adult Education," *Adult Education*, vol. VII, no. 3, Spring 1957, p. 135.
[3]Sherif and Sherif, *op. cit.* Chapters 15-18 constitute an excellent and ample discussion of most of the points touched on in the present brief review.
[4]Gordon Allport, "Attitudes," *Handbook of Social Psychology*, Carl Murchison, (ed.), Worcester: Clark University Press, 1935.

other psychological phenomena sharing the same general nature, and third, to analyze the properties or measureable dimensions of attitudes. Empirical research in adult education then might proceed from a solid conceptual base to investigate such crucial questions as (a) correlations with or effects of, such variables as age, sex and educational status upon attitudes, and (b) the possibilities and means for attitude change, as well as the implications of such change.

The above sequence is an ideal progression and tends to obscure the actual interplay of various steps of theory and research; however, it will serve as a broad outline for the ensuing discussion and may help to orient the adult educator in a field having contributions from many sources, broad practical applications and somewhat unequal developments.

THE NATURE OF ATTITUDES

The major significance of attitudes in social psychological research, together with the fact that, necessarily, they can be studied only indirectly, illustrate the familiar paradox that the very strength of a field may also be its weakness. That is, the many formulations of the concept of attitude by theorists, with their various measurement specifications, as contrasted with the common everyday usage of attitude and related terms, result in an all-embracing conception which can be of little practical use in dealing with problems of education. Of the above extremes, i.e. either too many uncoordinated specifications, or too generalized and unanalytical usage of the term "attitude," the writings of adult educators seem to lean toward the latter.

On the basis of a series of theoretical definitions of attitudes, Allport in 1935 attempted to abstract their common element; this he labelled "readiness for response."[5] He included in his review of research the very early work of German laboratory psychologists, in which "attitude" denoted a motor set. His own definition of attitude was "a neuro-psychic state of readiness for mental and physical activity." Before examining the slightly different wording of the basic quality of attitudes found in more recent writings, it is useful to point out the significance for adult educators of Allport's formulation.

Attitudes and controversial issues. Common usage usually restricts itself to speaking of attitudes about more or less controversial content areas, and adult educators often concern themselves solely with problems of assessing or changing these particular attitudes. Such emphasis is of great social significance, as will be brought out, but it is equally

[5]Allport, *ibid.*

important to realize that attitudes as dynamic psychological factors determining various response activities, i.e. as "readiness for response," are involved in all learning situations. Attitudes may be as significant in determining the responses of adults to, and conversely the effects of history, language or mathematics courses, as they are in regard to race relations education. It is true that most of the research to date has concentrated on the effect of attitudes on learning of controversial material. Levine and Murphy[6] studied the learning and forgetting by two groups of college students, one known to be pro-Communist and one anti-Communist, of two prose passages which conveyed pro-Communist and anti-Communist sentiments, respectively. The learning curve was based on the correctness of reproduction of the passage after hearing it at weekly intervals for four weeks; the forgetting curve was based on recall without hearing the passage again at weekly intervals of five weeks. It was found that the *amount* of learning was greater and forgetting less when the groups were exposed to material congenial to their previous attitudes, although the *rate* of learning and forgetting, as indicated by the shape of the learning and forgetting curves when plotted on a graph, was similar regardless of the bias of the prose content. It is too much to infer that this study affords a scale for the measurement of bias. It does put the adult educator on notice that biases can retard learning.

Functional nature of attitudes. Recent formulations of the nature of attitudes emphasize that they are *organizations of psychological processes with respect to aspects of the individual's world.*[7] Today it is axiomatic that an internal organization, i.e. a structured psychological field, has dynamic selective properties with regard to new stimulus situations. Thus, while this newer definition retains the implication of "readiness for response," at the same time it also implies the functional nature of attitudes.

The organization of psychological processes and the consequent functional nature of attitudes provides the basis for the primary importance of an understanding of attitudes for adult education—this is the thesis that attitudes do not form or change simply as discrete cognitive units, but that for any one *individual* or for any *group* attitudes exist in functional interdependence with other attitudinal, motivational and value components. It follows from this that adult education programs aiming at attitude change must be prepared for

[6]Jerome Levine and Gardner Murphy, "The Learning and Forgetting of Controversial Material," in *Readings in Social Psychology,* Maccoby, Newcomb, Hartley, (eds.), New York: Henry Holt, 1958.

[7]For example, Sherif and Sherif, *op. cit.;* David Krech and Richard Crutchfield, *Theory and Problems of Social Psychology,* New York: McGraw-Hill Book Company, 1948.

the resistance offered by existing attitudes and must provide adequate functional settings for the proposed attitudes.

Since, especially in the educational setting, the functional nature of attitudes is a key conception, it is worthwhile to repeat here the distinction made in the discussion of motivational research between the *genetic*[8,9] and the *immediate* psychological approach to study. For example, although there may be evidence that an adult's positive attitude toward education was formed as an internalization of his parents' expectations and requirements of him, the present existence of this attitude may serve a different function, with differing consequences—perhaps it is a means for a feeling of security in the face of rapid societal change, and as such may be more effective that the original function in motivating the individual to apply the knowledge he receives from his educational experiences.

H. Brewster Smith,[10] in his analysis of data from a study made in 1947 using intensive interviews to discover the structure and function of adult attitudes toward Russia, was able to distinguish the following possible functions which attitudes may fulfill:

> [Attitudes] may reflect or express the person's central values (their *value* function). They may show consistency with his characteristic ways of reacting (their *consistency* function), or perhaps gratify indirectly his basic needs (their *gratification* function). They may form part of his attempt to construct for himself a stable and meaningful world within which he can order his life (their *meaning* function). Finally, they may serve to express his identification with and promote his acceptance by his favored social groups (their *conformity* function).

[8]Krech and Crutchfield, *ibid.* See chapter on "Motivation to Learn."

[9]The *genesis* of attitudes is a question of theoretical interest; its actual nature is not readily open to research, but some such formulation is necessary as a basis for the study of the modifiability of attitudes. The following is taken from Allport's postulation of four psychological conditions for the formation of attitudes, with brief explanations:

1. *Integration* of specific responses of a similar type. A discrete and isolated experience does not engender an attitude because in itself it lacks organization in memory, meaning and emotion.

2. *Individuation* or differentiation of responses from primordial general approach-avoidance responses.

3. *Trauma* or the impact of dramatic experience.

4. *Adoption* ready-made from the attitudes of parents, teachers, peers, etc.

Allport, *op. cit.* Hartley, Hartley and Hart point out that the fourth condition, as listed, is probably a case of the general context of reference group influence, within which the first three processes of attitude formation may take place. E. L. Hartley, R. E. Hartley and C. Hart, "Attitudes and Opinions," in W. L. Schramm, (ed.), *The Process and Effects of Mass Communication,* Urbana: University of Illinois Press, 1954.

[10]H. Brewster Smith, "The Personal Setting of Public Opinions: A Study of Attitudes toward Russia," in *Public Opinion and Propaganda,* D. Katz *et al,* (eds.), New York: The Dryden Press, 1954.

Empirical research in adult education may determine the *present* function of an individual's attitude, using the present attitude as an independent variable, which, regardless of why it was first acquired, is now a determinant of the individual's future reactions; in turn, these new reactions or experiences may act back on the relevant attitude, changing its content or its immediate function. Leonard Doob incorporates this "two-way" consideration when he defines attitudes as "implicit drive-producing responses."[11]

Attitudes distinguished from other psychological phenomena. The fact that attitudes are *learned* responses, and may influence further learning, establishes them as *sociogenic* motives.[12] For example, the existence of a positive attitude toward American foreign policy may motivate an adult not only to answer positively on a questionnaire about this matter, but also it may motivate him to participate in an educational program on foreign policy. The affective tone of attitudes, their positive or negative aspect, also implies their goal-directed nature. It is important for adult educators to realize, however, that the extent to which any particular attitude is motivating, or in other words, the requisite *strength* of an attitude and the needed *external conditions* for it to be expressed in action, can be determined only by research. The crucial problem of the relation of attitudes to action and the difficulties of studying this relation are taken up in Chapter XIV.

Attitudes may be distinguished further in that they are not "free-floating" but are always formed in relation to objects, ideas or persons, unlike the so-called personality traits of all-pervasive nature, such as skepticism or honesty, and unlike momentary motivational or emotional sets. It is in these terms that attitudes may most clearly be seen as a focus of adult education—because attitudes are object-oriented through processes of social learning and are relatively stable, they are both crucial and accessible to the aims of education, but are effective only to the extent that unlearned psychological determinants do not interfere or are "held constant" with regard to educational aims.

One further distinction, that between *attitudes* and *interests,* should be mentioned here. The theoretical formulation thus far covers both these subjects, and insofar as there is a distinction, it seems to lie primarily in the historical usage of the two terms in research. "Interests" were an important topic in early writings on psychology, but hardly appear at all, even as a subtopic, in more recent works. The great surge in public opinion polls and attitude research seems to have

[11] Leonard Doob, "The Behavior of Attitudes," *Psychological Review,* vol. 54, 1947.
[12] See Sherif and Sherif, *op. cit.,* especially pp. 207 ff.

taken over the conceptual realm of interests, while greatly elaborating and refining it.

A consideration of the emphases found in attitude and interest research, respectively, indicates that the latter has become a subtopic or a "dimension" in the study of attitudes. Studies of interests probe either positive or negative orientations of persons to aspects of their environment, and thus yield the affective base of attitudes; or they seek to know degrees of interest, in a sense comparable to the "saliency" dimension used in attitude research. However, attitude research generally considers also the cognitive formulation within which positive or negative feelings are embedded.

It is understandable that adult educators have tended thus far to focus on the study of "interests," in the light of their basic and pressing concern for the initial participation of adults in educational programs; this emphasis will be illustrated in the next chapter. However, to the extent that there has been a deficiency in the study of attitudes in the field of adult education, the problem is more closely related to the issues discussed in the chapter on Evaluation. For the present, it is important to see that the *qualitative* success of adult education, whether in terms of any one individual's learning or in the larger terms of social change, requires an understanding of the nature of adult attitudes, their formation and modifiability, which is more comprehensive than what is usually meant by "interest" research.

THE DIMENSIONS OF ATTITUDES

It has been indicated that adult educators tend toward over-generalized usage of the term "attitudes." The root of the problem seems to be that adult education attitude research does not go farther than ascertaining their positive or negative dimensions; there are other dimensions which, if known, might serve to highlight the wide variations of attitudes among a population, and might help to explain variations in the effects of educational programs among a group which is generally favorably inclined to the program.

Attitudes and behavior. As was indicated also, attitude research differs from interest research largely in terms of making a distinction between one's cognitive or intellectually perceptive view of an object and his affective view of it. This distinction is of utmost importance because it puts into researchable terms the basic questions adult educators must ask in evaluating their efforts—what is the relation of one's knowledge about the world around him to his feelings about it, his policy orientation toward it, and ultimately his actions? Does an increase in his knowledge bring about a change in his affective reactions?

H. Brewster Smith, in the study cited above, found that certain consistent relations do hold between aspects of one's cognitive orientations and aspects of his affective reactions, in this case, toward Russia. One of the cognitive dimensions which was elicited by careful questioning was the *time perspective* of particular attitudes, i.e. whether they are grounded in long-run or short-run considerations. It was found that respondents in 1947 were more optimistic about United States relations with Russia in the short run or "the next few years," than when their long run perspective was tapped by a question concerning the "next 50 years."

Attitudes and information. Another cognitive dimension is the *informational level* of an attitude. Smith found that there was no consistent relation between respondents' informational level about Russia and the affective *direction,* whether pro or con, of their attitude toward Russia. However, those who were well informed were more optimistic in their time perspective regarding relations with Russia. Another affective dimension, *intensity* of concern about Russia, was found to be associated with a high level of information, most likely in a reciprocal relationship. The converse of this relationship points up clearly the practical problem for adult educators—those who held the most stereotyped and least-informed view of Russia also showed relative lack of concern about Russia.

Smith's study also found that various dimensions of persons' attitudes toward Russia were functionally related to their dominant life values and to the breadth of their interests, defined by a cosmopolitan rather than a personal or family orientation of their interests. These various dimensions of attitudes are, as already noted, actually all interdependent parts of a unified whole which can be analyzed only by careful research. Undoubtedly, further study will be able to distinguish other and perhaps more important cognitive and affective dimensions than those mentioned here. The value of making these somewhat artificial distinctions lies primarily in clarifying the relationship between external influences such as education, propaganda or everyday socialization processes, and the formation or modification of attitudes.

Conceptualization of dimensions of attitudes. Various writers have specified different lists of dimensions of attitudes. Hartley, Hartley and Hart[13] indicate the following:

Direction—Is the attitude for or against?
Degree—How much so?
Intensity—How strongly do you feel about it?
Salience—How important is it among all your attitudes?

[13]Hartley, Hartley and Hart, *op. cit.*

Krech and Crutchfield[14] mention *precision* or clarity of perceptions, and *specificity* or degree of interrelation with other attitudes, as two important cognitive dimensions along which attitudes may vary among people. They also point out that although the salience of an attitude as usually measured may indicate the *importance* of it in some cases, in others it may only indicate the conscious awareness of a relatively newly-acquired or changing attitude; truly important attitudes, such as respect for democratic values, may be so ingrained as to be habitual and thus less accessible to open-ended questioning.[15]

CORRELATES OF ATTITUDES

If there is one thing that the many polls and surveys conducted throughout the United States have established, it is that attitudes are related to other attributes of individuals. If this were not the case, there would be no need for the highly complicated sampling techniques which confront the uninitiated. However, it is not just that attitudes differ from person to person, but that they differ *systematically,* depending upon an individual's attributes and his location within the social structure. Hence, findings with regard to almost any attitude under investigation are presented only after the researcher has investigated the "breakdowns" with regard to subgroupings determined on the basis of age, sex, income, education, urban or rural and regional residence and other conceivably influential social factors.

The researcher makes such breakdowns because he knows from previous experience that even when a population is divided evenly on an issue, it might be, for instance, that most women are for it and most men against it. Such specifications reveal a great deal more than do the original figures alone, and good research is always looking for them. Once found, they offer important clues to those planning adult education programs and courses.

As stated above, such findings necessitate certain methodological considerations; however, there is the parallel theoretical question which asks why subgroups should differ systematically with regard to attitudes. Researchers usually are not prepared to answer this question

[14]Krech and Crutchfield, *op cit.*

[15]The complexity of attitudes and their multi-dimensional nature has had a great deal to do with the development of methodology and measurement techniques in the social sciences. If attitudinal differences were always a simple matter of pro and con, there would be no need for such devices as Guttman and Likert scales. The widespread and successful use of many complex instruments is testimony to the validity of the above conceptualizations. To the extent that adult education research is concerned with studying complex attitudes, it must utilize appropriate instruments which do not over-simplify the attitudes studied.

See in particular, B. F. Green, "Attitude Measurement," in G. Lindzey (ed.) *Handbook of Social Pychology,* Cambridge, Mass.: Addison-Wesley Publishing Co., Inc., 1954.

with precision. However, to the extent that answers are forthcoming, they state that it is not sex, age, or income *per se* which "causes" the differences and similarities observed. Rather, it is the differential experiences one undergoes by virtue of age, sex or income which have influenced the attitudes or have set the stage for influencing them.[16]

Attitudes and educational status. Following the above line of reasoning, there is one category of findings which should be of particular interest to adult educators: namely, the finding that attitudes differ systematically from one educational level to another. This is particularly true with regard to attitudinal questionnaire items which are most relevant to democratic values and philosophy. Clear examples of this variation can be found in terms of civil liberties, authoritarianism, ethnocentrism, racial tolerance, and comparable issues. In each case there are data representative of the total adult population of the United States which show rather dramatically that adults with less education tend to have less regard for civil liberties, less tolerance for groups other than their own, and more authoritarian and ethnocentric attitudes.[17]

It is rather clear from such findings that adults with more education have internalized and comprehended democratic philosophy far better than have their less educated peers. No responsible social scientist would infer from this that education "caused" the differences found, but he might well infer that adults with more formal education have had relevant experiences which are different from those of the less well educated. The question for adult educators at this point is

[16]It should be noted that attitudes have been studied with regard to their relationship with and function for personality structure. Under an assumption of unity of personality, attitudes are regarded as one manifestation of the whole person. Some early research attempted to relate scores on various Thurstone Attitude Scales with scores on measured interests and personality tests. *The Authoritarian Personality* is probably the best and most comprehensive example of attitude research which is based on personality, or rather, psychoanalytic, theory.

Adult educators concerned with particular programs should note that the studies vary in the extent to which they were able to find correlations between an attitudinal factor and other psychological variables, and such correlations often seem to be a function of the tests used; in any case, the *content* of an attitudinal "personality factor," such as conservatism-liberalism, may vary considerably with the larger social situation and with one's subjective relation to his reference group.

Examples of this type of study are: R. Pintner, "A Comparison of Interests, Abilities and Attitudes," *Journal of Abnormal and Social Psychology*, vol. 27, 1933; Leona Tyler, "Relationships Between Strong Vocational Interest Scores and Other Attitude and Personality Factors," *Journal of Applied Psychology*, vol. 28, 1945; T. W. Adorno *et al.*, *The Authoritarian Personality*, New York: Harper and Brothers, 1950.

[17]This is such a consistent finding that selection of documentary evidence must necessarily be arbitrary. However, see S. Stouffer, *Communism, Conformity and Civil Liberties*, Garden City, New York: Doubleday and Co., 1955; Sherif and Sherif, *op. cit.*; and R. Christie and M. Jahoda (eds.), *Studies in the Scope and Method of "The Authoritarian Personality*," Glencoe, Ill.: The Free Press, 1954.

whether or not adults who have had similar amounts of formal education, but differing amounts of adult education, differ systematically with regard to democratic attitudes. What sort of job adult education is doing with regard to many important democratic goals will remain a matter of conjecture until research is conducted along these lines.

MODIFIABILITY AND CHANGE OF ATTITUDES

Houle, in his account of the Armed Services' educational program, presents research evidence that the attitudes of adults may be changed, at least to some extent, by the provision of factual information.[18] However, Tuckman and Lorge found that a course on the Psychology of Adults, presented in general factual terms, did not lower the general amount of agreement with unfavorable and factually incorrect attitudinal items about old people and older workers embodied in a questionnaire.[19] The relation of new information to attitude change is more fully discussed in the chapter on Evaluation, but it can be seen here that attitudinal change does not rest on the basis of information per se. A more significant determinant is the nature and degree of the adult's ego-involvement in the material to be learned. For example, Tuckman and Lorge point out that the older people in the above-mentioned course showed the least modification of incorrect opinions; for them the course may even have served to reinforce pre-existing attitudes, by pointing out physiological changes of the aging process with which the older group already were identified. If this interpretation is correct it indicates a problem for adult educators due to students' misinterpretation of experience which in this case led to a rejection of known facts.

Elements in communication. Probably the best research model for studying attitude change in an educational setting is to be found in Hovland, Janis and Kelley, *Communication and Persuasion,* though these authors were primarily concerned with effects of mass media.[20] They structure the problem of attitude change in terms of:

1. the communicator
2. the stimuli or content of the communication
3. the audience predispositions
4. the effects, or audience responses.

[18]Cyril Houle and others, *The Armed Services and Adult Education,* Washington: American Council on Education, 1947.

[19]J. Tuckman and I. Lorge, "The Influence of a Course on the Psychology of Adults on Attitudes toward Old People and Older Workers," *Journal of Educational Psychology,* vol. 43, 1952.

[20]C. Hovland, I. Janis, and H. H. Kelley, *Communication and Persuasion,* New Haven: Yale University Press, 1953.

They point out that two other relevant variables in the communications learning process may be the *medium* of communication and the *situation* in which it is conducted. They indicate that although the learning process may be the same with regard to persuasive communications in everyday life as in educational situations, still some of the problems of initiating learning are undoubtedly avoided in the educational setting, to the extent that the audience accept their status as students, with the concomitant implications for their receptiveness to the communication.

Many of the topics which Hovland *et al.* emphasize in their studies of opinion and attitude change are covered elsewhere in this report and need not be detailed here;[21] at this point a few of their relevant findings with respect to the *stimulus* are summarized: The major research issues with respect to the content of communication designed to influence attitudes are (1) the effects of motivating appeals, especially "fear-arousing appeals"; and (2) the effects of differential organization of material, especially explicit vs. implicit statement of the conclusions of the argument, presentation of one side of the issue vs. two sides, and "primacy" vs. "recency" effects of the order of arguments.

The question of whether "emotional" or "rational" appeals are more effective in changing attitudes, although debated in the field of adult education[22] and often studied outside the field, is far from settled and will probably remain uncertain at least until operational definition of the key terms is achieved. Hovland *et al.* cite studies which have found that both emotional and rational appeals can be motivating. The conditions for the relative superiority of each cannot be specified without careful content analysis in terms of semantic meaning; furthermore, research distinctions must be made among the three possible aspects of audience motivational response to the communication, i.e. their motivation to (1) pay attention to the verbal content, (2) to comprehend the message, and (3) to accept the conclusions or change their attitudes.

"Fear-arousing appeals," those which depict unfavorable consequences if the message is not accepted, e.g. by pointing out the dangers of cancer if routine examinations are not made, were found to be most effective if the "threats" were not out of proportion to the possible steps to avoid danger, and if both dangers and precautions were

[21]See the chapter on "Adult Learning" for studies dealing with the communicator; chapters on "Motivation" and "Interests" for studies dealing with audience predispositions; and chapter on "Evaluation" for studies emphasizing the effects or audience responses.
[22]See for example, Max Birnbaum, "Mind and Emotion in Adult Education," *Adult Education*, vol. VII, No. 3, Spring 1957.

carefully specified rather than presented in general terms. Where the affective reactions or anxiety produced were out of proportion to the positive recommendations, there was likely to be a "boomerang" effect, in that the audience would discount the good intentions of the communicator and thus avoid the whole issue, or would even form conclusions opposite to those suggested.

Studies on the superiority of drawing conclusions explicitly as against leaving them to be inferred, with regard to the acceptance of these conclusions, show that no general rule may be applied. The evidence points to the hypothesis that where there is a relatively *complicated* series of arguments on *impersonal* issues, conclusions should be stated explicitly; conversely, where the arguments are familiar or simple for the audience, it is best that conclusions be inferred. These two points have definite applicability to the pedagogy of adult education.

The question of whether it is more effective to present one side of an argument or both sides to bring about attitude or opinion change also seems to rest on several conditions. It was found that among people initially favorable to the suggested attitude, presenting one side was more effective; among those initially opposed, the presentation of both sides, with positive conclusions, was more effective.[23] A breakdown according to the educational level showed that the better educated responded more favorably when both sides were presented, whereas the less educated changed their opinions more when only one side was given.

In addition to the communications learning factors, the dimensions of attitudes mentioned earlier, e.g. salience, intensity, should be taken into consideration as relevant to attitude change. Why is it, for example, that among a group of adults who are negative toward an issue, some will change their attitudes to a greater extent, more rapidly, or more permanently, than will others exposed to the same educational program? Adult educators may further their understanding of such situations by future research into the differing dimensions of initial attitudes.

The correlates of attitudes have also been found to be relevant to differences in the modifiability of attitudes. For example, Lorge[24] found that the attitudes of older age groups tended to become more firmly fixed and were less amenable to change than were those of

---

[23]For further evidence relating to this point see Chapter II, page 15, and the "Audio-Visual" section of Chapter IX.

[24]Irving Lorge, "The Thurstone Attitude Scales: II: The Reliability and Consistency of Younger and Older Intellectual Peers," *Journal of Social Psychology*, May 1939.

younger subjects with the power factor of intelligence controlled. However, this finding with regard to the individual attribute of age cannot be interpreted to mean simply that age caused fixity on the particular attitudes that Lorge studied, which included attitudes toward communism, patriotism and birth control. There is the further question of whether this finding would hold for attitudes pertaining to areas of content which are less "time-bound" than the above issues. It would be particularly important for some of the practical problems of adult educators to have more research concerning the relation of age and the modifiability of attitudes.

Groups and attitude change. Significant studies are now being done with regard to *group* as well as individual correlates of attitudes. For instance, Kelley and Volkart found that the extent to which a group member's attitudes will be influenced by a communication, the content of which runs counter to group values, is inversely related to how highly he values his membership in the group.[25] Duncan and Krietlow, also, found that the more cohesive or homogeneous a neighborhood area was as to certain cultural attributes, i.e. religious and ethnic group affiliation, the less likely that area was to adopt new attitudes and techniques,[26] as was noted in Chapter II.[27]

For the adult educator, the primary implication from the above discussion is that attitudes do not form or change simply as discrete cognitive units. This generalization does not preclude the efforts of adult education to carry on specific programs of factual information, but rather it calls for the integration and enlargement of these efforts, on the basis of empirical knowledge gained from more refined attitude research in adult learning situations.

[25] H. H. Kelley and E. H. Volkart, "The Resistance to Change of Group-Anchored Attitudes," American Sociological Review, vol. 17, no. 4, 1952.

[26] J. Duncan and B. Kreitlow, "Selected Cultural Characteristics and the Acceptance of Educational Programs and Practices," Rural Sociology, December 1954.

[27] The relation of individual or group attributes to differential rates of attitude change may be best explained by the functional relevance of attitudes for the people that hold them. Thus there may be strong resistance in educational situations to change of attitudes which are crucial for the maintenance of group structures, for carrying out social roles, or for fulfilling personality needs.

CHAPTER V

ADULT INTERESTS AND EDUCATION*

The interests of an adult which lie outside his occupation determine to a considerable degree how he spends his leisure time, assuming that both the opportunity and the motivation to pursue his chief interests are present. The concern of the adult educator in adult interests is therefore practical and immediate. In effect he is competing for the time investment of concrete individuals in some educational activity within delimited possibilities.

SOME BASIC CONSIDERATIONS IN THE AREA OF INTERESTS

Philosophers, psychologists and social theorists have filled the literature with speculations and insights about the function of interests in human life and have produced a plethora of concepts, many vague, some contradictory. However, to the adult educator, three questions appear basic:

1. What are adult interests? This question is basic to any others, but it is often asked alone. A descriptive answer in terms of one community, of which there are many examples,[1] can be useful, especially for administrative purposes, but any dynamic implications about the

---

*This chapter was written by Corinne Kirchner.
[1]For example, H. Barron, *A Study of Adult Educational Interests and Programs in Salt Lake County*, Ph.D. dissertation, University of Utah, 1954; R. A. Wilkins, *A Study to Determine the Adult Education Needs of Providence, Rhode Island*, Ph.D. Dissertation, Boston University, 1955.

educational process which might be drawn from it extend its scope into at least one of the following research questions.

2. How do adult interests affect participation, learning, or more generally, personal and social adjustment? This general formulation subsumes a variety of important questions, each with its own specifications, some discussed elsewhere in this report.

3. How may adult interests be aroused, sustained, modified or changed? The methodological significance of these questions will be discussed on pages 67-68; their practical significance emerges to the extent that interests may be found to have independent positive effects in the processes of educational activity or personality adjustment. If interests do play a part in, for instance, educational participation, then it is important to know to what extent they may be aroused or modified to this end.

Research seeking to answer these questions has proceeded from several sources: (1) Surveys by practitioners in various fields of participation, i.e. librarians, radio program planners, vocational counselors, etc.; (2) Studies concerned with interests as related to other characteristics of individuals as psychological entities. The emphasis is upon the uniformities of interests as compared with some psychological variable, and the aim is to uncover the precise nature of interest as a human capacity. This is primarily the domain of psychologists and with them seems to lie the burden of the definition of interests, as distinct from or related to motivation, needs and attitudes. (3) The study of interests has also been approached by sociologists concerned with variations in interests according to social group characteristics; with regard to the individual, the emphasis is upon the variation of interests according to his social roles. The more refined research in this field, as it has developed and as it contains significance for adult education, takes into account the established concepts from each of these approaches and applies them to the study of interests.

Research considerations. In 1935, Professor Wayne Dennis presented an overview of the research on adult interests.[2] His critique is relevant not only because it touches on all the analytic points to follow, but also because the major works by Thorndike, Thurstone, Fryer and Strong, on which Dennis bases his judgment, have not been superseded or supplemented to any great extent. Dennis holds that the study of human interests is the study of one's choice of activities; in education, the problem is to determine under what conditions educational activities will be chosen over other activities. In order to point up what

---

[2]Wayne Dennis, "Adult Interest as Related to Education," *Interests and Abilities of Adults and Techniques of Adult Education*, University of Virginia, 1935.

he feels are the weaknesses of the work of the psychologists, and in terms of his behavioral definition of interests, Dennis concludes that activities are the best indicators of interests, and that they can be known better by direct observation than by laboratory tests. Dennis argues that psychological interest tests show only what people will *say*, not what they will *do*. Harriet O'Shea, writing at about the same time, finds that most of the writing on interest had been done by educators rather than psychologists, whereas "interest should properly belong in the field of psychology for the basic steps of defining its nature.[3] The conflict here is more apparent than real. Obviously, the first step is to have a definition of the area under consideration; equally important, however, and perhaps preceding this step, is Dennis' emphasis on the purpose for which research is being conducted.

Definitions of interests. The discussion above has pinpointed several significant questions. How are interests defined? How are they measured? What is the conceptual framework for the research? In the previous chapters on "Motivation" and "Attitudes" the general nature of the psychological determinants of behavior was discussed; some of the problems of objective measurement of these subjective phenomena were highlighted. It was shown that the definition of these phenomena depends largely on how they are measured. Ralph Berdie follows this principle in his definition of interests:

> Interests are defined as factors within an individual which attract him to or repel him from various objects, persons, and activities within his environment. It is primarily an affective concept.[4]

This definition has been abstracted from many different studies. In any one study, the measurement may not be appropriate to a preconceived definition of interests, or it may not be possible to generalize any one specific technique or finding to another study based on a different conception.

Berdie's formulation requires further consideration. Firstly, interests are always attached to external or environmental factors, i.e. "objects, activities, or persons." In any one situation where interests are to be measured, it is necessary to analyze it into its component environmental factors before conclusions may be drawn about the total situation. Especially is this clear in adult education, where the activity of

[3]Harriet O'Shea, *A Study of the Effect of the Interest of a Passage on Learning Vocabulary*, Teachers College Contributions to Education, No. 351, New York: Teachers College, Columbia University, Bureau of Publications, 1930.

[4]Ralph Berdie, "Interests," *Encyclopedia of Psychology*, New York: Philosophical Library, 1946.

education and its components, the teacher or other persons in the class, or the subject matter may all elicit varying degrees of interest.[5]

The converse of the environmental factors, as indicated in the definition of interests, are the "factors within the individual" which must be distinguished from other factors, such as motivation and attitudes. The problems of making these distinctions have been discussed in previous chapters, but it is well to note here Fryer's conclusion that measurement has isolated motivation and interests as distinct kinds of psychological activity. In his words, motivation is the "driving energy of stimulation" while interest is the "acceptance or rejection aspect."[6]

Berdie elaborates his definition of interests by providing also alternate operational definitions:

> *Subjective expression of interests*—This definition puts the emphasis on the feeling component (pleasure or pain) which is inferred from observations of behavior interpreted as liking or disliking.
> *Objective expression*—This puts the emphasis on gross motor components inferred through observation of behavior involving an approach to and a choice of alternatives equally available.[7]

Criteria for studying interests. Berdie further indicates the various criteria that have been used to study the subjective or objective expression of interests:

1. attention (sometimes used synonymously)
2. process of choice
3. persistence
4. success (complicated by ability and opportunity)
5. differential remembering
6. learning
7. emotions or feelings

These criteria themselves seem to require further study: is there a perfect correlation, for instance, between interest and the choice of, or persistence in, an activity—if not, what other factors may enter into these correlations? In addition to these questions, it is necessary for the adult educator seeking to uncover adult interests to decide on the best indicators to be used—are subjective tests (evaluations made by the individual under study) or objective tests (observations made by

[5]Cf. Alvin Zander, "Student Motives and Teaching Methods in Four Informal Adult Classes," *Adult Education*, Oct. 1951, which attempts to analyze the educational setting; the more refined research on reading interests also makes a distinction between "subject matter interest" and interest in reading activity within these areas.

[6]Douglas Fryer, *The Measurement of Interests*, New York: Henry Holt and Co., 1931.
[7]Berdie, *op. cit.*

the investigator) more definitive for an understanding of interests? To date, subjective tests have been most widely used, and a discussion of the problems in their construction can be found in Fryer's book, already cited.

The classification of interests represents one way some of the research problems, indicated briefly above, might be systematically tackled. Berdie's analysis indicates that the classification of interests is made on the basis of "interest objects" and the various categories of these objects. Correlations are then usually sought between these categories and certain personal or social characteristics. However, in spite of the significance of classification for the construction of reliable indicators, this aspect of the research has generally been left to impressionistic groupings. Fryer makes the criticism that no systematic method was used in selecting items for most interest inventories, and that as a result there is probably a sampling error in them because no one knows how representative of the distinguishing interests of two or more social groups the selected items are.[8]

Classification of interests. Even if rigorous deductively logical reasoning is used to form sub-categories of interests, research has not investigated whether individual perceptions of interest categories, which can only be empirically established, are true to preconceived categories. Such research might reveal that the very classification of interests which is valid and meaningful for the adults being tested may vary according to socio-psychological variables.

A study by Guilford *et al.*, which marks the beginnings of systematic classification, has as its stated purpose a knowledge of "basic interest dimensions" and coordinately defines interests in terms of categories —i.e., interests are the "generalized behavior tendency of an individual to be attracted to a certain class of incentives or activities (including aversions)."[9] A series of interest tests containing 33 hypothesized primary factors with 100 subtests was given to a group of airmen and a group of Air Force officers with age and education controlled. Among the findings, it was possible to identify 17 factors, six of which were common to both groups, six only for airmen and five only for officers. The content of the identified factors indicates that six or seven were definitely directed to vocational stereotypes, while a total of 19 factors were found to be "basic interest" factors, some having broad vocational implications. The author's conclusion about the natural classification of interests is,

[8]Fryer, *op. cit.*
[9]J. P. Guilford, P. R. Christensen, N. A. Bond, M. A. Sutton, "A Factor Analysis of Human Interests," *Psychological Monographs, General and Applied*, vol. 68, no. 4, 1954.

> The structure of the domain of interests . . . includes a limited number of vocationally oriented variables superimposed upon or differentiated from a broader base of general interest variables that have non-vocational implications as well.

Such research serves to clarify the definition and measurement of interests, and is basic to any real progress toward understanding the role of interests in developmental processes. The latter, more dynamic, emphasis of research may be discussed by envisaging the conceptual framework within which study may proceed.

The conceptual framework. The dynamic role of interests may be studied for either of two theoretical purposes, which have been indicated also as two of the major practical questions which the adult educator puts to this subject—By what factors are interests modified, and how do interests modify or influence various other processes? Experimentally, these different questions place interests differently within the standard research design. In the former, interests are considered as the "dependent variable." Where the "independent" or controlled factors are, however, age or aging, sex, race, socio-economic status, etc., the correlations which may be found cannot be interpreted as purely cause-and-effect relationships. It is more likely that there is a third or outside factor that is causing the correlations. For example, the history of adult education itself illustrates the significance of social conditions and cultural expectations in "causing" the acquisition of interests traditionally associated with certain age groupings and the social roles appropriate to these ages. Intensified research into the correlation of interests with age seeks to determine the limits to which cultural expectations about age are rooted in the inherent nature of age and aging—it attempts to discover what *is* inherent.

Where the variation in interests is to be studied in relation to an independent variable such as a discrete educational program, the conceptual framework may conform more closely to the experimental model, as set forth in the chapter on Evaluation.

Research on the dynamic aspect of interests is also concerned with the extent to which interests may modify the process of educational participation and/or the learning that may occur in an educational situation. Here the interests are considered an independent variable. Given a group with certain interests, and a control group without such interests, what are the differences in the learning which occurs in the two groups?

Although it is useful to conceptualize the research in this way, and thus to clarify the need for control groups at appropriate points, the nature of the concept of interests as a phenomenon of the total personality makes it such that its true dynamic role is probably alternating continually between the socalled "independent" and "dependent" variables in any situation. This is indicated by what Thorndike calls the "forward and backward effect" of interests in which the existence of an interest not only modifies future behavior but also acts back on its own personality context.[10]

TYPES OF INTEREST

Review of studies. Cause-and-effect relationships between interests and other socio-psychological variables may be impossible to isolate completely, but research to date has indicated many significant correlations which have practical implications for adult educators. It would be possible to review the ensuing studies in terms of the historical development of the field, which would also illustrate a line of theoretical evolution. However, this presentation will follow, primarily, a classification by general situational areas in which interests have been studied in order to stress their practical significance. The areas have been suggested by the emphases of the studies themselves rather than by an *a priori* ordering of the field. These areas are: Interests and vocations; leisure; reading; participation in programs; and learning.

Interests and vocations. Edward K. Strong pioneered in the formulation of an interest inventory for the study of vocational interests. Strong's work is not merely of historical importance but represents lasting contributions to the knowledge about interests in general. "Strong's Vocational Interest Blank," with its wide range of items and several scoring keys, has been validated by much research and practical use since its conception in the early 1930s.[11] Strong used this test intensively on a group of college freshmen and a group of seniors who were retested at intervals up to ten years, and again after 22 years.[12] The

---

[10]E. L. Thorndike, *Psychology of Wants, Interests and Attitudes,* New York: D. Appleton-Century Company, 1935.

[11]E. K. Strong, *Change of Interests with Age,* California: Stanford University Press, 1931. See Fryer, *op. cit.,* for an account of the development of Strong's tests up to 1931 and D. Super (*Avocational Interest Patterns,* California: Stanford University Press, 1940) for a bibliography of the validations of Strong's test by other researchers.

[12]E. K. Strong, "Permanence of Interest Scores over 22 years," *Journal of Applied Psychology,* 35, 1951. Because this is a longitudinal study, the findings throw some light on age change as well as on the nature of interests. R. Kuhlen points out that most knowledge about aging is about "age differences" rather than "age changes" since the majority of studies are cross-sectional, i.e. they compare different individuals, with possibly different cultural contexts, at different ages rather than the same individuals at different ages. Kuhlen shows the need for more longitudinal studies, but at the same time indicates one difficulty which pertains to them—namely, that most of the tests themselves are culturally determined and may become outdated when used at a later time. Cf. R. G. Kuhlen, "Age Differences in Personality During Adult Years," *Psychological Bulletin,* 42, no. 6, June 1945.

primary finding is that approximately the same rank-order of occupational interests is maintained over one to 22 years. Interest scores are found to be about as permanent as I.Q. scores. Much of the change that does occur in specific interests represents a shift from the "carefree" to the "careful"; where downward shifts occur they are in the area of interests related to physical skills and daring. There is a decrease from age 25 to 55 in social interests, with an increase in individual interests. Those factors which were found to affect the permanence of interests are: (1) The age at the time of the original test—Interests change rapidly from age 15 to 25 and then very slowly to age 55, so that the seniors at the time of the original test displayed more permanence than did the freshmen; (2) The interval between test and retest—The longer this interval the more opportunity for change, although it is still slight; (3) The pattern of marriage and child-rearing.

Strong's tests, although keyed to distinguish among vocational groups, obviously shed light on the more general basis of interests, as might be expected in line with the finding by Guilford et al., given above. However, it is important to note that Strong began by defining the interests he was to study as those which are relatively stable.[13] This is not to invalidate his findings, but only to show that care must be taken in interpreting them. Fryer's conclusion from his extensive review of research is that some interests are very stable while others may be extremely transitory. Strong was concerned with those interests which are related to a major social role of his subjects, i.e. occupation, and this must be kept in mind. More studies are necessary concerning the stability of interests as associated with various other social roles, making clear whether stability is used as a criterion to any extent in the definition of interests.

At about the same time as Strong's early research, E. L. Thorndike was embarked on an extensive study of adult interests, under laboratory conditions and not necessarily with vocational emphasis. Thorndike made the important basic statement that interests could be studied experimentally; however, he did not distinguish among "wants, interests, attitudes, and emotions."[14] He attempted a kind of longitudinal study by asking a group of men in their 50s and 60s to indicate on a questionnaire what their interests had been at ten-year intervals from the age of 20. He found a slight decrease in the volume of inter-

[13]E. K. Strong, *Vocational Interests of Men and Women*, California: Stanford University Press, 1943.

[14]E. L. Thorndike, *Psychology of Wants, Interests and Attitudes. op. cit.*

ests from the 20s to the 50s, with most of the decrease in physical activities, and with no decline in interests related to learning.

These findings may have been influenced by difficulties of recall or by a coloring of memory in terms of the mens' later situations, but Strong found also, in a cross-sectional study of professional men ages 20 to 60, as much versatility of interests in the old as in the young, although the interests were different. Upon analysis of all of Strong's data, it was seen that the interests best liked at 25 tend to increase, while those least liked tend to decrease.[15]

Thorndike found experimental evidence that all of the following techniques were possible for modifying interests, but each was effective only to a limited degree, depending largely on the individuals: contiguity, suggestion, imitation, "conditioning," associative shifting, selection by rewards.[16] These, of course, also are associated with learning processes, and whether or not Thorndike's classification is the best possible, the major import for adult educators of his findings is that interests are learned and may be modified, even for adults. His experiments showed further that repetition *per se* may either increase or decrease the strength of an interest, depending on the change in the nature of the object and its associations—which is to say in effect that, due to the forward and backward effect of interests, there may be no such thing psychologically as pure repetition of a stimulus.

Interests and leisure. Donald Super's study of avocational interest patterns stems directly from the work done with Strong's Vocational Interest Blank.[17] Super indicates that since avocational interests had been used to help in discriminating between vocational interests, and the tests for the latter had been validated, he feels justified in extending the use of Strong's test to the study of leisure interests. Super's main purpose was to determine empirically the psychological role of avocational interests, and thus to test the contradictory theories that avocations function as a "balance" for vocational activities, or that they are "supplementary" to vocational interests. The hobby groups used were: model engineering, instrumental music, amateur photography and stamp collecting. The scoring keys for only the first three groups were found to distinguish among the respondents, 288 adult males and 200 high school boys. With respect to his various questions about avocations, Super found different patterns among the hobby groups. The hobby of music and of model engineering (if the individ-

---

[15]E. K. Strong cited in Pressey, Janney and Kuhlen, "Development and Change of Interests with Age," in *Life—A Psychological Survey*, Chapter 7.

[16]E. L. Thorndike, *Adult Interests*, New York; Macmillan, 1935.

[17]D. Super, *op. cit.*

ual was in a nontechnical vocation) usually were chosen before the vocation; photography and model engineering (if the individual was in a technical vocation) usually were chosen after. Different hobbies attract men at different ages. The amount and reasons for dissatisfaction with their vocations also vary among people with the different hobbies. In general, more older men preferred their jobs to their hobbies than did younger men. Super concludes that neither the theory of "balance" nor of "contribution" is adequate and he proposes an "individualized" theory which would make the psychological role of avocations depend on the present needs of the individual in a given situation and the possible ways of satisfying those needs.

A British study, using both questionnaires and interviews, attempted to isolate the influences of age and intelligence on the leisure interests of a group of women.[18] Three age groups, 20, 20-24, and 25+ were used, with five broad IQ groups in each. The general findings support the earlier generalization that the "span" or number of interests does not change with age, though the content does. Further, the span of interests correlated positively with intelligence. The authors indicated a suspected tendency that the content of the interests of women with higher IQs is similar to the interests of the older, "more mature" groups, and the interests of the low IQs are similar to those of the younger groups.[19]

The factor of IQ as it relates to hobbies is generally neglected in the research on adult interests in this country, possibly because of the difficulty of obtaining IQ data for most groups of adults who are not in the Army or some formal educational program. A study of high school students which does include the IQ factor must therefore suffice.[20] Questionnaires were given to a sample of 2,106 boys and girls coming from four schools and covering more than four years time in one of the schools. Among other findings, some relation was found between IQ and certain hobbies, with reading, music, art and writing characteristic hobbies of the students with high IQs, and sports characteristic of the lower IQs. This finding, taken together with Thorndike's and Strong's data showing physical activities to be greater interests of the young than the old, and reading, writing and other individual, sedentary interests more common to the older age group, would appear to support the tendency discovered in the British study.

[18]J. W. Reeves and Pat Slater, "Age and Intelligence in Relation to Leisure Interests," *Occupational Psychology* (London), 21, July 1947.
[19]The ranking of the specific interests as reported in this study is not noted here because of the different social context and facilities in Britain.
[20]George Davis, *The Prevalence of Hobbies and their Educational Significance*, Ph.D. dissertation, Iowa State University, 1937.

Davis also found, among the high school students, that those with higher IQs tended to have more interests, but that the persistence of hobbies showed little relation to IQ. Another of Davis' questions which is generally neglected in the research with adults, was intended to discover how interests were first aroused; the most frequent source was a similar interest of a friend, and the next most frequent was the family interests.[21]

The majority of these findings are in line with common sense expectations. However, they have significance both in their own terms and as related to the data on participation in adult education discussed in the next chapter. Given the often demonstrated relation between education and income, in itself not unrelated to IQ, the frequent finding by agricultural extension and workers' education studies as well as others, that adults of lower education and income status participate less in adult education activities than do others suggests two things: (1) More attention might be given to program-planning designed for these lower status groups, and (2) Until further advances are made in this direction the easy optimism of some adult educators as to the contribution of adult education to producing desirable social changes may need to be tempered.

A large-scale study of leisure activities was conducted by the National Recreation Association in 1934.[22] A questionnaire was used to investigate the use of leisure hours by 5,000 people, aged 20 to 60. It was found that participation in musical and educational activities increased with age, but all others decreased in frequency of participation. This study did not take into account the various factors that may affect participation, but it did make the refinement of distinguishing between the "desire" to participate and actual participation; it found that "desire" also decreased with age, but less markedly than did actual participation.

In 1952 a smaller but more intensive study of recreation and the aging process was carried on and to investigate the distinction between

[21]A study of British adult students elicited information about the origins of their interest in natural science and psychology. The findings showed differences between the two subjects and between the sexes. In natural science, those who had had science in school marked school as the most frequent source, with books and lectures also important; those who had not had science in school marked books and lectures to a lesser degree and often did not answer; for men their jobs and books were important. In psychology, the most frequent sources were books and magazines and influences of friends; for women, their jobs and influences of relatives were more important. Flood and Crossland, "Origins of Interest and Motives for Study of Natural Sciences and Psychology among Adult Students in Voluntary Courses," *British Journal of Psychology*, 18, June 1948.

[22]National Recreation Association, *The Leisure Hours of 5000 People*, 1934 cited in Kuhlen, "Age Differences in Personality During Adult Years," *lec. cit.*

desired and actual participation.[23] The sample consisted of adult men, ages 20 to 59, having a range of income from 0-$7,000 and different levels of education. Baley found that the higher the income group the fewer the recreational activities that were liked, the more individualistic these activities were and the more the men enjoyed "conversing" or the "exchange of ideas." Baley indicates that this finding is probably a function of age, the older men having the higher incomes.[24] In general, actual participation was of a sedentary nature. The greatest discrepancy between desired and actual participation occurred in sports or the more active interests, and this discrepancy increased with age. The reasons that were given for discrepancies varied between the active and sedentary interests and with age, but the dominant reason for all groups was "lack of time," followed by "health," "lack of money," "lack of facilities," and "lack of knowledge or skill." From the point of view of adult educators, it is interesting that "lack of knowledge and skill" declined with age as a reason for discrepancy between actual and desired participation in sedentary activities, except for a sharp increase in this reason at ages 50 to 59. Baley's interpretation is that at the later age there are more opportunities for participation available because of more time and money, and therefore lack of knowledge becomes a mere apparent deterrent.[25]

INTERESTS AND READING

The research discussed thus far indicates that reading as a sedentary, individualized activity does not lose its interest through the adult years, and may even increase as the more active and social interests decline. This generalization is significant for adult educators as Gray and Munroe point out in introducing their now classic work, *The Reading Interests and Habits of Adults*,[26] since the process of adult education generally requires a wide use of reading. Also from this point of view, reading is an important concern more because research shows that a large number of adults are not interested in reading or do not read well, than because many do.

Reading a major leisure time activity. A survey of 17 cities with interviews given to a sample population in 1946 found that 41 per cent named reading as a favorite sparetime activity and that more named

[23]J. A. Baley, *Recreation and the Aging Process*, Ph.D. dissertation, Ohio State University, 1952.
[24]*Ibid.*
[25]*Ibid.*
[26]W. Gray and R. Munroe, *The Reading Interests and Habits of Adults*, New York: The Macmillan Company, 1929.

74   AN OVERVIEW OF ADULT EDUCATION RESEARCH

reading than any other activity.[27] Although this finding is presented
in positive terms, the proportion may well seem to be low to an adult
educator. Furthermore, studies by *Business Week* in 1953 show that,
in the distribution of recreation time and money, reading has dropped
while spectator amusements are at the top of the list and many of the
active arts, such as "do-it-yourself" projects, have flourished.[28] Lester
Asheim maintains that the social context for these statistics reveals a
"society whose value is on action rather than thought."[29] Where reading is done it is valued for immediate rewards rather than "delayed"
rewards of intellectual satisfaction.

Some factors influencing reading. Gray and Munroe point out the
two major stimuli for research in reading as significant for adult education:

> Experience has taught that before desirable reading habits can
> be established on the part of many young people much information
> is needed concerning their present reading activities and the in-
> fluences that have determined their development.[30]

> Of even greater significance than the amount read by adults is
> the character or quality of the material that is read.[31]

The authors review many studies of reading habits in order to glean
some generalizations from them and follow this by a report of two
community case studies of their own. Newspaper reading is found to
be almost universal among adults, followed by reading of magazines
and then books. Amount of education, occupational status, and residence (urban rather than rural) are correlated positively with the
amount of reading done. Men read newspapers more, while women
are greater readers of magazines and books. There is also a positive
correlation between a variety of interests and the amount of reading.

To these general findings, Gray and Munroe add the insights taken
from a series of case studies or "reading histories" of several individuals.
In the authors' words, there are "almost as many types of development
as there are cases studied," but it is possible to identify certain factors as
playing important parts in the formation of reading interests. Thus, environmental factors often seem to predominate and the influence of parents and friends is important, especially if there is a strong emotional

[27]"What . . . Where . . . Why . . . Do People Read?" N.O.R.C., University of Denver,
Report no. 28, 1946.
[28]*Business Week*, (September 12 and 19, 1953) cited in Lester Asheim, "What do Adults
Read?" *Adult Reading*, D. H. Clift *et al.*, (eds.), 55th Yearbook of the National Society for
the Study of Education, Chicago: University of Chicago Press, 1936.
[29]Asheim, *op. cit.*
[30]Gray and Munroe, *op. cit.*, p. 13.
[31]*Ibid.*, p. 264.

tie involved. However, sometimes individuals seem to read "in spite of their environment" or in order to escape from it. The authors point out that it might be revealing to analyze in this way cases of individuals who almost never read, but who seem to have superior environmental advantages.

Specific interests vary. Following the Gray and Munroe survey by two years, and devoting itself to the subject interests of readers, was Waples and Tyler's *What People Want to Read About.*[32] Although the former study did make the important distinction of indicating that different people read different parts of newspapers and different kinds of books or magazines, Waples and Tyler undertook to classify the content of reading interests in a more intensive manner. They compiled a wide and carefully categorized list of reading topics and presented this in questionnaire form to their various groups of respondents. Analysis of the findings showed that interest was greatest in reading about the "self," that is, in topics related to characteristics of the specific groups. Furthermore, interest in a topic such as "Personal Development" seemed to vary inversely with success in meeting the problems involved. Waples and Tyler found that reading interests could be differentiated by the following factors, in decreasing order of importance: sex, amount of education, occupation, size of community (rural-urban), age, geographic environment, and time spent in reading. There are studies that have indicated that those who read the most do not necessarily read the *best.*[33]

It was found that "biography" appealed to all groups, but that the subjects of biography vary with the same factors as reading in general. Some of the specific topics which were found to be of greatest general interest were "the next war," "labor and the labor market," and "developments in the automobile industry." Two topics of at least some interest to all groups were "international attitudes" and "personal hygiene." Among the major sex differences that were found, there was low feminine interest in business matters but high in topics related to personality, with a contrary trend for men. Some of these topics are dated but doubtless there are modern equivalents.

Accessibility influential. Waples followed up this fruitful survey with another important investigation whose purpose was to show the dif-

[32]D. Waples and R. Tyler, *What People Want to Read About;* American Library Association and University of Chicago Press, 1931.

[33]P. F. Lazarsfeld and R. Wyant, "Magazines in 90 Cities—Who Reads What," *Public Opinion Quarterly,* I, October 1937, and R. W. Tyler, "The Study of Adolescent Reading by the Progressive Education Association," in L. R. Wilson (Ed.) *Library Trends,* Chicago: University of Chicago Press, 1937, cited in D. Waples, B. Berelson and F. R. Bradshaw, *What Reading Does to People,* Chicago: University of Chicago Press, 1940.

ferences between stated subject interests and actual reading and to determine the factors operating in this relation, especially the controllable factors.[34] A checklist of subject interests was given to a sample of factory workers and college students, both men and women; the resulting data were then ranked according to their popularity. Actual reading of newspapers for a two-day period was recorded by the respondents on a special check list; magazine and book reading were recorded in diary form for a two-week period.

The findings with respect to the amount of reading support those of earlier research in that newspapers were most widely read by both sexes, but more by men; the reading of nonfiction books was negligible for factory workers; and the total nonfiction reading was more for men. Comparing next the areas of subject interest with actual reading, Waples found some real discrepancies and, from his data, was able to conclude that *accessibility*, rather than subject interest, was the major factor in determining actual reading. The data showed that of the 23 subjects most interesting to men, nine were not read about in magazines, books or newspapers, with similar figures for the women.

Although it might seem regrettable that such discrepancies were found between interests and actual reading, still the fact that they were due to the reader's acquiescence to what was put before him inclined Waples to see this as an encouraging picture insofar as accessibility is a "controllable" factor. However, Lester Asheim, writing almost 25 years later about Waples' findings, paints a rather gloomy picture of a sort of vicious circle,[35]

> Studies . . . have uncovered the interesting and rather disturbing fact that interest is less important as a factor in determining what a person will read than is accessibility. In other words unless the reader is very strongly motivated, he is likely to read what is there whether he is particularly interested or not . . . People tend to choose for reading what is at hand. The producers of printed media tend to publish more and more of the kinds of things that have been chosen by readers in the past. Which means that an apparent demand could be created for something which the producers have made available, rather than what readers would select if they had unrestricted choice.

Choice of titles important. There will be noted in the above the qualification, "unless the reader is very strongly motivated." Still an-

[34]D. Waples, "The Relation of Subject Interest to Actual Reading," *Library Quarterly*, II, January 1932.
[35]Asheim, *op. cit.*

other factor which may influence reading habits is that which Schramm identified as "index cues"—"Reading presents itself to our attention in the form of materials organized around index cues. These cues form our way of scanning the environment and may or may not accurately represent the content.[36] A study which illustrates the part played by this factor aimed to discover the influence of changed titles upon the sale of the popular and inexpensive series of "Little Blue Books" from one year to the next (1925-26 to 1926-27).[37] Examples of the original titles followed by its successor, with the sales for one year of each, follow:

The King Enjoys Himself	8,000	Pen, Pencil and Poison	5,000
The Lustful King Enjoys Himself	38,000	Story of a Notorious Criminal	15,500
Ten O'Clock	2,000	Patent Medicine and the Public Health	3,000
What Art Should Mean to You	9,000	The Truth About Patent Medicine	10,000

The conclusion drawn from these figures is that the highest interest, at least for Little Blue Books, is in sex and related topics, and next in various areas of self-improvement; the latter is interpreted by Professor Wayne Dennis as encouraging for adult educators. However this may be, the validity of the findings is lowered in the absence of any control groups, such as an equal number of copies printed again under the original title the second year, or an equal number of books with titles changed away from "sex" and "self-improvement" compared with those changed toward these areas.

"Index cues." Unfortunately, this study represents practically the only work on "index cues" in contexts other than that of commercial advertising. For the present, it is useful to consider Schramm's conceptualization of the field for purposes of research in reading, in which "index cues" are an important factor. In brief, Schramm is concerned with the question of "why adults read" and says that for the individual this question must be answered by studying the factors in the

[36]W. Schramm, "Why Adults Read," *Adult Reading*, D. H. Clift *et. al.*, (eds.) 55th Yearbook of the National Society for the Study of Education, 1956.
[37]Haldemann-Julius, *The First Hundred Million*, cited in Dennis, *op. cit.* The modern phenomenon of "paperbacks" with general physical, including economic, availability and wide popularity as judged by sales for many classical and nonfictional works, offers generous possibilities for further study of adult reading interests on a national scale, especially as related to the factor of index cues and their psychological availability.

"instant of decision" as to whether or not a given selection will be read. The factors, graphically, are as follows:

Content to → be read	Index cues →→	Decision ←	Personality ← Characteristics	Active Environment
(May be perceptually different for different readers.)	(May or may not accurately represent content and differ widely in availability over time and among individuals.)		(Chiefly relevant skills, motivations, values and intelligence.)	(Competition for attention, factors of comfort in reading, values and mores of society.) [38]

Schramm points out, "it is unrealistic to hope to be able to describe in detail the total situation . . . for each individual, so a model is necessary to structure the field and analyze information from it." This he calls the "fraction of selection— $\frac{\text{Expectation of reward (motivation)}}{\text{Effort required (accessibility-skill)}}$."
The "effort required" involves physical availability of reading materials, which must be studied according to patterns of distribution.[39] It also involves "psychological availability" on the part of the individuals to the extent that their predispositions permit their perception of materials that are physically available. Also to be considered in relation to availability for any one individual is his skill in reading. The converse of this is the "readability" of the book, a topic considered elsewhere in this report. These individual aspects of availability may be studied in relation to certain social characteristics as sex, age, education.

Reading motivations. Motivation also may vary according to social group variables, but determining the actual motivation of an individual is not so easily studied in an objective manner. People may read the same things for vastly different reasons, and conversely, with varying effects. Some of the problems of studying motivation have been discussed in a previous chapter. From the point of view of subject

[38]Schramm, *op. cit.*
[39]Waples *et al.*, *op. cit.*, describe patterns of distribution. They state in part, "Differences between actual and desired reading, then are traced to differences in accessibility to the desired publication; and differences in accessibility are traced to variations in the patterns of distribution. Hence we are obliged to find the causes of such variations. Variations may arise from the nature of the people involved or from the nature of the distributing agency. . . . The nature of the community accounts for the relative support given to the existing agencies and in part of the character of their holdings. The nature of the agencies explains the patterns of distribution which result from the objectives and practices of the particular agencies."

interests, when one has determined the major classification of motives that are at play in the reading of any group, he can then ask to what extent these motives are satisfied by reading in different interest areas, or conversely, which interest fields best satisfy the various motives. A study with this purpose used a questionnaire derived from 134 possible motives, compiled with the advice of more than 55 libraries, and measured against 13 subject interest fields.[40] The data from about 1,800 forms showed that the dominant motives do vary significantly by subject fields; "recreation" was found to be the highest motive for reading fiction and poetry, and was also high for essays, drama, and biography. "General information" was the highest motive for the fields of biography, travel, sociology and philosophy-religion. Other high motives were "job efficiency" and "school assignment."

The author found no relation between particular occupation and reading motives. Grouping the answers by sex, "general information" was found to be more important for men, and "recreation" more important for women. Among the motives, a significant difference was found between those that cut across various subject interest fields (e.g. "recreation" and "information") and those peculiar to one field only (such as "hobby" for reading in Fine Arts).[41] The author indicates that the motive, "To make up for lacks in your schooling" is important to adult education, but that in this study it showed hardly any importance for reading in the various subject interests.

INTERESTS AND PARTICIPATION

The study of adult interests for the purposes of understanding and predicting participation in programs involves much more than a simple one to one relationship between stated interest and participation, as has already been implied. First, there is the methodological problem of the validity in the construction of the tests used to measure interests. However, Professor Dennis' criticism that psychological tests "show what people will say but not what they will do," may be but further invitation to psychological study of such discrepancy as may exist. Dennis' formulation, "What are adult interests in order to know what they will participate in" must be refined to ask, "Will adults participate in the areas of their declared interests?"

It was shown above that, at least in the activity of reading, accessi-

[40]H. L. Butler, "An Inquiry into the Statement of Motives by Readers," *Library Quarterly*, X, January 1940.

[41]This is an urban study. For a detailed study of reading interests and motives among rural people, see P. M. Houser *et al.*, *Rural Reading Habits*, Bulletin A69, Agricultural Experiment Station, University of Maryland.

bility may be a more determining factor than subject interest. Other variables involved in the relation of stated interests to participation, are all the socio-economic and demographic factors discussed in the next chapter. There is also evidence that although the volume and general content of interests do not alter greatly with aging, nevertheless there is a trend away from more social interests to individualized ones. The implications of this last finding for education may be either positive or negative, depending largely on the methods and techniques of education involved. One wonders also whether the relatively new Golden Age clubs, one result of the recently developed interest in the aged, have checked, where successful, the trend toward individualized interests. Many of these clubs have educational activities. Research to date, however, has majored on the psychological and physiological aspects of aging. With the rapid increase in the number of persons over 65 years of age, a broadening of research concerned with this age group, both relative to adult education and the broader aspects of participation, is highly desirable.

Educational versus other types of participation. The primary research emphasis for adult educators concerns the bearing of interests on *educational* participation rather than on participation in general, although this distinction is difficult to make and invites further investigation in its own right. To what extent will a stated interest incline a person toward or away from educational activity as compared with noneducational participation in that field? In this connection there is the experience of a community education program built around stated interests which was conducted some years ago in the model village of Radburn, New Jersey. Radburn is particularly interesting because it had a highly selective population so that the socio-economic differences which might affect participation were kept at a minimum. The program was promoted as one of "popular discussion" with trained leaders, rather than "education." It was found that in every case the per cent of those who expressed interest and actually participated was lower than those who only expressed interest, although in some cases actual participation was higher than the per cent who expressed interest. It was suggested that precisely because of their previous interests, many people were not satisfied or stimulated by a program aimed at the general community, which often did not reach their own levels of knowledge in the respective fields.[42] The implied

[42]Robert Hudson, *Radburn: A Plan of Living,* New York: American Association for Adult Education, 1934. An identical result and interpretation emerged about the same time from an unpublished paper by a student of the senior author based on several hundred participants in The Home Economics Extension program of Kansas State College.

solution seems to indicate a more restrictive and graded program than is currently accepted for adult education purposes.

An alternative solution, which also imputes limited value to stated interests for community program-building, is suggested by Cyril Houle et al.[43] The authors found that programs built on interest inventories of individual men and women frequently were not as successful as those which studied patterns of values created by immediate social groups. To illustrate, they cite the case of a group of Army buddies who wanted to take courses together; their choice of particular courses was dependent on group values rather than individual interests. Thus community surveys, especially those which analyze existing social patterns and groupings, would seem more significant in program-building than are "interest finders."

Interests, needs and participation. A study whose purpose was to discover the "educational needs" and "educational interests" of adults by means of a questionnaire, gives promise of a new approach for disclosing the reasons for discrepancy between interests and educational participation.[44] However, the items "Suggested courses" and "Courses they would attend if offered" were used rather ambiguously as criteria for "needs" and "interests", respectively. The major interpretation the author made of his findings, though interesting, does not shed any real light on the question implied in the purpose and merely underlines the need for further research—i.e. he found the greatest need was for more information about existing programs, since a high proportion of suggested programs and those which people "would attend if offered" were being offered at the time.

The interrelation of interests and needs is most apparent when one is studying actual participation. A study which recognizes this fact was concerned primarily with testing a scientific method of adult counseling, that is, of discovering interests with a direct view to participation.[45] The theoretical framework for this study emphasized two aspects of the definition of interests, with a different indicator to measure each:

1. Fundamental tendency or drive, (need) which was measured by observation by trained observers of an individual's behavior in a group. It was found that most fundamental needs centered around

[43]C. Houle *et al.*, *The Armed Services and Adult Education*, Washington: American Council on Education, 1947.
[44]Perdue B. Graves, *An Investigation of Adult Education Needs and Interests in Topeka*, Ed. D. dissertation, University of Kansas, 1949.
[45]T. F. McFarland and D. E. Sonquist, "Interests as a Basis for a Program in Adult Education," *Religious Education*, 25, September 1930.

patterns of shyness and over-sensitivity with a smaller number around suspicion, depression and day-dreaming.

2. Activity or objective interests *which are a means of satisfying the former drives or needs,* measured by means of a check list of activities given to 439 incoming members to the YMCA.

In this well-designed study, the subjects were equated on 10 factors (age, education, former "Y" membership, etc.) so that the participation differences found were reflections of the counseling methods being tested. The methods were:

    a. trained secretarial counselor with free interview
    b. trained counselor with tests or measures for interests
    c. volunteer lay counselor with interview
    d. volunteer counselor with tests.

It was found that for eliciting interests the "trained counselor with tests," i.e. the most scientific method, was the most effective, with the others following in order of scientific elements, down to the finding that even the lay interview method was better than no system at all. Classes were formed on the basis of a file kept of the interests that were checked. An initial count showed an average of 62 per cent attending the activities they had checked; however, over time, the attendance of those who had no counseling dropped to 39 per cent, while those counseled went up to 73 per cent.

An evaluation of this multi-faceted research program showed that the reasons or motives for attendance varied, but in general they were limited and isolated, reflecting a "low level of expectancy" as to what the YMCA might offer the members in terms of their basic interests. This was in contrast to the ideals and goals expressed by administrators and was due, according to analysis, to the "activity-oriented" rather than "member-oriented" program before counseling. In the authors' words, "The process of raising the level of expectancy in a community [concerning what adult education programs have to offer as meaningful for individuals] must come by increasing the range and quality of the interests of members."

J. P. Leagans also points out the proper and limited place of interest-oriented programs, in another context and a more philosophic base:[46]

> . . . Extension people must recognize and meet the interests (expressed desire to learn, study or gain more information about some object in the environment which he believes will give him satisfaction) of farm people. They must use the known interests as "springboards" for developing further interests; for their responsibility is

[46]J. P. Leagans, *Educational Interests of Farm Operators in North Carolina as Related to Work of Agricultural Extension Service,* Ph.D. dissertation, University of Chicago, 1948.

not . . . merely to "serve" the people, because this is saying in reality
that the *actual* is the same as the *ideal*.

Fryer points out another limitation of "stated interest" tests in that
their validity is lowered when a person is asked whether he is interested in things he knows little or nothing about.[47] In certain vocational settings, Fryer indicates, orientation programs are used to raise
the validity of interest tests which are given later.

Potential interests versus stated interests. James and Montross re-
count their experience with a group of farmer and laborer couples
living in isolated rural conditions, who had organized a group and
then appealed to the University Extension for guidance in developing a program that would help them "better themselves." By interview and questionnaire, information was obtained about their formal
education, reading habits, travel, etc., all of which were rather limited.[48] An interest inventory was also given. It was found that "wild
life," "home decorating" and "world affairs" appeared in order of most
preference, with "fine arts," "public speaking" and the "problem of
communism" most rejected. There was little consensus, but the first
two preferences were clearly related to the group's daily experiences.
At a trial meeting four films were shown—two about wild life in Africa,
one about Eskimos (foreign peoples) and one about history. The
wild life films elicited but brief interest, but the Eskimo film led to
much discussion and a whole program was built around films and
discussion of the problems different foreign peoples have to face and
their solutions. The authors state, "Obviously, the group could not
have anticipated that the 'foreign peoples' subject would sustain its
interest since it had had little or no past experience upon which to
make such an assumption."

The issue may be re-stated as that of "stated interests" versus "potential interests." It seems related to the finding in the Radburn study
that people were already too familiar with their stated interests to desire to pursue them further in educational programs, at least at such
a general level that little or no interesting, new facts accrue.

Some suggestions for further research. The conclusion from these
difficulties should not be construed as an impasse precluding interest
research for program-planning, and leading to "trial-and-error" meth-

[47]Fryer, *op. cit.* E. May points out an implication of the fact that people know what they
are interested in only in terms of what is psychologically available to them. If one defines
interests operationally by "process of choice," then "Ignorance is a limitation on freedom of
choice." May, *Experiments in Methods in Adult Education,* Ed. D. dissertation, Teachers
College, Columbia University, 1937.

[48]B. J. James and H. W. Montross, "Focusing Group Goals," *Adult Education,* Winter
1956.

ods. One flaw in the latter approach is illustrated by the fact that the farmer group, above, did *not* become interested in the subject of history simply by being exposed to a film about it. Furthermore, it could be argued that while the extension of interests is an admirable aim in program-planning, this would have no effect unless there is initial participation which must be based somehow on existing interests. A possible solution is represented by those interest inventories which elicit "rejections" and thus provide one way of arriving at an area of delimited but still flexible interests. Future research suggests itself in the form of studies which would assess the possibilities of eliciting interest in "rejected" subjects,[49] both for initial participation and later program-building, by using various index cues, methods of teaching the material, and various presentations of the material in contexts of student motivations.

Approaching the problem of determining potential interests from the basis of stated preferences, research might proceed along the lines of the factor analysis method of determining "interest clusters," in which one interest might be inferred from another on an empirical basis. Is there such a thing as a "compatibility-incompatibility" continuum of interests, so that the existence of certain stated interests precludes or hinders in varying degrees the acquisition of other interests, and if so, what are the components of such a continuum? Related to this, is there any "heirarchy" of interests, along which the acquisition of certain ones would be necessarily basic to others?[50]

Especially useful for an understanding of adult educational participation would be a functional study of interrelationships between individual interests and needs, the external opportunities for pursuing these interests, and the pressures in the social environment to take advantage of the opportunities. This research could be done in terms of differing educational levels of adults.

INTERESTS AND LEARNING

The previous section has indicated the importance of the possibility of learning interests for the purpose of stimulating educational participation. But, even assuming that the quality of programs participated in is high, what is the value for the individual of participation

---

[49]Thorndike's studies, mentioned above, indicate that simple repetition and even learning *per se* will not consistently alter interests in a positive or negative direction. What other variables besides simple "familiarity" and "acquisition of information" are involved in the variations in interests that do occur, and can these be used to effect a positive interest from a former rejection?

[50]See Waples, *et al., What Reading Does to People,* for similar suggestions about further study of readers' "predispositions," pp. 89 ff.

per se? With reference to reading for example, the question of ultimate importance was not simply what is read, but what is the relationship of reading interests to the *effects* of reading. With respect to
program participation, this aspect emphasizes the learning that may
or may not result. What is the influence of interest in a subject on
the learning of it?

It is generally accepted that interests are positively correlated with
learning—that as a result of an interest one will learn well or more
efficiently and that by learning more about a subject, one will become
interested. These statements invite investigation. It is clear that
variations in ability play a part in variations in learning, and the
question becomes one of analyzing the relation of interest to ability,
assuming that the two can be distinguished objectively and studied.
The theoretical value of such attempts for throwing light on the personality structure is apparent. The more immediately practical purpose is to determine to what extent adult education guidance workers
can predict a potential participant's ability in a field from a knowledge
of his interests.

Interests and ability. The difficulties of studying the relation of interest to ability, as well as the state of current knowledge on this problem, may become clear by examining a series of studies which seek to
extend and refine each other's methods. This series was triggered by
Thorndike's early attempts in the study of interests, and particularly
by his research in 1919 reporting the high correlation of +.89 between
interests and abilities as based on self-estimates.

Bridges and Dollinger, a little skeptical of this figure, followed in
1920 by using "more objective tests of ability" than self-estimates.[51]
Students at the beginning of the semester ranked their interest in their
present courses, regardless of marks, and then estimated their ability.
At the end of the term marks were obtained and the following positive
correlations were computed: .60 between estimated ability and interest; .25 between interest and grade rank; .28 between estimated ability
and grade rank. The authors' conclusions are : (1) Interest and *estimated* ability are related because the subjective perception of one
determines perception of the other, and (2) Neither interests nor estimated ability is a good indicator of *true* ability, or actual marks.

Thorndike countered that both "grades" and the use of "present
courses" were subject to too many chance factors affecting self-ratings
of ability and interest respectively; he felt that *rank order* of grades

[51]J. W. Bridges and V. M. Dollinger, "The Correlation Between Interests and Abilities in
College Courses," *Psychological Review*, 27, July 1920.

compared to *rank order* of interests, based on general interest in sub-jects over several years, were more reliable indicators.[52]

In 1927 Fryer took up this problem, and by re-examining and modifying Thorndike's method, secured much lower correlations.[53] He felt that interest and estimated ability ranks influenced each other when obtained on the same day, and that suggested subject headings for interests forced higher correlations. By correcting these points and obtaining grades, which though not perfectly objective indicators of ability are more so than self-estimates, Fryer found that the correlation between rank interest and estimated ability ranged from $+.50$ to $+.70$; that the predictive value of interests for grades was only 5 per cent better than chance; of estimated ability for grades was 8-14 per cent better than chance; and that both were lower in certain guidance situations where courses have not been encountered at all.[54]

The foregoing studies have all emerged from college credit situations which do not provide a direct parallel to the adult education program; they have been used because of the lack of comparable research in adult education. Two reasons may be suggested for this deficiency: (1) The general lack of measures of ability given, or even sanctioned, in certain traditional adult education programs; (2) The lack of "perfect" control groups for this research, since the noncredit adult program by its nature supposedly contains only persons interested in the subjects they are taking. These conditions, however, need not remain forbidding to those who realize the potential value of research into the relation of interests and abilities in the field of adult education. With respect first to point 2, it seems clear that while a control group of people who have no interest in the subjects may not be available, still there are sufficiently varying degrees of interest that comparison should be possible between the extremes. The absence of tests of ability also need not be a continuing obstacle; the value of introducing such tests lies beyond the immediate research purpose here recommended, as is pointed out in the chapter on Evaluation.

A more serious problem in studying the relation of interests and abilities in adults lies in the evidence that over time, interests may be

[52]E. L. Thorndike, "The Correlation Between Interests and Abilities in College Courses," *Psychological Review*, September 1921.

[53]D. Fryer, "Interest and Ability in Educational Guidance," *Journal of Educational Research*, 16, June 1927.

[54]T. A. Langlie studied the stated interests of first-year college students, comparing interests based on high school experience with "anticipatory" interests as each was related to the actual highest and lowest grade ranks at the end of the new courses. He found that the relation of "dislikes" based on high school experience to the lowest actual grade ranks was the most reliable; the least reliable, though positive, relation was between anticipated interests and best marks. Langlie, "Interests and Scholastic Proficiency," *Personnel Journal*, October 1930.

conditioned by existing and developed abilities and psychological rewards that have become attached to the latter. To the extent that this is true, adults may be subconsciously inclined to restrict their interests in terms of their expectations of possible failure in untried areas of ability, resulting from unhappy experiences in earlier, more competitive educational or social situations. Certainly these fairly well established influences suggest the need for intensive research into the possibilities of isolating adult interests and abilities in planning for future educational endeavors. One area of study might be to reverse the usual emphasis—that is, to determine the extent to which potential or possible interests might be predicted from inventories or established tests of abilities. It is possible that more could be · learned about adult interests if enrollments in adult education activities were studied in a number of communities and related to the age and sex of the participants, holding educational and socio-economic statuses constant. The hypothesis here is that if a sufficiently large body of data showed consistent patterns by age groups, knowledge as to the influence of age on interests might be enhanced to the advantage of program building.

As indicated, there also seems to be a need for further examination of the relation of interests and adult learning apart from ability. Holding constant the ability of any one person in a particular field, will his interest change, and in what direction, as he gains knowledge of the subject material? Is learning a true index of interest, and if so, is the converse equally true? Thorndike's work represents some tentative excursions into these problems.[55] Generally, his studies showed that neutral feelings will crystallize either positively or negatively with increased awareness about a subject, but that other changes cannot be predicted. He concludes that more depends on the nature of the subject and the new learning in relation to the individual, than on the simple fact of greater understanding. In the context of attitude theory and research discussed in the previous chapter, adult educators should pursue this finding and similar questions in terms of *functional* analysis of affective orientations to new cognitive learning experienced by different groups of adult students.

In summary—The body of research considered above represents a wide and varied field with many divergent emphases. However, all of the studies are subject to the basic theoretical considerations indicated at the outset—especially important is the extent to which subjective phenomena may be objectively measured and studied. Although

[55] E. L. Thorndike, *Adult Interests*, New York: Macmillan, 1935.

this generic problem may not be finally solved merely by clear definition of the concept and methods, certainly this is the most realistic way of first tackling it. Except where noted, the studies above have contributed to refinements both in the definition and measurement of interests. In this way they have arrived at generalizations that at best will be useful for the purposes of adult education both in program-planning and individual counseling, and at least are available for further testing and qualification.

It is important to keep in mind as an "over-all" generalization that none of the findings clearly justifies a cause-and-effect interpretation. Interests are always related to "interest objects," i.e. aspects of the environment; as such their meaning is culturally endowed and may vary with cultural change. The cultural context of adult education is, of course, fairly well-defined, and can be specified for any particular research program, but the process of adult education itself may, and indeed seeks to, alter its own cultural context. In this broader frame interests are a key factor, but their cumulative effect may be most practically worked with by emphasis on the understanding of each individual's interests in relation to his own personality and social setting.

PARTICIPANTS AND PARTICIPATION
IN ADULT EDUCATION*

The voluntary nature of adult education has made participation a major problem. From the inception of the movement the failure of many of those for whom programs were intended to take advantage of the opportunities provided has been a source of frustration for advocates of adult education.

Agencies and institutions have approached participation in a number of ways:

1. Extension of educational opportunities on a "take it or leave it" basis has characterized remedial programs and continuation schools nearly everywhere. This approach is also dominant in efforts to provide liberal education for adults who would submit to systematic study, as exemplified by the British tutorial class. In America the liberal tradition, modified to accommodate the conditions of adult life, is reflected in some university and evening college offerings and in "packaged" discussion programs.

2. A major approach assumes that adults will participate in programs and activities in which they have expressed a definite interest. It has found greatest expression in noncredit public school and community college programs and in the programs of private agencies.

*The first draft of this chapter was prepared by John S. Newberry, Jr.

3. Residential adult education, a recent adaptation of the Folk School movement, represents a wedding of the "interest" and "liberal" approaches. It seeks to utilize interests and experience as a means of integrating life and knowledge.

4. Particularly since World War II adult educators have stressed community action through citizen participation. In this approach participation in the community provides first-hand experience in the practice of democracy. Adult education then becomes inextricably linked to social participation.

This chapter first presents a description of the participants in formally organized adult education so far as available data permit and then reviews some findings of research relating to social participation which have implications for adult education.

The many agencies engaged in adult education, the diversity of their programs and of their clientele, and the episodic nature of adult participation make difficult even a rough description of "who participates." The problem is further complicated by the lack of any consistent policy of record keeping among the many agencies and institutions in the field.

Research approaches to participation in adult education. Two basic approaches have been used in studies of participation in adult education: (1) study of the characteristics of participants in particular institutions or types of institutional programs, and (2) sampling of a population or area to determine differences between participants and nonparticipants in various types of adult education. Each approach has been employed at several different levels.

Most of these studies are purely descriptive. They are of use to the agencies responsible for them but the great variety of situations considered and the differences in methods employed make generalization difficult. It is possible, however, to classify them under seven categories.

1. Studies of participants in a particular institutional program in a single community serve to supplement and corroborate trends identified in broader approaches. These are based upon total enrollments or upon more detailed study of samples.[1] This last approach has been

[1]L. Henderson, *The Magic City Teaches its Adults: Miami, Florida,* Miami: Lindsey Hopkins Vocation School, 1956; Studies using samples: L. K. McLaughlin, *Student Population in University of California Extension Classes,* Ed. D. dissertation, University of California, Los Angeles, 1951; J. R. Morton, *University Extension in the United States, A Study by the National University Extension Association,* Birmingham: University of Alabama Press, 1953; J. R. Nicklin, *Characteristics of Students Enrolled in Credit Courses in Television Offered by the University of California Extension, Southern Area,* Ed. D. dissertation, University of California, Los Angeles, 1955.

used frequently by the Agricultural Extension Service. The Extension Service studies do not differentiate participants as between those interested in vocational activities and others.[2] Use of institutional records permits the study of trends over a period of years but apart from statistical compilations little research in trends has been done.

2. Comparative study of students in particular programs which serve to identify constellations of related characteristics which differentiate participants in various programs.[3]

3. Community studies based upon a sampling to show the extent to which particular programs reach various segments of the population have the particular advantage of demonstrating the overlap of clientele among the various agencies.[4]

4. Studies comparing participation in adult education in corresponding samples drawn from selected communities, though made, have so far failed to isolate community factors related to the differences in participation found, because of inadequate research design.[5]

5. State-wide studies of adult participants in particular institutions or programs either based upon questionnaire returns or interviews[6] provide a fairly comprehensive picture of the population reached in particular states.

6. National studies of a single institutional type, agency or program include those: (a) based upon a questionnaire sent directly to participants,[7] (b) where the local institution actually conducts the studies,[8] and (c) these combining a variety of primary and secondary sources.[9] National reports of Extension Service activities and compilations of

---

[2]Persons interested in these surveys should secure copies of the annual reviews of all federal and state university research in this area which have been issued by the Extension Service, United States Department of Agriculture, Washington 25, D.C.

[3]S. R. Deane, *A Psychological Description of Adults Who Have Participated in Selected Activities*, Ph. D. dissertation, University of Maryland, 1949.

[4]A. A. Kaplan, *Socio-Economic Circumstances and Adult Participation in Certain Cultural and Educational Activities*, Contributions to Education No. 889, New York: Teachers College, Columbia University, 1943.

[5]L. E. Tomlinson, *Parental Participation in Selected Forms of Adult Education in Relation to Population Factors*, Ed. D. dissertation, University of Oregon, 1948.

[6]J. L. Davies, *A Study of Participant Interest and Ability in Adult General Education Programs in Iowa*, Ed. D. dissertation, Iowa State University, 1949.

[7]Great Books Foundations, *Great Books Under Discussion, A Report of the Programs in 1953*, Chicago: the Foundation, 1954; Morton, *op. cit.*

[8]H. Allison and H. Kempfer, *Private Home Study in the United States, A Statistical Study*, Washington, D.C., National Home Study Council, 1956; National Education Association, Division of Adult Education Service, *A Study of Urban Public School Adult Education Programs of the United States*, Washington, D.C.: the Association, 1952.

[9]E. B. Olds, *Financing Adult Education in America's Public Schools and Community Councils*, Commission on Adult Education Finance: Washington, D.C.: Adult Education Association, 1954; C. P. Loomis, *Rural Social Systems and Adult Education*, East Lansing: Michigan State College Press, 1953, Chapters 2, 3, 8, 10.

data from local and state studies by the USDA Extension Service provide fairly comprehensive information on some characteristics of users of the Extension Service.

7. The study of the distribution of participation in adult education on a nationwide scale was first attempted officially in a sample survey made in October, 1957 by the Bureau of the Census in collaboration with the United States Office of Education. The study included only participation in group or class type activities, omitting correspondence study, mass media, and individualized study. The results appear to vary considerably from those of a Gallup poll a decade earlier, probably because of differences in definition.[10]

SOME CHARACTERISTICS OF PARTICIPANTS IN PARTICULAR INSTITUTIONS, AGENCIES AND PROGRAMS OF ADULT EDUCATION

An examination of the results of the many surveys of participation suggests that however inclusive its goals, each organization enlists those individuals who are attracted by its program, and its clientele. It might almost be said that each program attracts those it was foreordained to attract. Thus questions of attitudes, interests and motivation discussed in chapters three to five, inclusive, of this report, are at once seen to relate to participation. This is illustrated by the contrasting experience of the public school and certain other agencies. The school tends to enroll a larger proportion of young adults and a considerably smaller proportion of persons over 50 years of age than are represented in the population served.[11] The Extension Service, on the other hand, reaches adults under 30 least effectively.

The explanation of this is not far to seek. The continuation program in urban schools and adult vocational agricultural courses in rural areas naturally attract, and indeed, are intended for young adults.[12] The Great Books program, as a contrasting case, draws predominantly from the middle-aged and the attrition rate is higher among the younger persons who enlist in this program.[13]

Educational status influences participation. In general, the Exten-

---

[10]Preliminary findings of the survey are reported in a recent article by John B. Holden. The survey sample comprised 35,000 households in 330 sample areas selected so as to be representative of the nation as a whole. The study covered organized educational activities in which the individual had participated three or more times within the previous year. Each individual was recorded only once, thus eliminating "overlap." Holden, "A Survey of Participation in Adult Education Classes," *Adult Leadership*, April 1958. The Gallup Poll was reported in the *Adult Education Journal*, April 1945.

[11]National Education Association, *op. cit.*

[12]Henderson, *op. cit.;* Deane, *op. cit.;* Davies, *op. cit.*

[13]Great Books Foundation, *op. cit.*

sion Service reaches proportionately more people with high school and some college education than those with either more or less education. Functionally illiterate people are least effectively served. Moreover, as the amount of education increased the percentage of farmers availing themselves of more than one medium of Extension instruction, such as attending meetings, reading bulletins, listening to broadcasts, increased sharply.[14]

Public school clientele. Public schools on the other hand serve a significantly larger per cent of those with less than a high school education than do other urban programs. Doubtless one reason for this is the considerable number of younger persons who left school before finishing but who now find high school graduation a prerequisite for many types of jobs and hence return to finish.[15] An examination of the records of a number of school programs suggests that persons with high school graduation or more, enrolled in public school adult education classes, are primarily interested in hobbies, cultural subjects, and civic and public affairs forums. As would be expected, those using university extension services have an above average amount of education. Only five per cent had not completed high school. Almost two-fifths were candidates for the bachelor's degree. Junior college adult education appears to attract persons of educational and economic status midway between those reached by public schools and university extension.[16]

Socio-economic status and participation. Socio-economic status is another determinant of participation in adult education programs. As early as 1936 M. C. Wilson, in a summary of studies in 32 states, determined that the Extension Service reached farm owner families proportionately four and five percentage points better than farm tenant families; families on large farms, variously defined, 11 per cent better than those on small; and persons with a high school education or more, 10 per cent better than those with less. Extension appears still to serve middle status groups more effectively than those of lower status but there is considerable local variation. Studies comparing "disadvantaged" areas with those having high economic resources indicate that the proportion of population reached by Extension is

[14]M. C. Wilson, *How and to What Extent is the Extension Service Reaching Low Income Families?* Circular 376, Washington, D.C.: Federal Extension Service, 1941; C. P. Marsh and A. L. Coleman, *Communication and the Adoption of Recommended Farm Practices,* Lexington: University of Kentucky Agricultural Experiment Station, 1954.

[15]Henderson, *op. cit.*

[16]G. Myrdal, *An American Dilemma,* New York: Harper and Bros., 1944; H. Sorenson, *Adult Abilities,* Minneapolis: University of Minnesota Press, 1938; National Education Association, *op. cit.*

as great in disadvantaged areas as elsewhere. It is least successful with agricultural laborers, especially immigrant laborers and their families.[17]

The general success of the flexible pattern of organization adopted by the Cooperative Extension Service is illustrated by the lack of any marked regional differences in reaching rural people. The national coverage is unquestionably more complete than that of any other agency or institutional type in the field of adult education. Although the proportion of poorly educated and low status persons served is less than that of better educated and higher status groups, the success of Extension with "underprivileged" groups compares favorably with that of any other organized form of adult education. Because of the size of the program there is no question that many more people of low status and little education are reached by Extension than by any other single agency.

Institutions are selective of clientele. Adult participants in the public school programs tend to come from middle and lower middle status groups in urban areas to a greater extent than do participants in other formal adult educational programs. This is in sharp contrast to participants in university extension activities, only one in five of whom reported incomes of less than $3,000 and more than three-fourths of whom held full-time jobs.[18]

Few programs of voluntary agencies have been carefully studied even in terms of a careful description of the clientele and its participation. Two exceptions to this statement are the nationwide study of its participants by the Great Books Foundation and the intensive study of 2,000 participants in the Los Angeles metropolitan area discussion group program, described in Chapter 10.[19] Both of these programs drew heavily from the better-educated segment of the population with above average incomes. Compared to other formal adult education programs, they are most selective with respect to education, economic status and occupation.

[17]H. F. Lionberger, *Information-seeking Habits and Characteristics of Farm Operators,* Research Bulletin 581, Columbia: University of Missouri Agricultural Experiment Station, 1955; Wilson, *How and to what Extent . . . op. cit.;* M. C. Wilson and G. Gallup, *Extension Training Methods and Other Factors That Influence the Acceptance of Agricultural and Home Economics Practices,* Circular 495, Washington, D. C.: Federal Extension Service, 1955; L. Scantland, C. A. Svinth, and M. Taves, *A Square Look at Extension Work in Spokane County, Washington,* Extension Bulletin 463, Pullman: State College of Washington, 1952.

[18]Olds, *op. cit.;* Henderson, *op. cit.;* McLaughlin, *op. cit.;* Myrdal, *op. cit.*

[19]A. Kaplan, *A Study of the Liberal Arts Discussion Program for Adults in the Metropolitan Los Angeles Area,* White Plains, New York: The Fund for Adult Education, 1958, dittoed.

The data thus far presented establish the fact that some agencies are selective of their participants, and that there is also considerable diversity among the participants in adult education. An examination of the descriptive studies of library users, enrollees in correspondence study and viewers of telecast courses sponsored by university extension divisions, which have pioneered in this area, reinforce these impressions.[20] There are no studies of participation in the educational programs sponsored by churches, organized labor and business and industry.[21] However, on the basis of the research reviewed for this chapter and of the preliminary findings of the trial census of adult education, some tentative conclusions can be advanced as to the extent and intensity of participation in formal programs of adult education in the United States.[22]

SOME GENERALIZATIONS WITH RESPECT TO PARTICIPATION

Participants in formal adult education constitute a distinct minority of the total adult population. The census study estimated the total number of participants at 8,270,000 or 7.8 per cent of the out-of-school population above the age of 14.

Vocational classes popular. Vocational classes are clearly the most popular among those reached by the census. They enlisted 35.3 per cent of those participating in adult education. "General education" was second with 13.9 per cent, closely followed by classes in civic and public affairs, 12.9 per cent, and home and family life with 12 per cent. Recreational skills attracted 11.1 per cent. Just under 2 per cent

[20]B. Berelson, *The Library's Public,* New York: Columbia University Press, 1949; A. Campbell and C. A. Metzner, *Public Use of the Library and Other Sources of Information,* Institute for Social Research, Ann Arbor: University of Michigan, 1950; Allison and Kempfer, *op. cit.;* C. R. Hughes, *The Influence of Some Selected Factors upon Completion of Correspondence Study,* Ed. D. dissertation, University of Florida, 1955; Micklin *op. cit.*

[21]Adult education under the last-named auspices is perhaps the most rapidly developing area in the whole field and the one about which least is known. Over four-fifths of about 350 industries studied by Clark and Sloan were conducting formal adult education programs. One corporation offers 1,000 separate courses in which 6,500 students are enrolled. The annual budget is $45,000,000. By no means all of these courses are vocational, even when that term is broadly interpreted. Clark and Sloan's study is the first inquiry into this field. Cf. H. F. Clark and H. S. Sloan, *Classrooms in the Factories, An Account of Education Conducted by American Industry,* New York: New York University Press, 1958.

[22]The word tentative is ascribed to these conclusions for several reasons. One is the lack of research in the areas just noted. A second is the discrepancy between the results of the trial census and the Gallup poll of over a decade earlier, doubtless due to differences in definition. A third is the fact that by definition the census excluded many types of adult education, as for instance the activities of the Extension Service, about which, fortunately, a large amount of data exist. It included only class and formal group programs and activities of a primarily educational nature, and individuals were represented as participating in only one activity. For source of census data reported by Holden in following paragraphs see footnote 10.

were in Americanization classes and the rest, 12.9 per cent, in all other types.

"Liberal" courses appeal to special groups. There is some evidence that a relatively larger proportions of women, older adults, better educated persons, and professional personnel participate in so-called "liberal" subject areas—especially in activities which do not carry "credit." Proportionately more men (and to a somewhat lesser extent, employed women), younger adults, and those in technical, skilled, semiskilled and unskilled occupations are enrolled in vocational courses or in credit courses taken with dominantly vocational motives.

Distribution of participants varies by characteristics and agencies. The participants are drawn in disproportionate numbers from certain segments of the population:

(a) The proportion of participants relative to population increases steadily with education. Holden reports that only 1.4 per cent of the functionally illiterate were participants, but that 25.5 per cent of those with "more than four years of college" were enrolled. Amount of formal schooling appears to be the most significant determinant of participation in all forms of adult education which have been studied. Educational level is highest in university extension and Great Books programs. Cooperative extension and the public schools reach relatively larger groups of the less well-educated.

(b) Occupation also appears to be highly related to participation in adult education. Holden reports that the professional-technical group of employed persons constitute 25 per cent of the participants and only 8 per cent of the nonparticipants. Clerical and sales workers, a larger proportion of the population, account for about the same number, 24 per cent, of participants.

University and Great Books programs draw a higher proportion of professional and technical personnel than do other programs. The degree of participation by occupation appears to be directly related to the educational requirement of the occupation. Laborers, for example, represent only four per cent of the participants but 10 per cent of the nonparticipants in the labor force. Correspondence courses and public school programs generally include a broad range of occupational groups.

(c) Economic status or income is also significantly related to participation in formal adult education, although it appears that much of this relationship may be attributed to the related factors of education and occupation.

(d) Participation in adult education decreases with age. Holden reports that 13.6 per cent of those between 14 and 19 are participants,

32 per cent of these are enrolled in public school adult classes and 30 per cent in private trade and business schools. The largest number of participants for any 15 year span are in the 30 to 44 age group. Although only 2.8 per cent of the population 60 to 74 participate, there are over half a million participants over 60 years of age. Much of this decline in participation with age may be attributed to factors other than physiological age; notably education and decline of occupational interest.

Of the programs reviewed, Cooperative Extension and the Great Books serve proportionately more persons over 45. Correspondence and university programs (other than television courses) reach comparatively few older persons.

(e) The census survey found a regional difference in the ratio of participants to nonparticipants: in the West, the ratio was 14 to 100, as compared to 8 to 100 in all other regions.

Much of the inequality of participation by region and by state in particular programs may be attributed to differences in the financial support provided at the state level for institutional programs such as the junior college, the public school and the public library. When funds have been provided, people participate in large numbers and relatively more of the groups not otherwise effectively reached become participants.

There are marked differences between rural and urban areas in patterns of participation in formal adult education. The Cooperative Extension Service is unquestionably the major institution for adult education in rural areas. Public school, university, library and package discussion programs are dominantly, though not exclusively, urban.

Accessibility promotes participation. There is some evidence that accessibility and proximity to centers for adult education increases participation. This was quite evident in the Springfield, Massachusetts, study and has been noted in a number of Extension and library surveys. Associated with this finding is that by Houle which indicated that in the armed services the more persons knew about the availability of adult education programs, the greater was the amount of participation. Basically, however, both retention and recruitment rested on the excellence of the program.[23]

An active minority participates in several forms of adult education and utilizes many of the services of particular institutions. This minority is drawn largely, as one would expect, from those groups from which come disproportionate numbers of the participants.

[23]Kaplan, *op cit.;* C. Houle and others, *The Armed Services and Adult Education,* Washington: American Council on Education, 1947.

Participants in adult education are drawn from those groups which are exposed to a number of media for the diffusion of knowledge. They are more apt to be active users of the library, of museums, and the media of mass communication. Even more significantly, they are more apt than nonparticipants to be discriminating users of these media. Participants come largely from those groups which are active in formal associations.[24]

Characteristics of nonparticipants. Those who are not being reached by adult education, then, are also less effectively reached by other means of disseminating knowledge. As this group includes a disproportionate number of those who enter adult life without adequate educational preparation, a challenge is presented to adult educators to find means of reaching a group which represents a continuing drain upon the resources of society.

Those who have less than an eighth grade education, over 55 years of age, laborers and service workers, and those with low economic status and subsistence level of living are likely to participate less in adult education. Negroes and certain nationality ethnic groups participate less than do white and native stock.

The data presented above indicate among other things that socioeconomic factors play a part in influencing participation in adult education, and that participants are also active in other social organizations and activities. Thus a representative study of participants in general adult education programs in Iowa reported that almost two-thirds were members of three or more community organizations and seven in ten had been officers in at least one.[25] It is therefore a tenable hypothesis that the findings of social scientists, especially of sociologists, with respect to social participation and its attributes hold significance for adult educators.

SOCIAL PARTICIPATION

Because of the paucity and limited scope of research on participation in adult education, and on the assumption that broader studies of social participation will have applicability, the discussion turns to an examination of some of this research. Interesting parallels will be seen.

To the adult educator the various forms of social participation have several significant connotations. They should be regarded as: (1) actual or potential means of educating the participants, (2) channels

---

[24]Kaplan, *Socio-Economic Circumstances* . . .; Lionberger, *op. cit.;* Campbell and Metzner, *op cit.*
[25]Davies, *op. cit.*

of communication through which the adult population of the community may be reached and around which programs of adult education may be organized, (3) possible competition for organized programs of adult education, and (4) as legitimate and major objectives of adult education. In a democracy the dissemination of the skills and knowledge requisite for effective social participation must be a primary concern of all educative agencies.

Concepts, definition, and classification. Social participation has been variously defined, usually in purely operational terms. Participation, in effect, is defined by the particular aspect of behavior studied and the particular items used as criteria of participation.

For the purpose of this report, social participation is defined as interaction with others in a socially defined relationship wherein the roles of those participating are more or less structured and mutually understood. The relationship must involve some exchange or transmittal, although direct personal contact is not always required. Social participation also implies some degree of purposive effort and ego-involvement on the part of the participant. Casual contact and routine "transactions" are, therefore, excluded, as is interaction in the course of gainful employment.

Participation may be classified according to the nature of the social relationship (formal, informal), the kind of organization or group (church, formal associations), and the type of activity (attendance, reading, visiting.) [26]

The extent of social participation. Church membership and participation in religious organizations are generally the most widely reported forms of contact with formal organizations[27] in all popula-

[26]Students of participation differ in the way in which they classify particular activities. O. D. Duncan and J. W. Artis, for example, classify certain activities *semi-formal* participation which Brown or Anderson classify as *informal*. Cf. Duncan and Artis, *Social Stratification in a Pennsylvania Rural Community*, Bulletin 543, State College: Pennsylvania State College Agricultural Experiment Station, 1951; E. J. Brown, *Elements Associated with Activity and Inactivity in Rural Organizations*, Bulletin 574, University Park: Pennsylvania State University Agricultural Experiment Station, 1953; W. A. Anderson and H. E. Smith, "Formal and Informal Participation in a New York Village," mimeographed Bulletin 28, Ithaca, New York: Cornell University Agricultural Experiment Station, 1952.

[27]W. A. Anderson, *Social Participation of Rural Nonfarm Adults*, Ithaca: Cornell University Agricultural Experiment Station, Bulletin 928, 1958; M. Axelrod, *A Study of Formal and Informal Group Participation in a Large Urban Community*, Ph.D. dissertation, University of Michigan, 1954; J. Hostetter and W. G. Mather, "Participation in the Rural Church," Paper no. 1762, Journal Series, State College, Pennsylvania, Agricultural Experiment Station, 1952; H. F. Kaufman, *Participation in Organized Activities in Selected Kentucky Localities*, Bulletin 528, Lexington: University of Kentucky Agricultural Experiment Station, 1949; R. Payne, *Organizational Activities of Rural Negroes in Mississippi*, Circular 192, State College: Mississippi State College Agricultural Experiment Station, 1953.

tions which have been studied—with the possible exception of urban men. In no population studied have churches involved all adults. There is always a fraction of the population varying from small to substantial, without any contact with the church. According to the annual compilations of the National Council of Churches this fraction is growing less.

Participation in formal associations has been widely and intensively studied in many parts of this country and in communities of all sizes and types. Because of the comprehensiveness of data available and because formal associations have considerable significance for adult education, they will receive major consideration.

A substantial portion of every population studied had no contact whatever with any formal association. The per cent of nonparticipants varies considerably within and between areas studied. Anderson's recent study found little difference between farm and rural nonfarm adult participation. About one person in eight had a zero score on the Chapin Social Participation Scale. Between one-fifth and one-fourth appears to be closer to a modal average. In some situations the proportion runs close to twice as high. Participation involving more than nominal contact with formal associations tends to be even more restricted. Within particular associations the number of those who attend regularly, serve actively, and take more than passing interest in the affairs of those association constitutes a decided minority of the membership.[28]

The studies demonstrate quite conclusively that the popular notion of America as a "nation of joiners" is patently untrue. The "joiners", in reality, constitute a minority of the population. Adult educators cannot assume therefore, that formal associations accurately represent all of the community. There remains a substantial segment of the population which, if it is to be reached, must be approached by other means.

A distinct type of formal participation includes those activities of corporate associations in which participants serve without the usual prerogatives of membership. Volunteer service is a characteristic form of participation in institutionalized health and welfare agencies. Also included are such quasi-governmental activities as Civil Defense.

[28]Axelrod, op. cit.; R. Payne and H. A. Kaufman, Organizational Activities of Rural People in Mississippi, Circular 189, State College: Mississippi Agricultural Experiment Station, 1953; Anderson, Social Participation of Rural Nonfarm Adults; A. Rose, Union Solidarity, Minneapolis: University of Minnesota Press, 1952; R. M. Dimit, A. T. Wink and M. E. John, Factors Associated with the Success of Pennsylvania Granges, Bulletin 566, Pennsylvania State College, Agricultural Experiment Station, 1952; G. M. Beal, "Additional Hypotheses in Participation Research," Rural Sociology, XXI, September-December, 1956.

David L. Sills' study of the volunteers who served in the local activities and organizations of the National Infantile Paralysis Foundation represents the only definitive study of this type of participation. Sills demonstrates that in this organization, at least, the volunteers are drawn very largely from the "middle class." They were also active in other organizations—"seven out of ten belong to at least three organizations."[29]

Semi-formal participation is another category which includes attendance at activities and programs where participation does not imply more than temporary association with the sponsoring organization—fairs, theatricals, concerts, spectator events, and the like. Duncan and Artis found that this form of participation was somewhat more widespread than formal participation but less frequently reported than informal activities in a Central Pennsylvania community.[30]

It would seem that activities of this sort are at least potentially educational, and in view of the audience they appear to serve, may provide some fairly stiff competition for formally organized adult education programs. Many adult education activities of the "one-shot" variety—institutes, public lectures, forums and the like—resemble the types of activities here called semi-formal. Further research is needed in this area but is made difficult by the extremely short time span and the lack of continuing contact inherent in such semi-formal events.

Informal participation. Various forms of informal participation have been studied including: (a) participation with immediate family, (b) with extended family or kin group, (c) in the immediate neighborhood, (d) participation in cliques (autonomous groups) or with "friends," and (e) participation with fellow workers away from work. Despite some serious methodological limitations and incomplete coverage, research in informal social participation indicates quite conclusively that it is more widespread than other forms of participant activity. Among certain marginal groups informal participation represents virtually the only form of meaningful interpersonal contact. Even in urban areas of very low socio-economic level there appear to

[29] D. L. Sills, *The Volunteers: Means and Ends in a National Organization*, Glencoe, Ill. The Free Press, 1957.

[30] Semi-formal participation showed moderate correlation with socio-economic factors and status indexes, Duncan and Artis, *op. cit.* This finding is supported at least indirectly by other studies, although the data are not exactly comparable, W. A. Anderson, *Fringe Families and their Social Parcipitaion*, Bulletin 909, Ithaca, New York: Cornell University Agricultural Experiment Station, 1955; Kaplan, *Socio-Economic Circumstances. op. cit.*

be few social isolates.[31] Informal social contacts currently represent the only means by which adult educators may reach certain segments of the population in almost any community.

Activities which involve communication on a one-way basis, such as reading, radio listening, television viewing, and attendance at motion pictures, represent a very different type of "participation." They have considerable significance for adult education as channels of communication, as potential media of education, and as competition for programs, but will not be considered in this chapter.

Even this cursory summary conclusively shows that participants in formal programs of adult education and in formal associations, as well as major users of the more educational aspects of mass media, appear to be drawn from the same segments of the population. There remains a substantial fraction of almost any community which is not more than casually exposed to any of these educative or potentially educative forces but is regularly involved in various types of informal participation. It is important therefore to examine the factors associated with participation.

FACTORS ASSOCIATED WITH SOCIAL PARTICIPATION
CHARACTERISTICS OF PARTICIPANTS:

Occupation. The most nearly universal relationship found in studies of participation is the consistent positive association of formal participation rates and patterns with variables which are either correlates or measures of socio-economic status.[32] In urban communities occupation appears to be a major determinant of rates and types of formal participation. Professional-technical and managerial personnel participate in the widest variety of associations, have highest rates of participation and hold a disproportionate number of offices. They dominate memberships of professional, business and civic organizations. White collar workers are active in a variety of associational types, particularly social

[31]Axelrod, *op. cit.*; Anderson, *Fringe Families* . . .; Anderson and Smith, "Formal and Informal Participation . . ."; Anderson, *Rural Social Participation and the Family Life Cycle,* Part I, *Formal Participation,* Part II, *Informal Participation,* Memoires 314 and 318, Ithaca, New York: Cornell University Agricultural Experiment Station, 1953; F. Dotson, "Patterns of Voluntary Association Among Urban Working Class Families," *American Sociological Review,* XVI, October 1951; R. Vinter, *Social Goals and Social Participation Among Lower Class White Males,* Ph.D. dissertation, Columbia University, 1957; H. Doddy, *Informal Groups in Adult Education,* New York: Institute of Adult Education, Teachers College, Columbia University, 1951.

[32]There is considerable variation in the degree of association from community to community and the relationship never approaches a perfect correlation. Status variables which appear to be most significant in one community may be less significant than other variables in other communities. Kaufman, *op. cit.*; William G. Mather, "Income and Social Participation," *American Sociological Review,* VI, June 1941.

and cultural groups. Skilled and semi-skilled workers are chiefly active in labor unions and fraternal orders. Service and unskilled workers are least active, with memberships largely confined to veterans and certain beneficial fraternal associations for men, and church for women. In rural areas occupation remains significant for types of association participated in, but rates of formal participation are less uniform for occupational groups because the population is less sharply differentiated by occupation.[33]

Income. Income has widely been reported as significantly associated with active formal participation.[34] Some studies suggest that income *per se* is less significant than the social acceptance and heightened sense of civic responsibility which accompany higher income. Foskett, indeed, interprets social participation in terms of role theory, indicating that a good education or income creates expectations among others as to the behavior of an individual possessing these assets. Such pressure or the policy of an employing institution may therefore account for participation. Such considerations are not, however, a complete explanation for participation since the role theory does not take account of the interests of the individual or of the potential influence of his cultural background.[35]

Amount of schooling. The amount of formal schooling is almost universally reported as being highly significant to the extent, intensity and patterns of participation in formal associations both in most of the studies already referred to and in numerous others. Agger and Goldrich, for instance, in comparing two contrasting communities—Valley City, a retail trading center of 2,000 population and Boomtown, a growing industrial city of 16,000—found a positive and substantial relationship in both between socio-economic status and participation in community organizations and also that education is the index of socio-economic status closely related to socio-political participation.[36]

[33]Axelrod, *op. cit.;* W. Bell and M. Force, "Urban Neighborhood Types and Participation in Formal Associations," *American Sociological Review,* XXI, February 1956; H. Goldhamer, *Some Factors Affecting Participation in Voluntary Associations,* Ph.D. dissertation, University of Chicago, 1945; M. Komarovsky, "The Voluntary Associations of Urban Dwellers," *American Sociological Review,* XI, December 1946; Kaufman, *op. cit.;* Payne and Kaufman, *op. cit.*

[34]W. Bell and M. Boat, "Urban Neighborhoods and Informal Social Relationships," *American Journal of Sociology,* LXII, January 1957; H. F. Kaufman, *Prestige Classes in a New York Rural Community,* Memoir 260, Ithaca, New York: Cornell University Agricultural Experiment Station, 1944; G. A. Lundberg, M. Komarovsky and M. A. McInery, *Leisure, A Suburban Study,* New York: Columbia University Press, 1934; Mather, *op. cit.*

[35]Bell and Boat, *op. cit.;* J. M. Foskett, "Social Structure and Social Participation," *American Sociological Review,* XX, August 1955.

[36]R. Agger and D. Goldrich, "Community Power Structures and Partisanship," *American Sociological Review,* August 1958.

Participation in both church and nonchurch organizations increases with education. The striking increase in office holding with education reported by many studies indicates that organizational leadership is heavily concentrated among the better educated segment of the community.[37] The paramount importance of education to formal participation is shown by studies which find educational level to remain significant when other factors are held constant.[38]

While it is unlikely that all differences in formal participation between high and low educational groups may be attributed absolutely to education, effective formal participation does require certain communicative and human relations skills which must be learned. It is probable also that those with more education are more highly motivated to participate and to assume leadership. Adult education, then, through dissemination of the skills and knowledge requisite for effective social participation can increase the size of the "active minority" in organizations and in communities. Further research is needed to determine what skills and knowledge are necessary to participation and to develop effective means of organizing and carrying out programs to disseminate them. It would seem, however, that "leadership training" is not a complete answer. "Followers" also need to learn how to be more effective members.[39]

The prominence of the professional, managerial and better educated in formalized organizations is sometimes interpreted as evidence that a "power elite" is in control. It has even been said in occasional speeches and promotional literature that adult educators must convince this "power elite" on whatever geographical level, of the desirability of adult education in order to have successful programs.

As stated in Chapter VII, there is no question but that the voters are not as committed to tax-supported adult education as they are to the traditional program of the public school. Nor is there any question but that persons of influence can assist in improving the support for adult education. It must be pointed out that, as already indicated, many of the individuals accorded superior status in their communities are already active participants in social organizations and in adult education activities, though other prestigeful persons are not. The research findings examined do not support extreme interpretations of

[37]Kaufman, *Participation in Organized Activities. . . .*; J. S. Newberry, Jr., *A Descriptive Study of Certain Aspects of the Membership of Formed Associations in a Southern Town,* Ph.D. dissertation, Florida State University, 1959; J. C. Scott, Jr., "Membership and Participation in Voluntary Associations," *American Sociological Review,* XXII, June 1957.

[38]Bell and Force, *op. cit.*; Duncan and Artis, *op. cit.*; Foskett, *op. cit.*

[39]M. G. Ross and C. E. Hendry, *New Understandings of Leadership, A Survey and Application of Research,* New York: Association Press, 1957, especially chapter 4.

the theory of a power elite as related to adult education participation. Without denying the obvious fact that there are power, or at least, pressure groups at all levels, it seems quite clear, as later sections of this chapter will indicate, that there are many influences bearing upon both participation in adult education and its status in the community.

So far as the individual is concerned, however, there is conclusive evidence that his social standing in the community profoundly affects his participation, no matter how his social position is measured.[40]

The low to moderate positive association of informal participation with measures of socio-economic status reported in some studies[41] is of less significance than the universal finding that among people of low socio-economic status and with little formal education, informal participation is widespread—often being the only habitual form of interpersonal communication.[42]

The extent and nature of reading, discriminating use of mass media, and "constructive" use of leisure are all positively associated with status factors—occupation and educational level appear to be particularly significant.[43]

Age. Age differences have widely been found to be associated with differences in rates and patterns of social participation. Participation in formal associations is generally low for youth and young adults of both sexes, increasing sharply in the late 20's and early 30's. From about age 35 to age 50 formal participation remains fairly constant with a peak of activity falling somewhere in that period. The onset of the decline of participation appears to vary from community to community from shortly over 50 to well past 60.[44] Participation in the

[40]Composite indexes constructed from socio-economic variables: Axelrod, *op. cit.*; W. L. Warner and P. S. Lunt, *The Social Life of a Modern Community, I. The Yankee City Series,* New Haven, Conn.: Yale University Press, 1941, Rating of local judges: Brown, *op. cit.*; Kaufman, *Prestige Classes* . . . ; Self-rating by informants: Anderson, "Formal and Informal Participation . . .", and *Rural Social Participation* . . . ; Brown, *op. cit.*

[41]Brown, *op. cit.*; Duncan and Artis, *op. cit.*; Axelrod, *op. cit.*

[42]Anderson, *Fringe Families* . . . ; "Formal and Informal Participation . . ."; and *Rural Social Participation* . . . ; Bell and Force, *op. cit.*; D. C. Hay, "A Scale for the Measurement of Social Participation in Rural Households," *Rural Sociology,* XIII, September, 1948; Vinter, *op. cit.*

[43]Campbell and Metzner, *op. cit.*; A. C. Clark, "The Use of Leisure and its Relation to Levels of Occupational Prestige," *American Sociological Review,* XXI, June 1956; Lundberg *et al., op. cit.*

[44]Axelrod, *op. cit.*, p. 56; Kaufman, *Participation in Organized Activities* . . . , S. Mayo, "Age Profiles of Social Participation in Rural Areas of Wake County, North Carolina," *Rural Sociology,* vol. XV, September 1950; P. Taietz and O. Larson, "Social Participation and Old Age," *Rural Sociology,* XXI, December 1956.

[45]Hostetter and Mather, *op. cit.*; Kaufman, *Participation in Organized Activities* . . . ; Taietz and Larson, *op. cit.*

church and in leisure organizations persists longer and may even increase after 60.[45] Older persons in good health and those in upper economic or education brackets[46] tend to retain and even to increase participation in formal associations after 60. These findings, together with those by Foskett[47] that most of the association between age and "community participation" was accounted for by other factors, strongly suggest that age *per se* is not a serious barrier to participation.

Sex. Differences in the participation patterns of men and women have been widely reported. The most nearly universal difference appears to be the much greater participation of women in church and church-related organizations. In populations which are at least moderately heterogeneous men usually participate more heavily than women in nonchurch formal associations.[48]

Differences in participation between the sexes are more evident when participation is examined within the context of other variables. Socio-economic status, urban influence and ethnic background appear to affect the patterns of participation of women much more than those of men. Among middle-class urban populations women are frequently reported to attend meetings more regularly, but men tend to be members of more organizations.[49]

Except in metropolitan urban areas married persons are consistently reported to be higher formal participants than single persons, especially the widowed or divorced.[50]

Family cycle. Couples with school age children tend to be more active than those in pre-child or early-child stages and one-parent families are least likely to participate. Apparently the various stages in the family life cycle do not operate uniformly in conditioning formal par-

[46]Bell and Force, *op. cit.;* I. Webber, "The Organized Social Life of the Retired: Two Florida Communities," *American Journal of Sociology,* LIX, Jan. 1954.

[47]Foskett, *op. cit.*

[48]Axelrod, *op. cit.;* Hostetter and Mather, op. cit.; Kaufman, *Participation in Organized Activities.* . . .

[49]Anderson, *Fringe Families* . . . ; Axelrod, *op. cit.;* Kaufman, *Participation in Organized Activities.* . . . Kaufman found that women in rural areas of Kentucky and in lower socioeconomic categories were much less active in non-church associations than men, but that as urban influence and social status increased women approached, and in some instances even exceeded, men in non-church formal participation. Kaufman, *ibid.;* W. H. Key, *Rural-Urban Differences in Social Participation,* Ph.D dissertation, St. Louis, Washington University, 1953; Status-urban: Axelrod, *op. cit.*

Among foreign-born and first generation Americans of various ethnic backgrounds males approach American patterns of participation in the community much more closely and much more quickly than do females. Kaplan, *Socio-Economic Circumstances* . . . ; N. L. Whetten and A. W. Green, *Ethnic Group Relations in a Rural Area of Connecticut,* Bulletin 244, Storrs: Connecticut State College Agricultural Experiment Station, 1954.

[50]Axelrod, *op. cit.;* Goldhamer, *op. cit.;* Komarovsky, *op. cit.*

ticipation since there are real differences among the various studies on this point. Informal participation shows even less uniformity in relation to the family life cycles. Patterns of participation tend to "run in families." Rates and types of participation of husbands, wives and their children tend to be similar. Greatest family uniformity is probably in church participation but all aspects are influenced by family patterns.[51]

Greater use of activities involving the entire family might be made in urban areas. Interest in organizations and programs is reinforced by joint family participation. Attendance then acts to preserve family solidarity rather than as yet another divisive element. The organization of family programs through neighborhood and community centers in urban areas, particularly in neighborhoods where family informal participation is high, would appear to be one way of reaching many people not now involved by formal associations or organized adult education.

Length of residence. Length of residence has been found to influence formal participation in all communities at all points on the rural-urban continuum. The time required for newcomers to reach participation rates of residents varies from community to community. One study found the time required was significantly shorter in urban rather than rural communities in Kentucky.[52] The time required for migrants to assume participation patterns of residents also varies within a single community. Significantly, migrants from environments similar to that of the new community adjust more rapidly and those in upper-status brackets adjust more quickly than migrants from dissimilar environments and those in lower-status brackets.[53]

Patterns of informal social participation could well be utilized in

[51]Anderson, *Fringe Families* . . . ; "Formal and Informal Participation . . ."; and *Rural Social Participation* . . . ; Payne, *op. cit.*

The advantages of joint family participation have been recognized for many years in certain forms of adult education, particularly in rural areas—witness the Chatauqua, the Grange and the Farmer's Institutes. The Cooperative Extension Service through its emphasis on the "family farm" has recognized the reinforcing effect of programs involving the entire family. "Family night" programs blending social, religious, and educational activities are increasingly being utilized by churches and to some extent by other formal associations.

[52]Kaufman, *Participation in Organized Activities.* . . .

[53]B. G. Zimmer, "Farm Background and Urban Participation," *American Journal of Sociology*, LXI, March 1956. Zimmer found that not only did migrants to a midwestern urban center from rural areas require longer time to approach formal participation rates of nonmigrants than migrants from urban backgrounds, but that migrants from farms were slowest to "adjust" and the longer they had farmed the slower was their rate of adjustment.

Newberry, *op. cit.*, found in Thomasville, Georgia that length of residence within the general area was more significant to formal participation than either length of residence in the community or in the immediate locality.

developing programs of adult education and other services to assist migrants, particularly those in lower socio-economic groups, in preparing for and adjusting to urban life.[54]

Out-migration from urban areas to suburban and fringe areas suggests other problems for adult education. The evidence that migrants to fringe areas and suburbs do participate in local associations and assume leadership in fringe organizations at rates equal to those of long time residents suggests that county agents and other adult educators could utilize these migrants as resources for developing their programs.[55]

Urban—rural—suburban differences. There is abundant evidence that participation in formal associations outside the church is relatively more widespread in urban than in rural communities. Kaufman's data from localities ranging from rural open country to a city of 60,000 in Kentucky provide convincing evidence of this point.[56] A restudy of a Pennsylvania rural community found that increase in characteristics reflecting urban dominance was associated with increasing extent and rates of formal participation. Further evidence is provided by studies which show greater formal participation and less reliance upon informal participation in the more urbanized areas of a single county.[57] The considerable increase in federal programs in rural America since 1933, such as rural electrification and soil conservation, all of which work through local committees or organizations, has also increased rural participation.

There is some evidence that the relationship between formal participation and urbanization is not linear. William Henry Key compared participation in six areas of interaction within sample localities in open country, village, town, small cities, and large urban centers. He found that "the high point of participation in secondary groups came in the small urban locality groups while the low point of par-

---

[54]Zimmer's findings, *op. cit.,* suggest that such programs might be undertaken in areas experiencing heavy out-migration of rural people—among rural Negroes in the Cotton Belt, for example—and in urban areas receiving heavy in-migration.

[55]Anderson, *Fringe Families . . .* ; C. E. Ramsey and R. Damley, *Some Effects of Fringe Migration on Channels of Communication,* Rural Sociological Bulletin 51, Ithaca, New York: Cornell University Agricultural Experiment Station, 1957. Cf. also, University of Connecticut series, *Studies in Suburbanization.*

[56]Kaufman, *Participation in Organized Activities. . . .*

[57]R. C. Buck and L. A. Ploch, *Factors Related to Changes in Social Participation in a Rural Pennsylvania Community,* Bulletin 582, State College: Pennsylvania State University Agricultural Experiment Station, 1954; E. S. Grigsby and H. Hoffsommer, *Rural Social Organization of Frederick County, Maryland,* Bulletin A-51, College Park: University of Maryland Agricultural Experiment Station, 1949; H. W. Reicken and N. L., Whetten, *Rural Social Organization in Litchfield County, Connecticut,* Bulletin 261, Storrs: University of Connecticut Agricultural Experiment Station, 1948.

ticipation in primary groups came in the same area." He attributed the greater participation in formal associations found in small cities to "the absence of either spatial or social isolation."[58]

Axelrod's findings in Detroit suggest that it is only in the upper socio-economic and highest educational categories of the metropolis that formal participation and participation with friends tend to supplant family and neighborhood interaction as the primary forms of social participation.[59]

Within a metropolitan area there is evidence of sharp neighborhood differences in patterns of participation due to residential segregation on socio-economic, ethnic, and family factors and to variation in degree of "dominance" of the urban center over neighborhood economic and social organization. Studies of social participation in urban areas have demonstrated that the ecological approach has particular applicability to neighborhood patterns of participation.[60]

Participation patterns in suburban and fringe areas show considerable variability. They reflect some survival of rural patterns, modified by rapid increases in special-interest participation according to the occupational, educational, cultural, religious and family characteristics of the residents.[61]

[58]Key, op. cit. There was a positive linear relation of urbanization to "participation at work" and a negative linear relation to "neighboring." The other four types: formal participation, friends, extended family, immediate family—showed the relation quoted above.

[59]Axelrod, op. cit. Other supporting evidence: San Francisco, Bell and Boat, op. cit.; Springfield, Mass., Vinter, op. cit.; New Haven, Conn., Dotson, op. cit.

[60]In urbanized areas and cities where Census tract data are available (100,000 or more population) the charactertistic patterns of participation in each tract can be predicted quite accurately according to the incidence of population and housing characteristics within the tract. Census tract typologies such as the Shevsky-Bell typology appear to be particularly useful instruments for predicting participation. Bell and Boat, op. cit.; Bell and Force, op. cit.; S. Greer, "Urbanism Reconsidered: A Study of Local Areas in a Metropolis," American Sociological Review, vol. XXI, February 1956.

Where Census tract data are not available many other sources may be used to delineate neighborhoods. Kaplan demonstrated the utility of ecological study of participation for the reorganization of public school adult education in Springfield, Massachusetts. Kaplan, Socio-Economic Circumstances . . . ; also see, S. Reimer and J. McNamara, "Contact Patterns in the City," Social Forces, vol. XXXVI, December 1953.

[61]Anderson, Fringe Families . . . ; Lundberg et al., op. cit.; W. T. Martin, "A Consideration of Differences in the Extent and Location of the Formal Associational Activities of Rural-Urban Fringe Residents," American Sociological Review, vol. VI, June 1941; Ramsey and Damley, op. cit.; N. L. Whetten, Studies in Suburbanization, Ill: Wilton, A Rural Town Near Metropolitan New York, Bulletin 230, Storrs, Connecticut State College Agricultural Experiment Station, 1939.

The tendency for commuters and recent arrivals to split participation between the city and the fringe (or suburbs) may retard development of instrumental organizations. Cf. Anderson, Lundberg et al., Martin, cited just above, and A. H. Scaff, "The Effect of Commuting on Participation in Community Organizations," American Sociological Review, XVII, April 1952.

The findings underline the necessity for careful study of the social, economic and ecological charateristics of the community and its people in order to determine the patterns of participation, communication, and interaction which are likely to be effective in reaching and involving the various elements of the population in educational programs and activities. Where the community is undergoing fairly rapid change, continuing study of patterns of participation is essential. There are also regional differences in participation.

Cultural backgrounds. National background appears to have considerable influence on participation. British, Scandinavian (except Finnish) and German foreign-born approach or even exceed native Americans in participation in formal associations. Low rates of formal nonchurch participation and high family, kin, and neighborhood participation are reported for both foreign-born and first generation ethnics of Polish, Central European and Latin (American and European) origin. Ethnic groups living in relative isolation tend to preserve their traditional patterns of social participation.[62]

A recent study of two contiguous ethnic-cultural groups, Danish and Polish, vividly illustrates the problem of adult educators working with contrasting cultural heritages. The Danes placed a high value on education, their younger adults having a median number of years of schooling completed beyond high school. There were several reading circles and a public forum. Its lectures in the community hall were well attended. Participation in the Extension Service was high. The median family belonged to between three and four organizations. Social and cultural participation was a group value. The neighboring Poles, on the other hand, were family-centered and suspicious of persons from outside the group, thus blocking educational efforts. They had low organizational participation. Their youth completed only the minimum education required by the state.[63]

Religion. Differences in formal participation according to religious preference are reported in urban, rural and suburban studies. Catholics tend to be less active than Protestants in formal associations outside

---

[62]Kaufman, *Prestige Classes* . . .; Kaplan, *Socio-Economic Circumstances* . . . ; B. Kreitlow and J. A. Duncan, *The Acceptance of Educational Programs in Rural Wisconsin*, Bulletin 525, Madison; University of Wisconsin Agricultural Experiment Station, 1956; N. L. Whetten and E. C. Devereux, Jr., *Studies of Suburbanization, I: Windsor: A Highly Developed Agricultural Area*, Bulletin 212, Storrs: Connecticut State College Agricultural Experiment Station, 1936; Whetten and Green, *Ethnic Group Relations.* . . .

Among people of foreign ethnic background it is generally impossible to separate the influence of religion as it constitutes a significant element of the common culture. Kreitlow and Duncan, *op. cit.*

[63]H. Pedersen, "Cultural Differences in the Acceptance of Recommended Practices," *Rural Sociology*, March 1951.

of the church but somewhat more active in church and church-related organizations. Membership in all kinds of organizations, taken together, is usually greater among Protestants.[64]

Protestants expressing preference for denominations or professing beliefs which fall at the "church" end of a church-sect typological continuum (Episcopal, Presbyterian, Congregational, etc.) tend to be more active in formal associations outside the church than those whose beliefs or preference fall toward the "sect" end of the continuum (Pentecostal and other "Fundamentalist" sects) .[65]

The differences in participation according to religion or ethnic background undoubtedly reflect socio-economic factors so that all of the differences observed should not be attributed to differences in denominational preference or belief.

Within the Negro community formal participation closely parallels the results already described, except that formal participation among low status Negroes appears to be more widespread than among whites of corresponding status.[66]

The reader will have already realized that so far as comparative data are available, participation in adult education programs and organizations and participation in the whole complex of social organizations on the community level show many similarities. This, as already indicated, suggests that the findings of the broader studies of the totality of social participation summarized in the preceding pages have wide applicability to adult education.

The factors so far considered, however, are "static" because they are not subject to immediate change through the efforts of any particular organization or agency. They are chiefly of concern to the adult educator because they indicate that the distribution of patterns of social participation in the community is associated with certain characteristics of the population. If the adult educator can determine how these characteristics are distributed, both proportionately and spatially, in

[64]Urban: Goldhamer, *op. cit.*; Komarovsky, op. cit. Suburban: Whetten, *Studies in Suburbanization, I* and *III*. Rural: Anderson, "Social Participation . . ." Kaufman, "Prestige Classes. . . ."

Two urban studies found Jewish white-collar workers (Goldhamer in Chicago) and skilled workers (Komarovsky in New York) to be more active than non-Jews of the same occupational groups.

[65]Anderson, "Social Participation . . ."; Brown, *op. cit.*; Duncan and Artis, *op cit.*; Russell R. Dynes, "The Consequences of Sectarianism for Social Participation," *Social Forces,* vol. XXXV, May 1957; Whetten, *Studies in Suburbanization, III*.

[66]Gunnar Myrdal summarizes the literature on Negro formal associations and participation, *op. cit.*, pp. 952-55. Kaplan, *Socio-Economic Circumstances . . .* ; Mayo, *op. cit.*; Payne, *Organizational Activities of Rural Negroes.* Among rural Mississippi Negroes educational level is extremely significant to formal participation.

his particular community, he can *predict* within certain limits the forms of participant activity which involve each particular segment of the population and organize programs and activities utilizing these behavior patterns.

Dynamic factors. George M. Beal has criticized the preoccupation of participation research with "static factors." He proposed ten "dynamic factors" which, when tested, proved to be significant to the participation of a sample of members of Iowa cooperatives.[67]

For the adult educator dynamic factors are important because they define the relationship of the individual to the organization and because "group members, leaders, and professional workers can bring about change in them." There is evidence, furthermore, "that it is possible to bring about changes in participation by changing 'dynamic factors'."[68]

The extreme variety of purpose, structure and operation of formal associations makes it highly unlikely that the factors will be equally significant for all associations.

The kinds of participation required to fulfill the functions of the association are quite different for different types of associations so that it has been necessary to develop special instruments to measure participation for the study of dynamic factors.[69] The following propositions, however, appear to have broad, if not universal, applicability.

1. Active participants have an image of the purpose of the organization more in keeping with the stated goals and the "official" image than that of inactive members. The degree of activity of the participant is related to the importance he ascribes to the objectives of the organization.

2. Active participants are more likely than inactive members to believe that they derive benefits from membership. The benefits considered "greatest" by active participants are more apt to be in keeping with the central or over-riding purpose of the organization than are the benefits considered greatest by inactive members.

3. Active participants have more detailed and accurate knowledge[70]

[67]Factors tested included knowledge of the organizational structure, purposes and function; identification with the cooperative; satisfaction with service; belief that the member had a "say" in the running of the cooperative, and other items specifically related to the function of cooperatives and the conditions of participation in them. Beal, *op. cit.*

[68]Beal, *ibid.*

[69]*Ibid.*; Rose, *op. cit.*

[70]Sills, *op. cit.*, found that many volunteers and some chapter heads in local National Infantile Paralysis Foundation organizations tended to perceive the Foundation as a federation of independent local organizations despite its obvious and well publicized structure (pp. 214-24). This striking exception to the proposition results from the operation of factor no. 4.

of the organization than do inactive members: its structure, major charter provisions, names of incumbent officers, relation of the local to headquarters, and history.

4. Active participants are more apt to believe that they have a share in the process of decision making in the organization than do inactive members. The "belief" is more important than the actuality of democratic control as is shown by Sills' findings.

5. Active participants recognize responsibility to the organization and to its program. Inactive members are more apt to show little concern for the organization and its objectives.

6. Active members identify themselves with the organization. They are more likely than inactives to refer to it as "my club" or "our program."

7. Active participants are more likely than inactive members to be on terms of friendship or intimacy with others in the organization. They tend to select members as "best friends," are more apt to have persons in their immediate family and relatives who are also members of the organization or its auxiliary groups, and are more likely to report that many or all of their neighbors are members than are inactive members.[71]

It is evident that the key to participation is the relationship of the individual to the group.

Adult education for participation, therefore, must operate at two levels: (1) the level of the individual member in order to strengthen or change the individual's conception of the purpose, structure and function of the group; (2) the level of the group in order to bring the realization of the need for change to those who have influence over major decisions. Participation may be changed by altering the purpose, organizational structure, or functional operation of the group, or by altering the motivation of the individual. Because of the limitations imposed by "static" factors, the first course is much more likely to produce rapid change in participation behavior. It is not always necessary to change the purpose, structure, or function of the group so long as the individual's conception is changed, nor will change in the organization necessarily result in change in participation unless the individual's conception also undergoes alteration.

Application of "dynamic factors" to adult education. When control

[71]Among the studies that support these conclusions are: Beal, *op. cit.*; Rose, *op. cit.*; W. S. Folkman, *Member Relations in Farmers' Purchasing Cooperatives,* Bulletin 556, Fayetteville: University of Arkansas Agricultural Experiment Station, 1955; S. Lipset, M. Trow and J. Coleman, *Union Democracy: The Internal Politics of the International Typographical Union,* Glencoe, Ill.: The Free Press, 1956; Dimit *et al., op. cit.*; Dynes, *op. cit.*

of the direction of the program or activity is not widely and democratically distributed identification with the program and with the offering agency is inhibited. Activity will take place only in terms of the specific benefits and satisfactions derived. When, however, participation also means a measure of control over direction of the programs and responsibility for development and achievement of its goals, the participant will tend to identify himself more closely with the group and its objectives. His motivation for participation is thereby increased.

At the same time the institution (or the teacher) loses a measure of control over the process and direction of the activities of the group. The passive conception of participation frequently expressed by adult educators (class attendance, public relations, etc.), by community planners (limited advisory committees), and by organizational personnel (docile membership), may well reflect a feeling of insecurity resulting from partial recognition that active participation involves a transfer of control from the "leader" to the group.[72]

METHODS OF PARTICIPATION RESEARCH

Thus far nothing has been said as to the research methods employed by those studying participation. They vary so considerably that a note on this topic is desirable. Formal participation, particularly in formal associations, has been subjected to the most intensive and widespread study.

Participation has been approached through the study of the distribution of participation behavior in particular populations. Except for certain rural studies in which interviews were obtained from virtually every household in the area studied,[73] participation studies have utilized some form of sampling. Some earlier studies, particularly in urban areas, used samples "of convenience" so that results are not generalizable beyond the immediate sample. Some recent studies are excellent examples of careful application of sampling techniques.[74]

[72]The almost total lack of awareness of the dynamic aspects of participation found in a survey of directors of urban redevelopment projects and of adult education directors in cities having such projects, together with the limited community participation and very restricted neighborhood participation reported in all but a very few of the programs indicates that "education for participation" has received little application in one important area of community action. Gerda J. Lewis, *A Study of Citizen Participation in Urban Renewal and its Relationship to Adult Education*, Ph.D. dissertation, Cornell University, 1957.

[73]Buck and Ploch, *op. cit.*; Mayo, "Age Profiles . . .", and Mayo and Marsh, "Social Participation in the Rural Community," *American Journal of Sociology*, vol. LVII, November 1951.

[74]Komarovsky, *op. cit.*; Goldhamer, *op. cit.*; Axelrod, *op. cit.*; Bell and Boat, *op. cit.*; Bell and Force, *op. cit.*; Sills, *op. cit.*

Types of research designs. Participation studies follow one of four general designs: (1) the cross-sectional study utilizing a sample selected to be representative of the total population;[75] (2) the comparative study selecting samples differing significantly—often with other factors controlled—so as to show the effect of the particular factor studied;[76] (3) selection of a population representing an extreme with respect to some characteristic;[77] (4) studies of the relation of individual members to particular organizations or types of organizations and of "dynamic factors." Supporting data and case study corroboration are provided by studies of community, and county, social organization.[78]

Methods of measuring participation. Earlier studies relied upon membership and officership as indexes of participation in formal organizations. Recognition that membership constitutes a very low order of participation resulted in the use of other criteria such as attendance, contributions, and serving on committees. F. Stuart Chapin combined these items, weighted so as to give a better representation to more intensive forms of participation, into a Social Participation Scale.[79] Although the Chapin Scale has been more widely used than any other index of participation it has never achieved universal acceptance.

Measurement of informal participation has been attempted from two general approaches which are sometimes combined: (1) participation in certain kinds of activities;[80] (2) contact with certain groups or types of groups.[81] Studies of "interaction" utilize "contacts" without regard to the nature of the relationships.[82] Composite[83] indexes

[75]Axelrod, *op. cit.*

[76]The effect of urbanization: Kaufman, "Participation in Organized Activities . . ." Greer, *op. cit.;* Socio-economic status and familism: Bell and Boat, *op. cit.;* Bell and Force, *op. cit.;* Cultural homogeneity: Kreitlow and Duncan, *op. cit.*

[77]Old age: Taietz and Larson, *op. cit.* Low socio-economic status: Vinter, *op. cit.*

[78]Beal, *op. cit.;* Folkman, *op. cit.;* Lipset *et al., op. cit.;* Rose, *op. cit.;* Sills, *op. cit.;* Grigsby and Hoffsommer, *op. cit.;* Warner and Lunt, *op. cit.;* Kaufman, "Prestige Classes . . ."; Reicken and Whetten, *op. cit.;* Whetten, *Studies in Suburbanization, I* and *III.*

[79]F. Stuart Chapin, "Social Participation and Social Intelligence," *American Sociological Review,* vol. IV, April 1939.

[80]Anderson, "Fringe Families . . .", "Formal and Informal Participation . . . ," *Rural Social Participation . . . ;* Brown, *op. cit.;* Hay, "A Scale for the Measurement . . ." and Hay, "The Social Participation of Households in Selected Communities of the Northeast," *Rural Sociology,* vol. XX, June 1950.

[81]Axelrod, *op. cit.;* Key, *op. cit.*

[82]Reimer and McNamara, *op. cit.*

[83]Composite formal-informal scale: Hay, "A Scale for the Measurement . . ."; "Community Participation Scale" combining participation in civic organizations, voting, attendance at public meetings and discussion of issues: Foskett, *op. cit.;* Combined index of formal, informal and cultural participation: S. A. Queen, "Social Disorganization and Social Participation," *American Sociological Review,* vol. VI, June 1941.

combining several types of participation to show "total participation" appear to be of doubtful value.

When separate scales are constructed for various aspects of participation and applied with care they become useful tools for studying differences in participation behavior among groups or populations.

Conclusion: summary and interpretation. The tremendous expansion of all forms of adult education in the past 35 years has not succeeded for the most part in bringing education to those who, from the point of view of society, are most in need of it. To a very large extent, present adult education programs are educating the educated. This failure in no way negates the essential worth of these programs. In a rapidly changing social order continuing education is necessary to keep even the highly educated abreast of change.

It is evident, however, that often expressed goals of adult education are not now being realized: (1) only a minority of the population continue their education into adult life, and (2) the ideal of life-long learning is achieved by relatively few. The serious social consequences of these failures are shown in the evidence that those inadequately served by formal adult education are also less frequently and less effectively exposed to other means of disseminating knowledge.

The evidence that those not involved by either formally organized adult education or by formal associations are participants in various types of informal groups suggests that this failure of adult education may be attributed, in part at least, to reliance upon patterns of organization not well adapted to the needs and experience of those with limited education and low socio-economic status, which may even thwart the aspirations of this group. This hypothesis is supported by evidence that approaches which have attempted to utilize existing patterns of interaction, notably the Cooperative Extension Service, have enjoyed at least a measure of success in reaching "disadvantaged" adults. If adult education is to broaden the base for participation it must move away from traditional institutional approaches and concepts of participation. Research is needed to discover whether the better-educated participate more because their previous experience prompts them to seek solutions to needs through traditional and familiar patterns; while the less-educated, with less experience in organized education, do not perceive that pattern as the way to solve their needs.

The great variability in patterns of participation both within and between communities found in studies of social participation indicates that if adult education is to progress beyond "hit or miss" organization and methodology it must be based upon careful, detailed and continuing studies of the population to be served and of existing patterns of organization and interaction.

The need for effective participation and an informed membership, common to all formal associations, presents the adult educator with an opportunity to serve community associations and at the same time to make effective use of the community associations network. Education for participation and for leadership must deal with those factors which govern the relationship of the individual to the group. The role of the adult educator is two-fold: first to assist leadership in improving participation by providing: (a) better programs, (b) accurate knowledge of the organization and its purposes, (c) training and experience to develop skills necessary for effective participation; and second to convince leadership that there is greater security in status derived from member satisfaction and the achievement of organizational objectives than in status based upon title, position, outmoded structure and traditional procedures.

The adult educator then must become an expert in *process*. He must function as an agent for change by assisting many different kinds of groups to recognize their problems and needs, set goals, plan and carry out programs to meet these goals. The processes of adult education applicable to any organized group, therefore, must become a major concern of the professional training of adult educators.

Some needed research. In addition to a few suggestions for research given earlier, certain other problems need study. Ways should be developed to systematize the gathering of data on the characteristics of participants in order to develop comprehensive and comparable statistics. There is a great need for research directed toward developing simplified and reliable means of determining the essential characteristics of populations for use by adult educators who are not social scientists. Considerable progress has been made, particularly in the utilization of ecological approaches to community study, but the techniques so far devised are not so direct or "fool-proof" that they can be applied with any assurance of reliability by anyone who is not trained in social research. A basic problem is to discover how to enlist and hold adult groups widely differentiated in terms of their varying educational, cultural and socio-economic backgrounds. Controlled experiments with differing groups, using varied approaches, materials and teaching methods are called for.

There is a continuing need for experimental research to perfect ways of adapting existing patterns of interaction to educational situations. In this connection, life history case studies of participants and nonparticipants equated in terms of socio-economic and educational statuses, age and sex might prove very valuable. The objective would be to gain insight into factors predisposing an individual toward either a positive or negative attitude toward the learning process, and to secure his evaluation of programs experienced. Cooperation of the subjects would, of course, have to be secured and perhaps compensation given.

The value of this approach is in part because participation has thus far not been studied from the viewpoint of the participant or potential participant. Such a study might also help to determine whether or not participants choose different kinds and degrees of participation in adult education with reference to some system of priorities or values inherent in their mainfold relationships with others. In other words, if participation is selective, what are the bases for selection among individuals of various types?

Research relating to social participation must focus increasingly upon the relation of the individual to the group. There is need for greater refinement of concepts and for differentiation of types of organizations according to the nature of the participant behavior required.[84]

Progress in developing education for participation would be speeded by research, uncommitted to theoretical tenets incapable of being tested, designed to isolate the learned components of leadership and participation skills.

[84]William M. Evan has presented a model for an empirical approach to the classification of organizations according to the incidence of three "dimensions of participation" among their members. The dimensions advanced are: "activity," "the distributive aspects of decision making," and "shared purpose." W. M. Evan, "Dimensions of Participation in Voluntary Associations," *Social Forces*, vol. XXXVI, December 1957.

ORGANIZATION AND ADMINISTRATION OF ADULT EDUCATION

Up to this point the discussion has been concerned with matters related to the participant in adult education: his ability to profit from educational activities and the relation of his interests, attitudes and motivations to his participation. Many of the pertinent research findings presented, and most of the theoretical considerations, have been culled from psychology, social psychology and, especially in the preceding chapter, from sociology.

The present chapter begins the discussion of factors of major concern to the adult educator: organization and administration of adult education, effectiveness of various techniques and methods used by adult educators, problems of program planning and leadership training, and the use of discussion as an adult educational tool. The final chapters in this section will be devoted to the place of groups in adult education and to the community as the locale of adult education activities and its influence upon them.

In few, if any, areas of adult education has there been less definitive research than in its organization and administration.[1] Much of what

---

[1]Studies in this area by the Agricultural and Home Economics Extension Service might be considered an exception. These are not dealt with in this report, since in this particular, Extension is highly atypical among adult education agencies. Its structure has been determined by law, the Smith-Lever Act of 1914. It is a cooperative state-federal nationwide agency.

has been done consists of purely descriptive data such as faculty status, title, salary and size of staff of directors of adult education in public schools, evening colleges or university extension divisions.

ADULT EDUCATION ADMINISTRATION IN PUBLIC SCHOOLS

Many descriptive studies of public school adult education are of this type, with special attention to curriculum and enrollment. One such study makes clear an important point in considering the administration of adult education in schools, namely, the great diversity among the states in their support of adult education. The availability of state aid greatly increases the incidence and amount of adult education in public schools. A questionnaire study by Mumma[2] covering 651 school systems in the middle Atlantic states, found that 82 per cent of the school administrators in Delaware and Maryland indicated that adult education was a responsibility of the school system. In the leading state, New York, only 60.2 per cent of the systems had a definite adult education policy adopted by the school board. In Pennsylvania, the low state, the figure was only 27.1 per cent. Comparably, Professor Andrew Hendrickson, in his annual reviews of the status of adult education in Ohio, has several times pointed out the sharp contrasts in enrollment and support between that state and its neighbor, Michigan.

Clark's study of adult education in the public schools of Los Angeles,[3] however, gives considerable attention to administrative concerns and since a number of the issues raised apply at least to some degree to other school systems and some other agencies, its findings are reported here at some length.

Adult education a marginal activity. Clark points out that one handicap of public school adult education is its marginal position in the system. It is a new activity and must compete for support with the long-established elementary and high school divisions. The idea that adult education has a claim on tax funds has not been accepted by the general public to nearly the same degree that the education of children and youth has been. In time of financial stress, therefore, support for adult education is under heavier attack than any other feature of the school system. In order to meet this attack, or indeed to answer legitimate questions as to budget, it is necessary to stress

[2]R. Mumma, "Public School Adult Education," *Adult Education,* October 1950; E. Olds, *Financing Adult Education in America's Public Schools and Community Councils,* Washington: Adult Education Association, U.S.A., 1954.

[3]Burton R. Clark, *Adult Education in Transition,* University of California Press, Berkeley and Los Angeles, 1956.

citizen demand for courses in the program. This means that adult education operates under what Clark calls an enrollment economy. The administration must encourage attendance and is often required to drop courses which do not achieve a predetermined enrollment or average attendance. This discourages administrative initiative in building programs based on sound educational principles; the pressure in both courses and teacher selection is to choose what will be popular.

Fees for courses. It is true that in many situations both in public schools and private agencies adults will pay for education. Holden found in Michigan[4] that individuals will pay more readily for adult education which will increase their earning capacity than for some other types. To a considerable degree they will also pay for courses that will provide satisfactions of a cultural or recreational nature. They are reluctant, however, to pay for offerings designed to improve home and community. Interestingly enough, when individuals were queried as to the use of tax funds for partial payment of various types of adult education, public affairs education was most frequently mentioned as a legitimate charge on the school budget. Vocational education came second, home and family life education third, followed by intellectual and cultural development and recreational skills. The only social factors influencing these results appeared to be family income and the educational status of the respondent.

Charging for adult education offerings in public schools is usually resisted by administrators, though some systems have adopted the practice. It adds to the administrative overhead cost and is therefore not a net gain. More important, it operates to reduce enrollment and hence to accentuate the insecurities of the enrollment economy.

Among other insecurities in public school adult education which Clark points out in the Los Angeles study referred to earlier is the fact that only in large cities is the administrative officer full-time; in others he is assigned to adult education as a secondary responsibility. Another problem is the fact that adult classes typically have no building of their own but must use structures designed for children and youth. Thus even the physical setting emphasizes the marginal or peripheral status of adult education.

Administrative objectives of adult education. Administrators have sought to meet some of the problems of the enrollment economy by

[4] J. B. Holden, *Factors Relating to the Financial Support of Continuing Education as Revealed by a Study of Selected Michigan Communities,* Ph.D. dissertation, Ohio State University, 1955. This study was conducted by trained interviewers in three different-sized communities. The results were tested for significance by the chi square technique.

all-inclusive statements of objectives. Clark quotes a statement of seven
specific objectives published in 1951 by the California State Department of Education and supported by the California Association of
Adult Education Administrators:

1. To make adults aware of their civic responsibilties to one another
   and to the community.
2. To make them economically more efficient.
3. To develop an understanding of the attitudes and personal adjustments required for successful home life and family relationships.
4. To promote health and physical fitness.
5. To provide an opportunity for cultural development.
6. To supplement and broaden educational backgrounds.
7. To provide for the development of avocational interests through
   opportunities for self-expression.

Comparable statements have been issued by public school adult
educators elsewhere. It will be noted that this statement is not only
very broad but also that only the second item concerns adult vocational education, which in many situations is the largest division of
the program. Given the situation, the breadth of these objectives is
both laudable and understandable. However, as Clark points out,
the more general or diffused the goals of an organization are, the
less chance there is that they will affect decision-making within the
organization. Decisions will be more influenced by daily pressures, in
this case by the enrollment economy. There is sociological evidence
to support this generalization. In public school adult education the
necessity for emphasis on enrollment and attendance means in effect
that the student body has a greater influence on program than the
professional personnel.[5]

ADMINISTRATION IN OTHER AGENCIES

This extended discussion of Clark's study has been included both
because of its intrinsic value and because, in the absence of comparable studies dealing with other areas of adult education, it has
implications for them. There have been a number of attempts to
group the manifold agencies of adult education into types. Spence
and Cass, for example, use nine categories or patterns.[6] For the purposes of this chapter, because of the small volume of research, it is

[5]Attention should be called to Chapter VI of Clark's study which deals with implications
for theory and policy and with recommendations. A review of this material is outside the
province of a report of this character since it goes beyond findings into interpretation. It is,
however, a most valuable, not to say brilliant, contribution of value beyond the area of
public school adult education.
[6]R. B. Spence and A. W. Cass, "The Agencies of Adult Education," *Review of Educational
Research*, June 1950.

sufficient to adapt slightly a classification used by Houle,[7] who identifies four major types of adult education agencies:

1. Agencies developed primarily for the education of adults, such as university and agricultural extension and correspondence schools.

2. Agencies developed for the education of children and youth, such as public schools, which out of a sense of the need have developed programs of adult education; this includes parent-teacher associations and colleges.

3. Institutions developed to serve the whole community in specific ways which have expanded their original programs to include adult education, such as libraries, museums and social settlements.

4. Agencies and institutions founded for noneducational purposes that have undertaken adult education in order to strengthen their major programs and to do their job better. Among these are labor unions, churches, cooperatives, business organizations and the agencies of health, welfare and recreation.

Administrative arrangements vary widely. In the absence of research dealing with the organization and administration of adult education in practically all of these agencies, it should be pointed out that except in the first category adult education occupies a position somewhat similar to its place in the public school. Many of the individual institutions in the third category, for instance, are not engaged in adult education at all beyond what is called for by a traditional interpretation of their specific purpose. Others have barely begun to take a large view of the field. Still others, like the Enoch Pratt Library in Baltimore and the Newark, New Jersey, Public Library, have programs of scope and vigor which have attracted national attention.

As in the schools, therefore, adult education in most of the agencies mentioned in the last two categories above is marginal or peripheral. Whether this has the same effect and causes the same problems as in public school adult education, only research can determine. Such research might well include some case studies of situations under categories two to four above, where adult education has been successfully integrated into the organizational and administrative structure of various types of agencies. A sufficient sample of such cases, if they can be found, might point the way toward the solution of the problems Clark mentions.

An interesting suggestion with respect to the organization of adult

[7]Cyril Houle and others, *The Armed Services and Adult Education,* American Council on Education, Washington, 1947.

education comes from a study by Hoffer[8] which compared two quite similar Michigan counties which, however, differed sharply in the conduct of the Extension program. In one, the Extension Service personnel attempted to set up their own separately organized groups throughout the county. In the other the agents worked through existing organizations as far as possible. The latter was much more successful in terms of participation and other tests of the effectiveness of Extension programs. Hoffer concludes that adult educational activities should be introduced into primary associations and institutions, since the people who belong to them are more likely to be interested and participate in activities which are a part of the program of their churches, labor unions and similar organizations, than they are to flock to a new agency which they often view with mild suspicion.

Obviously a single study does not prove the point and there are many successful Extension programs where this plan has not been followed. Hoffer's study does, however, suggest a method of organization which may be effective where many agencies compete for the available leadership and leisure time of the people.

An opinion study conducted by McClusky touches on this point.[9] It records the consensus of professional workers in public school adult education as to the administrative responsibilities for adult education.

These school men saw the duty of the local school to be:

1. To provide such adult educational facilities and services as the school can offer more effectively than other agencies.

2. To cooperate with and help nonschool agencies to increase the value of their educational services.

3. To see that some other agency than the school assumes the chief responsibility for coordination of nonschool adult educational activities.

These last two points raise the broad question of coordination of all adult education programs in local communities, often attempted through adult education councils. There is no question but that planning and coordination in adult education are necessary since the field's organization and administration are in a very chaotic state; this is inevitably so since so much adult education is an adjunct of agencies whose primary purposes are concerned with other activities. The efforts to effect coordination through councils are discussed in Chapter XIII.

[8] C. Hoffer and D. L. Gibson, *The Community Situation as it Affects Agricultural Extension Work,* East Lansing, Michigan State University, 1941; and C. Hoffer, *Social Organization in Relation to Extension Services in Eaton County, Michigan.*
[9] H. McClusky, "Adult Education in Public Schools," *Educational Bulletin,* University of Michigan, February, 1945.

PROGRAMS AND PROGRAM PLANNING

Programs of adult education are as varied as the agencies participating in the movement. If anything, there is even more variation in the procedures for deciding on the program to be offered. The very use of the word program by most adult education agencies is significant, for in conventional educational parlance, a program is technically the curriculum. This latter word, however, is restricted to public schools, adult evening colleges and university extension. Even these agencies, especially the last-named, do not invariably use the term curriculum to describe their offerings. It is apparent, then, that in the field as a whole, program is a more flexible, less restrictive term than curriculum. It is no accident that the narrower term is employed chiefly by those adult education agencies which offer courses for credit, even though they may have many noncredit offerings as well.

Properly speaking, the term program in adult education should be related to three different levels. At the *community* level, it relates to all educational activities for adults available in any given community. As such, in places which have them, program would be a major concern of councils of adult education, discussed in Chapter XIII. At the institutional level, program is obviously the concern of a single agency and relates only to what adult education opportunities the institution offers its own clientele. Finally, on the activity level, program relates only to the design of a single adult educational activity.

These categories are not used in this chapter since existing research has not made these differentiations, but the use of some such conceptual scheme in future program planning research would reduce semantic confusion and make possible more refined definition of both research issues and their attendant methodological problems.

Credit and noncredit university programs. Credit courses leading to certificates, diplomas or degrees must conform to the standards laid down for such awards, often by state authorities. Obviously such programs can be little influenced by teachers or students. Other agencies are equally insistent upon standardized content and procedures. The lifesaving courses sponsored by the Red Cross fit this pattern for obvious reasons. The Great Books Foundation, in the nature of the case, follows predetermined sequences based upon the classics it has selected. These are but two examples.

Probably because of this situation, there is very little research other than descriptive material dealing with adult education curricula. It is doubtless not without significance that the two agencies with the most flexible programs have engaged in more research dealing with program building than all others combined. These are the Agricultural and Home Economics Extension Services of our colleges of agriculture, and the parent education groups. It should be added, however, that many credit courses, perhaps especially above the high school level, are open to noncredit students on an auditing basis.

Some differences between credit and noncredit courses. So far as teaching personnel are available and demand exists, credit courses parallel the content of courses offered to day students in both public schools and colleges. Noncredit courses for adults in these institutions are greatly influenced by student demand as measured by enrollment and attendance. In public institutions high demand impresses the administrator and the appropriating authority. In private institutions such courses pay their own way and contribute to the overhead. These essentially economic considerations make it difficult to plan either a well-rounded program or a long-term one, which might prove its value, if tested, over the span of a few years.[1]

Harrison, however, attributes the different program designs of credit and noncredit curricula in evening colleges to differences in the age and maturity of the students.[2] He conducted a questionnaire

[1]Burton R. Clark, *Adult Education in Transition: A Study of Institutional Insecurity,* Los Angeles, University of California Press, 1956.

[2]J. W. Harrison, *Designing Educational Programs for Adults: A Comparison of Non-Credit and Credit Courses in University Evening Colleges,* Ph.D. dissertation, University of Chicago, 1957.

study which included teachers and students in both credit and non-credit courses, but based his analysis chiefly on replies from the instructors. While his instrument covered more elements than program design, such as location of classes, he found differentiating attitudes on a number of elements in program design between teachers of credit and noncredit courses. The latter favored accepting any student interested in a subject and permitting each to work at his own speed. They opposed giving examinations and requiring written papers. On all these points instructors in credit courses disagreed. Teachers of noncredit courses advocated interviewing their students and following their interests. On these points their colleagues were negative or undecided. In the main students agreed with their instructors but reversed them in that those in credit courses were more interested in practical applications than the older, noncredit students.

These and other differences, Harrison believes, sustained his hypothesis that the effectiveness of some elements in an educational program are affected by the maturity of the learner, though others are of equal validity for all groups. The noncredit group in his study was older. This is to say that the objectives and motives of students in noncredit courses are probably different from those taking classes for collegiate credit. They thus conform to the more usual type of adult education situation. It follows that the instructors must adapt their methods to audiences with somewhat different objectives.

SOME SAMPLE PROGRAMS

Many of the descriptive studies available use different methods and bases of reporting offerings available to adults, but a few samples may be given before turning to noncredit program building.

Public school cases. A recent study of adult education offerings in the public schools of Colorado revealed that half of the courses, 50.3 per cent, were vocational. Of these, 42.5 per cent were agricultural. General academic subjects stood second, 11.6 per cent, many of these leading to a high school diploma. Courses in public affairs followed closely with 9.8 per cent, but this tenth of the courses captured 43.0 per cent of the enrollment. The remaining offerings, in order, were concerned with the following areas of interest: fine arts, recreation, personal improvement, home and family life, and elementary education.[3]

The largest adult evening school in Los Angeles lists 99 courses,

[3]Thomas J. Gilligan and W. T. Van Orman, *Planning a State Adult Education Program in Colorado,* Denver, Denver University, Doctor of Education study, 1956.
[4]Clark, *op.cit.*

some of them given in several sections. These include 15 in English and speech—largely vocational in nature, such as commercial writing, but including speech correction, public speaking, and three literature courses; citizenship, civics, chemistry, bookkeeping, foreign languages, home decoration, music, real estate law and appraisal, psychology of personality, rug-making, shorthand, United States history. The smallest school in this system offered 27 courses, largely vocational or dealing with personal improvement.[4]

A university example. A list of nonvocational courses offered for adults, some for credit, some not, by two universities in eastern Canada in 1955 included painting, music and art in Europe, folk dancing, general economics, the Middle East, English composition, English novel, music appreciation, philosophy, religion, business and industrial psychology, child psychology, sociology, history of art, art appreciation, money and banking, garden flowers, current events, Soviet Russia, the state in economic life, personality problems, the art of shorter fiction, understanding ourselves, foreign languages, the individual and society.[5]

It must be remembered that in most colleges and universities courses offered adults through university extension or schools of general studies are open to both credit and noncredit students. Programs have been expanding, especially in the last decade or more, on both collegiate and high school levels. This is true even in the rural schools.[6]

Factors in successful public school programs. The descriptive studies alluded to do not tell how the programs, whether credit or noncredit, were determined. Spence and Shangold, however, examining the reports from the public schools of New York State, outside New York City—and this state has an extensive program for which state aid is available—indicate 18 factors related to the excellence of adult education programs in public schools.[7] They do not, however, define excellence nor do they discuss the relative importance of these factors which may be summarized as follows:

1. Awareness by the community of the need for the continuous education of adults.

[5]Roby Kidd, *Adult Education in Canadian Universities,* Toronto: Canadian Adult Education Association, 1956.

[6]H. Kempfer, *Adult Education Activities of the Public Schools,* Washington, D. C.: Office of Education, 1949; J. H. Kolb and E. deS. Brunner, *A Study of Rural Society,* Boston: Houghton-Mifflin Co., 1952, pp. 346-48.

[7]R. Spence and B. Shangold, *Public School Adult Education in New York State, 1944-1947,* Albany: University of the State of New York, Bulletin 1391, 1952.

2. Leadership of the program by the school's chief administrative officer.

3. Support by the board of education.

4. Financial support by the state.

5. An able director of adult education.

6. Supervisory help from the state department of education.

7. Recognition of responsibility of the local community to assist in developing the program.

8. Readiness of the school to work with organized groups in the community.

9. Broad involvement of the community in building the program.

10. Increasing use of qualified citizens under adequate staff supervision.

11. In-service training for all having responsibilities in the program.

12. Continuous evaluation of the program.

13. A wide range of offerings tailor-made to meet the needs of the community.

14. Willingness to take the program to the people where they are.

15. Use of a variety of appropriate materials, such as pamphlets, films, recordings, etc.

16. Adequate counselling of registrants.

17. Flexibility in schedule as to time of day, length of class period, and of unit or course, thus adjusting so far as possible to the needs of the participants.

18. Continuous research.

A later and more intensive study of adult education programs of selected urban school systems in the same state confirmed most of these points and added several others.[8] De Groat found, for instance, that an informal atmosphere permitting contact and sociability with persons of similar interests was a very real factor in winning a "success" rating. Classes small enough to permit some individual attention if desired by participants were important except in the case of forums on public affairs and of classes concerned with home and family life. These were relatively few in number but drew disproportionately large shares of the total enrollment.

Other "success" factors that emerged from De Groat's study were good teaching and counselling, adequate facilities, and in some cases, willingness of the school system to locate classes in more than one center, even in private homes.

[8] Fannie M. De Groat, *Elements that Seem to Contribute to Successful Adult Education Programs in Selected Public Schools in the State of New York,* Unpublished Ph.D. dissertation, Cornell University, 1952.

Both of these studies emphasize characteristics of the program examined in terms of "success." They could also be considered criteria by which the excellence of any specific program could be determined. Some of these points are sustained by the research of the more informal agencies to which we now turn.

SOME PROGRAM BUILDING PROBLEMS IN INFORMAL AGENCIES

Informal organizations face a variety of needs, motivations and intellectual habits among their potential constituencies, some of which create problems of a different order from those faced by formal agencies. One of the controlling elements is clearly variations in the amount of participants' free time and in the demands their vocations make.[9] These factors must be considered in any program design.

Bunge's experiment, based on interviews and questionnaires with business and professional men on Long Island, led him to distinguish several recognizable types among men in this group in terms of their attitude toward adult education. The first was composed of those who expressed a real desire to broaden their horizons but felt they could not find the time. The motivations of others in terms of leisure time activity were clearly not intellectual. Still others felt they could acquire whatever they needed through their social contacts and by experience.

At least one study among young adults gives some support to this contention. Harby discovered that a considerable amount of incidental learning took place among Civilian Conservation Corps enrollees in terms of the situation and from interpersonal contacts.[10] However, this was a controlled situation.

Bunge found much interest expressed in civic problems but few men budgeted their time to permit them to work systematically at these or other problems. Put more briefly, Bunge's findings describe the inertia against which adult educators have to work where motivations are not strong. They also indicate the competing claims of family, social life or favored recreations upon the time of men in professional and business occupations. Programs must be sufficiently interesting and purposeful to overcome these handicaps.

Surveys for program design. Several studies indicate that one way to erode inertia is to involve potential participants in program planning conferences or in local surveys. The major finding of one study covering four states showed that such conferences can be effective in

[9]A. Frederick Bunge, *An Experimental Study of a Process for Program Planning in Adult Education,* Doctor of Education thesis, Teachers College, Columbia University, 1955.
[10]S. F. Harby, *A Study of Education in the Civilian Conservation Corps Camps of the Second Corps Area,* Ann Arbor, Mich.: Edwards Brothers, 1938.

helping local leaders inventory adult education needs and resources and to evaluate and improve existing programs.[11]

Whether dignified by the term survey or not, studying the situation is unquestionably a useful device in promoting successful adult education programs. In a project sponsored by the State College of Washington, the entire County Extension Service staff visited families informally, "dropping in to get acquainted." This approach was consonant with rural values of neighborliness. The method contributed basic knowledge of the people and their needs and gave specific information as to the cultural and other social forces operating in any given situation. Incidentally, such visits also offered the opportunity to promote the existing program and to evaluate it.[12]

This is a time-consuming method and might not be practical in cities where the potential constituency is large and the staff largely part-time in contrast to the full-time workers of the Extension Service. On the other hand, the value of the survey process participated in by the adult educators themselves is amply attested. Brannon quotes an experienced county extension agent, judged to be successful by his director, who had opposed such a study, admitting after hearing the report of the survey, "I've worked in this county 15 years and had to come to a meeting to find out I did not know the simplest facts about my county and its people."[13]

One more such study is worth noting because it concerned a problem area of ten townships largely settled by foreign-born and foreign-stock Polish farmers where the level of living and educational status were well below the state average. Rural adult education through the Extension Service had not been very successful. A large, carefully selected sample of 200 homes was interviewed in the language of the interviewee's choice. Typically, the vocational part of the interview (agriculture) was in English but when the family and community were discussed the conversation lapsed into Polish. Among the findings was the discovery that the problems of these people were both technical and social and that they could not be separated. An understanding of the interrelationships of the two as viewed by the people was clearly of paramount importance to the adult educator.

[11]C. D. Jayne and J. R. Gibb, *Report of the Mountain-Plains Adult Education Project,* Washington: National Education Association, 1955. Also reported in summary form in *Adult Education,* vol. V, no. 4, Summer 1955.

[12]A. J. Erickson, *Listen to the People Speak,* University Park, Pa.: American Association of Agricultural College Editors, 1956, mimeographed.

[13]Luther H. Brannon, *The Role of the Oklahoma Agricultural Extension Division with Particular Reference to County Program Development,* unpublished Ph.D. dissertation, Harvard University, 1950.

The successful program initiated on the basis of this study therefore adopted a unified family approach focused on problems rather than on separate projects.[14] This finding lends some support to those who object to a sharp separation of vocational and nonvocational adult education. Such shifts from specific projects to problems increasingly characterizes the Extension Service.[15] Przedpelski and others state that an extra dividend from such studies is that the educators get to know people not as students or clients but as people.

Lay participation in program planning. Matthews, who analyzed 9,400 County Extension Service programs, found that close to two-thirds of these, 63 per cent, were developed by using committees representing all communities after possible programs had been discussed at community meetings, or by employing this device plus including representatives of other agencies.[16] This finding applied to both vocational and nonvocational activities.

The results of such planning procedures confirmed a finding by Jaccard[17] years ago to the effect that where the local people shared in the processes of program planning, attendance at the activities provided was significantly larger than elsewhere. Indeed Jaccard demonstrated in terms of counties that where 30 or more people participated in building the program attendance was relatively 3.8 times as great as where the number consulted was less than ten.

This philosophy of cooperative program building was tested for over a decade in the broad program of activities at Ogalby Park, Wheeling, West Virginia. While Dr. May's study is largely descriptive, the cumulative experience of this period is significant enough to give a few illustrations.[18] Effective use was made of self-surveys in planning activities. One survey of the membership of the various luncheon clubs of Wheeling uncovered a large and surprising number of hobbies which led to many educational activities in this area alone, as well as to many new friendships. A self-survey of music resources resulted in ten definite outcomes including a training program for church choirs, a concert series, and the organization of a music council. Involving people in an arts and crafts program, securing examples of local work,

[14]B. Przedpelski and others, *New Approaches for Agricultural Extension in Problem Areas,* Madison: Extension Service, College of Agriculture, University of Wisconsin, 1952.

[15]Brannon, *op. cit.*

[16]J. L. Matthews, *National Inventory of Extension Methods of Program Determination,* Washington, U.S. Department of Agriculture, Extension Service Circular 477, 1952.

[17]C. K. Jaccard, *Results of Organization Meetings in Kansas,* Manhattan: State College of Agriculture, 1931.

[18]Elizabeth E. May, *Experiments in Method in Adult Education,* New York, unpublished Doctor of Education thesis, Teachers College, Columbia University, 1937.

and moving the enlarged exhibit from an obscure location to a large former barn at the Park resulted in a 150-fold increase in the number of people viewing the exhibit. This and other results demonstrated, according to Dr. May, the value of bringing materials, exhibits and courses to an acceptable environment, rather than trying to force the adjustment of people to a new educational experience in a new and strange environment. This conclusion based on actual results suggests that many of those who say they would participate in adult education activities if conveniently located, one instance of which is given below, may be quite sincere.

There is practically unanimous agreement in all studies that the maximum involvement of potential and actual constituents in program building produces the best results. Richert, however, after a review of a large number of studies in social psychology, group dynamics and extension, cautions that merely securing representation of recognized groups and interests is not in itself a guarantee of successful program planning, if these persons do not possess perspectives beyond the boundaries of their own group. In addition, all program planning groups profit by some orientation in the planning process and "the formulation of group structure."[19]

Socio-economic influences on program. At this point a caution should be injected into the discussion. City wide or countywide programming, even when determined after wide, even structured consultation, can seriously neglect essential differences among neighborhoods or groups. Duncan and Kreitlow studied a number of pairs of rural neighborhoods as nearly identical as possible except that in each pair one had an ethnically homogeneous, the other a heterogeneous, population. They compared them as to attitudes toward and acceptance of 30 educational and 25 farming practices. The heterogeneous group was superior on almost all items. They had, for instance, higher educational goals and favored a broader school curriculum.[20]

This study and the previously mentioned one by Przedpelski clearly indicate the too seldom realized fact that socio-economic factors have a very real influence on the effectiveness of programs, as they also have on participation. One definitive study along these lines was based on a 5 per cent sample of the adult population in Springfield, Massa-

[19]M. Richert, *A Study of Factors for Consideration in Membership Selection of County Extension Program Committees,* unpublished Ph.D. dissertation, University of Wisconsin, 1957.

[20]J. Duncan and B. Kreitlow, "Selected Cultural Characteristics and the Acceptance of Educational Practices and Programs," *Rural Sociology,* December 1954. Cf. also, Edward Spicer, (ed.). *Human Problems in Technological Change,* New York, Russell Sage Foundation, 1952.

chusetts, which covered 5,000 persons distributed among 14 ecological areas defined by median education, economic status determined by automobile ownership, possession of a telephone, proportion filing income tax returns, proportion of native-born and occupational distribution.[21] Among these areas the median years of schooling, for instance, ranged from 6.6 to 11.9. Chi square values indicated that the differences were not chance.

It was found that geographic accessibility influenced attendance at five types of adult education activities studied. The lower the socio-economic status of the area, the higher was the proportion of persons who wanted such activities located within their neighborhoods. This was not merely a question of physical accessibility. Even more the factor of "psychological accessibility" was determinative. Persons from lower-status areas in unaccustomed surroundings had feelings of "not belonging" and of being unwelcome.

Formal programs such as lectures and courses attracted the better educated, economically advantaged persons from the higher ranking areas. Among these there was some overlapping of offerings. Increasing the number of possible activities resulted in increasing the aggregate attendance. While many of the factors covered in this study are discussed in the chapter on participation, this last finding has a definite bearing on program building, especially in situations where an attempt is being made to develop a coordinated program of adult education on a community basis.

Many rural studies point to the influence of socio-economic factors on adult education. Wilkening discovered that acceptance of new ideas and even of advanced practices in agricultural technology were largely a function of status factors or of factors clearly influenced by socio-economic status.[22]

While the results of such factors as those just discussed are revealed when participation is studied, the repeated demonstration in both city and country that those unreached by adult education programs fall into groups having similar characteristics raises the question as to whether program building in adult education has either neglected or failed to find ways to interest members of certain groups and statuses, and if so, why. Controlled experimental research would seem to be called for here.

[21]A. A. Kaplan, *Socio-Economic Circumstances and Adult Participation in Certain Cultural and Educational Activities,* New York, Teachers College, Columbia University Bureau of Publications, 1943.

[22]E. A. Wilkening, *Acceptance of Improved Farm Practices in Three Coastal Plain Counties,* Raleigh, North Carolina: Agricultural Experiment Station, Technical Bulletin 98, 1952.

The authors have found only one study that makes even an indirect approach to this question, a study of 12,000 enrollees in adult education programs in Austria in 1932.[23] It reported that office and sales personnel showed a strong affinity for courses in literature, art, philosophy and the social sciences. Metal and other skilled workers tended strongly toward mathematics, spelling and the natural sciences. For the former the manifest function of adult education was to increase general knowledge, the latent function, to assimilate the intellectual amenities of the middle class. For the latter the manifest function was to overcome recognized deficiencies, the latent function, socio-economic advancement.

Successful and less successful planning compared. Because no other comparable study was found, one other from extension sources deserves attention. In it, after an extensive review of the literature on program development—research, experiential and hortatory—Darter developed ten principles for program development and then tested them by intensive case studies of program development in 12 southern counties in two states which were ranked by administrators and supervisors as to successful or less successful programs.[24]

Darter found that the more successful agents, after getting the pertinent facts, emphasized the importance of developing the capabilities of the people, made planning itself an educational process, planned the programs with the local people, involving as many as possible in the process, and arranged the programs to get maximum coordination with other agencies. The philosophy of these agents emphasized the development of people rather than the conduct of educational projects.

The less effective agents were highly vocational in their approach, did no surveys of conditions either in communities or in the county, provided little educational experience, developed the program mainly themselves, used organized groups very little and provided for little coordination with other agencies.

As indicated, the programs developed by the first group of procedures were much more successful in securing participation and in their coverage of their potential constituencies than the latter.

Examples of programs from parent education. Lyle employed an intensive survey to develop a program of adult education in family life in one community. She secured data, largely by questionnaires, with

[23]L. Radermacher and E. Smith, "Occupation and Adult Education Courses," in P. Lazarsfeld and M. Rosenberg, (eds.), *The Language of Social Research*, Glencoe, Ill.: The Free Press, 1955.

[24]V. W. Darter, *County Extension Program Development,* unpublished Doctor of Public Administration thesis, Harvard University, 1955.

respect to the physical environment of a sample of homes, provision of books and magazines, pattern of family living, degree to which family members shared the responsibilities of home life and economic security, degree to which the family shared decisions on matters of interest to all members, amount of family encouragement to children to develop special talents, and degree of concern with respect to community, national and world problems.

The school in this community had both an adult education program and a forum with program and policies made by a citizens' council. On the basis of the knowledge of the community and its attitudes secured by the study, Lyle proposed 11 program modifications and listed 14 problems needing discussion.[25] There is no information on the subsequent use of this study by the community. The citizens' council obviously offered a recognized forum for the consideration of the suggestions and for bringing approved policy changes to the attention of the administrative authority, which could then act with citizen approval for changes made.

The use of advisory committees in program planning, as in this case, is one of the most nearly universal procedures practiced by adult education agencies. Schools, libraries, community colleges, the Cooperative Extension Service and many voluntary agencies all employ it to a greater or lesser extent. It is frequently an effective device for insuring a more democratic participation in program building than would otherwise occur. In some situations members of advisory committees even perform staff services at times, such as getting out publicity and helping with registration.

Use of counsellors in program planning. Another study tested the use of a counsellor in developing an adult education program in the field of family life which had suggestive results, especially in view of the theoretical emphasis by adult educators on the need for better advice to registrants.

A group of 145 Parent-Teacher Association members were used in this study. Sixty of them responded to questions on most pressing family problems and rated 29 problems culled from the literature in the field. The others had an hour's discussion with a counsellor, following which they checked the questionnaire and responded to an open-ended series of questions. This latter group produced an average of nearly five priority problems per individual. The other group averaged 1.21. The pattern and distribution of the problems was similar

[25] Mary S. Lyle, *Adult Education for Democracy in Family Life*, Ames, Iowa: Collegiate Press, 1944.

for both groups, but the use of a counsellor obviously stimulated a more far-reaching analysis. Personal adjustment problems rank first, marital problems second and problems of sexual adjustment third. This similarity lends an element of confidence to the use of the questionnaire, but clearly the use of a counsellor was more productive, and not merely in terms of the number of problems listed. An analysis of the interviews indicated that while the topics discussed in the Parent-Teacher Association meetings were of value to parents, their greater concerns lay below the level reached in these programs.[26] Hale concluded that counselling was needed as a supplement to an adult education program and that it would greatly improve programs.

Strong confirmation of this finding in general terms comes from the analysis of the experiences with the educational programs of the Armed Services in World War II. This showed that the need for counselling and guidance among adults of military age was great in terms of helping them to both analyze their educational needs and to select the most helpful learning experiences. Guidance was also needed in meeting basic personality problems. Houle and his colleagues concluded that an effective adult education program cannot be established without adequate guidance procedures.[27] This conclusion confirms the experience of the experimental program of the American Association for Adult Education in counselling persons on relief in the early years of the great depression. While Houle's conclusion may seem extreme in the light of many reasonably successful adult education efforts in which guidance has been minimal, it may be taken as established that adequate guidance of participants in adult education programs of any scope multiplies the positive effects and reduces the proportion of drop-outs.

Adult education and action programs. Considerations of a quite different sort are presented by two studies of the discussion of public affairs by adult education groups,[28] both of which were rated as successful. In the Canadian project, the Farm Radio Forum, materials are distributed to groups prior to the broadcast to which they listen; afterward they discuss and report their judgments. In Ohio the dis-

[26]C. B. Hale, *A Study of Parent-Identified Need for Education and Help with Family Life Problems,* University of California, Los Angeles, Doctor of Education project, 1954.

[27]C. Houle and others, *The Armed Services and Adult Education,* Washington, D.C.: American Council on Education, 1947. See also chapter on interests, pp. 111ff. for a discussion of counselling from that point of view.

[28]J. Nicol, A. A. Shea, G. L. Simmins, and A. Sim, *Canada's Farm Radio Forum,* UNESCO, Paris, 1954; J. Friesen, *The Role of the Ohio Farm Bureau Federation and Its Neighborhood Councils in Rural Adult Education,* Unpublished Doctor of Education report, Teachers College, Columbia University, 1948.

cussion is based on distributed materials only, which cover the major positions on each issue presented. Group discussions and decisions are reported to headquarters. The Ohio program enlists about one-third of the Farm Bureau membership—about 20,000 persons in some 1,560 groups. In both situations civic awareness has been increased and the recorded opinions are influential in legislative bodies. The Canadian program has a considerable urban audience. In both, participants share in program determination. In Canada, for instance, use is made of an annual questionnaire and provincial conferences capped by a national meeting. In Ohio the state office avoids program dictation; the state officers are "on tap not on top."

Such procedures in program planning have successfully sustained these programs for many years. In Canada, however, it has been found that the average group's life is only two years unless action within the local community eventuates. This may be in part because of the nature of many of the topics, such as cooperative hospitalization, improving rural schools, library service and the like.

This finding raises interesting issues and challenges one school of thought among adult educators. Should program determination allow for action? Is knowledge for its own sake enough? Apparently the Canadian and Ohio experiences differ in their answers to such questions. In Ohio the registering of group consensus or of group viewpoints on issues seems to be action enough. The issue is particularly acute in public affairs adult education. The adult educator engaged in this activity is supposed to be neutral. His function is to further understanding of an issue and the points of view with respect to it. If he shows bias, at least without warning his group of his own position, he is labeled a special pleader. If the program is tax-supported this is often a serious charge. Some would therefore ban the discussion of controversial issues in all tax-supported adult education.

On the other hand, a number of school systems and 40 state colleges of agriculture through their Extension Services have had public affairs discussion programs for many years and have included controversial issues. In one state consideration of the school situation by such groups reportedly carried the day for increased state aid to education and for enabling legislation which opened the way for school consolidation. It may not be without significance that the community action programs initiated by the listening groups in Canada typically related to local affairs and that the groups were wholly without official connections. On provincial and national levels action, if it occurred, resulted wholly from publicizing the results of the polls taken by the hundreds of local groups. Many types of adult education definitely aim at action by participants, nor are these wholly in the vocational field. Art, music and public speaking are illustrations. This whole area greatly needs research. Successful and unsuccessful programs of public affairs discussion should be studied and the causes of the outcomes determined. These could relate to methods employed, promotion and auspices of programs, types of support and other factors. One very interesting and significant descriptive case study of one program is "The Community Education Project" a report of the San Bernardino Valley College, California.[29]

Long-term programming. Some considerations bearing on this issue and on the values of long-term programming are suggested by Morrow.[30] She defines programming as "a problem-solving process in which methods of scientific analysis are applied to the present situation of the local people to plan a course of action that will lead to new and better situations." Morrow's hypothesis is that program designing is done too quickly, hence is apt to be based on trivial topics of immediate but momentary interest, and that it is usually not coordinated with previous learning or developed as a logical unit in a long-term educational effort.

In order to overcome this handicap, Morrow suggests, on the basis of field experimentation, that programs should be based on conference-determined over-all objectives and self-surveys; they should be discussed by potential participants, leaders and administrators. This committee process should result in setting up long-range programs of which each annual program would be a logical part. The procedure described was followed in some groups in one county and compared with other groups using traditional methods of program determination. The results initially favored the more intensive or long-term procedures, but final evaluation must await the end of the long-term program set by the experimental groups. The program provides for action both in the application of knowledge and in terms of progressing over several years through a predetermined program.

Summary. In sum, it may be said that research in adult education program planning clearly shows, at least in terms of informal and noncredit agencies, (1) that the situation and the problems inherent in it must be taken into account along with the objectives, interests and needs of the people; (2) that the participation of local people in developing the program on the basis of the facts should be secured;

[29]E. I. Johnson, *The Community Education Project, A Four-Year Report,* San Bernardino, California: San Bernardino, Valley College, 1957.
[30]E. Morrow, *Long Range Integrated Programming for Adult Education,* Unpublished Ph.D. dissertation, University of Chicago, 1957.

and (3) that the planning itself should become an educational process which will assist people to analyze their own problems and decide on those steps which will help toward their solution through education.

Further research needs. It would be advantageous to study the processes of curriculum construction employed by the more formalized adult education agencies, such as public schools, colleges, universities and university extension and especially to set up pilot projects in which some of the experience of informal agencies would be tested for applicability to these other institutions. In such a study particular attention could be given to the apparently high rate of dropouts, discussed elsewhere in this report, to determine whether more participation by students in program planning in the more formal adult education agencies would reduce the dropout rate. What determines the inclusion or elimination of a course? To what extent can institutions support courses designed to fulfill the claims of adult educators with respect to making more informed and therefore better citizens, if such efforts do not immediately win participant support? Apart from courses in English for foreigners and naturalization procedures, should programs be adapted for ethnic groups? Do varying social, economic and educational statuses require differentiation in program offerings? Experiments in reaching different status groups, perhaps especially with content known not to have had a wide appeal thus far to lower-status groups, could well be made.

What evidence exists indicates the value of better counselling for adult education participants. Advisement, counselling and registration procedures need study, both in terms of program improvement and in terms of the possible effect of improved procedures in reducing the proportion of dropouts and in improving administrative knowledge of what potential enrollees actually need. How many participants actually register in second or third choice courses and are eventually disappointed? Such research should examine the experience of some corporations which finance nonvocational courses for their employees where demand is sufficient. There is a tendency in adult education to shape programs on the basis of the reactions of current participants to the available offerings. Studies to appraise both the manifest and latent needs and interests of the potential public as well as the actual enrollees might result in expanded offerings and enlarged clientele.

Significant too in terms of program building would be a study on a comparative basis of the values persons of different ages, backgrounds, educational and socio-economic statuses attach to formal and informal adult education. What attitudes do people of these various characteristics have in relation to available educational programs and are they in fact aware of their availability? Inferentially such a study would also give a valuable clue to the impact of the several adult educational programs on the population.

Of a different order would be studies of the nonworking time of people of different ages and educational and socio-economic statuses and their use of that time. What are the actual or potential conflicts in the demands of family, social groups and organizations, and churches upon each of these categories of adults? How can adult education programs be adjusted to fit into the time available?[31]

Finally, the methods and design of several of the studies noted in this section could well be repeated in other and different situations to increase the validity of the findings or to suggest necessary amendments to them.

[31]Years ago the senior author directed a study in which about 3,000 adults were asked how they spent their leisure time, how much of it was mortgaged by organizational activities and what three things they would most like to do if in absolute control of their leisure. There was almost no relationship between actual and desired activities.

METHODS AND TECHNIQUES
IN ADULT EDUCATION

The literature of adult education seldom distinguishes between methods and techniques. In an as yet unpublished study at Florida State University, Professor Coolie Verner points out that the use of these two terms as synonymous is confusing in that it fails to distinguish between the role of the institution or agency and that of the adult educator.[1]

METHODS AND TECHNIQUES DISTINGUISHED

"As a consequence, confusion develops between the administrative function of the institution and the processes which facilitate learning. In addition, without distinguishing between these two roles, there is no conceptual scheme upon which to build a design for research into the effectiveness of the diffusion processes.

"Adult education is concerned with the diffusion of knowledge as a means of inducing changes in attitudes and behavior. An adult educa-

[1] The opening section of this chapter is a summary of his forthcoming study of this topic prepared by Professor Coolie Verner. It may be said that concern over precise definitions of the two terms, methods and techniques, is evidence of the growing maturity of a discipline. Professor Wesley Mitchell, for instance, addressed himself to this problem in several of his early annual reports as Director of the National Bureau of Economic Research in the 1920s, a period when modern economic research was beginning to develop rapidly.

142

tor, therefore, is an agent for change operating within the context of an institutional program. This program must have organization and be a planned effort to achieve learning through a direct relationship with the learner, rather than by chance as is true in the case of general diffusion through advertising, propaganda or mass media.

"When an institution or agency chooses to organize directed learning activities for the diffusion of knowledge is must select the way to accomplish this in terms of the importance of such a program to institutional objectives, the resources available for it, and the 'public' to whom the program is directed. This is an administrative decision that determines the kind of a relationship that will be established between the learner, the knowledge, and the institution itself. This is the *method* of adult education.

"Method, then, may be described as the relationship which exists between the learner, the knowledge, and the institution which has knowledge to diffuse in order to bring about changes in attitudes and behavior. In some cases, such as universities or public schools, the objectives of the institution may encompass knowledge in general; while, in other cases, as in health and welfare agencies, the knowledge to be diffused may involve specific changes in behavior.

"In general, the 'public' for whom institutions seek to provide programs may be individuals in isolation, organized groups, or the community as a whole. In structuring a learning situation for individuals, the institution may choose such methods as correspondence, internship, apprenticeship, or directed individual study. On the group level it may use discussion, classes, laboratory, assembly, exhibition or convention. When directed to the community, either fundamental education or community development programs may be used. Each of these methods describes a relationship for learning which the institution has established. An institution may choose, furthermore, a combination of methods in an effort to serve an expanded public.

"Once the method has been determined by administrative decision a second stage in the diffusion process comes into play. Within the context of the method, the agent (i.e. adult educator, teacher, etc.) seeks to facilitate the learning process by establishing a relationship between the material being diffused and the learner. To this end, the agent may employ a wide variety of established processes or invent new ones that, in one circumstance or another, prove useful in furthering learning. These processes are the *techniques* of adult education.

"Not all techniques can be used appropriately with all methods but some are useful with many methods. Thus, a university conducting a program of correspondence study (the method) would not use role-playing (a technique) ; however, an agency using discussion (a method) would use group discussion (the technique) or role-playing and 'buzz' groups. Within the framework of the assembly or convention method, for example, the adult educator might utilize lecture, panel, forum, or group discussion techniques.

"Because of the way in which the field has developed there are numerous instances of confusion and conflict in terminology, so that the same term is used to designate the method and the technique. Thus, discussion is used to designate the method as in 'discussion method' and to indicate the technique, as in 'group discussion'. Such duplication of words is inevitable in the evolution of a science where two concepts are similar in nature but not distinguished sufficiently early to prevent duplication.

"In addition, there are many instances in which the properties of a method or technique are ascribed to materials or devices that are actually adjuncts of a method or technique. Thus, the library is sometimes referred to as a method when it is actually the institution with knowledge in general to diffuse. In the case of the library it usually seeks diffusion to individuals and through its Readers' Advisory Service employs directed individual study as its method.

"Audio-visual aids, bulletins, and such are frequently referred to as methods when in reality they are devices or materials used by the agent to supplement some technique. Used alone, such devices cannot be considered either methods or techniques because they do not establish an organized direct relationship with the learner involving some direct exchange between the learner and the agent. In such instances they become processes for the general diffusion of knowledge rather than methods or techniques for adult education.

"Similarly, 'extension' is not a method although it is so described frequently by both university and agricultural extension personnel. University extension divisions use a variety of methods such as correspondence, classes and such. Agricultural extension uses individual and group methods of one kind or another. Actually the term extension merely indicates that the method is applied outside the normal organizational pattern of the institutions.

"So far as research is concerned, it is one thing to study the effectiveness of a method in diffusing knowledge and quite another thing to study the efficiency of a technique in facilitating learning. Thus far, most of the research in the diffusion of knowledge has been in terms of the general diffusion of knowledge not involving a direct relationship with the learner rather than on methods of adult education. Research in adult education, however, has concentrated on the efficiency of techniques in facilitating learning."

Early extension studies. An illustration of this last point is to be found in many of the early studies in agricultural and home economics extension. The time and dollar costs of various extension teaching techniques such as meetings, demonstrations, radio talks and the like were determined. Surveys were made to determine which techniques had resulted in changed practices or attitudes and a ratio of practices adapted to the cost of the techniques was worked out. Later this procedure was refined to determine variations by sex, education and socioeconomic status.[2] A summary of this research by Wilson and Gallup classified these techniques, or methods as these authors called them, into the following categories:

Individual contacts (counselling)
Group contacts
Media used in the conscious dissemination of ideas, information and
    techniques
Indirect influence or the spread of ideas resulting from the total
    effort.

An alternate classification these authors suggest is by the "form" or technique used, such as the spoken word through meetings, broadcasting or counselling, the written word through bulletins, leaflets, news articles, and the visual education aids.

This research by the Extension Service has determined that it takes on an average of two and one-half "exposures" before a new practice, attitude or idea is accepted. There are varying "intensities" in the force of the technique used.[3]

Effect of meetings. With the rising educational level of the rural population, meetings have become more important in achieving educational objectives and are preferred over other devices by the clientele.[4] Lectures at such meetings are considerably more effective if used with film strips or charts and supplemented by a discussion period than when used without these aids.[5]

Crile has recently summarized the results of research on meetings.[6] She found that the percentage of persons listing meetings as "the most

[2]M. C. Wilson and G. Gallup, *Extension Teaching* Methods, Washington, D. C.: United States Department of Agriculture, 1955.
[3]*Ibid.*
[4]W. C. Rohrer, *The Extension Service in Cecil County, Maryland,* College Park, University of Maryland, Agricultural Experiment Station, 1954.
[5]C. Hearne, *Factors Which Affect the Influence of Meetings as a Means of Extension Teaching,* Madison, University of Wisconsin, Unpublished M.A. thesis, 1932.
[6]L. Crile, *Findings from Research on Meetings,* Washington: United States Department of Agriculture, Extension Service, 1956.

helpful method of adult education" increased with the educational level of the respondents and that attendance at meetings was associated with income, education and the degree of listening to the radio broadcasts of the college of agriculture. The success of meetings understandably varied not only with the care given to promoting them, but also with the effectiveness of planning the meeting itself.

Crile also found that interpersonal contacts were educationally important on all socio-economic and income levels but that the lower the educational status the more important they became in the spread of new ideas.

Conversely the lower the educational status of the participants in a program the greater their desire for demonstrations or case materials in teaching about any topic.[7]

These studies show that multiple approaches are advisable especially in reaching persons with below average education.[8] The ever-present problem is to determine what methods or techniques are best for what kinds of people used by what sorts of teachers in what types of situations. To this end studies similar to those described might very usefully be undertaken by other institutions.

This has been done to a degree by the Department of Defense. A considerable number of its studies showed that the use of two techniques was better than one. Thus tests after the use of a lecture and film produced scores 20 per cent better than scores where only lecture or film had been used.[9]

With respect to other methods and techniques, the available research is both spotty and uneven, and much of it descriptive, especially of devices used by a skillful adult educator in particular situations and described on the basis of such experience, but with no data that permit generalizations as to wider applicability. Two areas of research with respect to methods and techniques in adult education are exceptions to this statement. These concern the use of audio-visual aids to teaching and the whole complex topic of reading as an aid to effective adult education. These will be discussed in the two closing sections of this chapter.

Role-playing. First, however, it is necessary to consider a relatively new device for which there is considerable enthusiasm—role-playing, mentioned also briefly in the chapter on Discussion. The theory be-

[7]Wilson and Gallup, op. cit.; Per Stensland, *Education and Action in an American Labor Union,* New York: Teachers College, Columbia University, Unpublished Ph.D. dissertation, 1950.

[8]H. F. Lionberger, *Low-Income Farmers in Missouri,* Columbia: University of Missouri, Agricultural Experiment Station, 1949.

[9]See Page 154 of this report for further support of this finding.

hind this device is that by assuming and acting out a "role" a participant will become better acquainted with and more sympathetic to the point of view, attitudes and considerations which in life actually influence the person whose role he impersonates. Thus a white person might play the role of a Negro excluded from a convention hotel in a discussion of whether meetings should or should not be held in hotels which have a color bar.

A typical report on role-playing as an educational device described its use with 24 young adult leaders in the field of public affairs. The experience demonstrated the arguments used with respect to the issues discussed and is said to have stimulated the interest of the participants and increased their sympathy for other viewpoints.[10]

The most thorough-going study of role-playing uncovered by the authors, which investigated its effectiveness in an Armed Services' leader training program covering 8,000 men, throws some doubt on the validity of the enthusiasm for role-playing.[11] It demonstrated that role-playing does not soften rigid persons sufficiently to participate in this technique unless ample time is used and more than two experiences are provided. Zander also discovered that role-playing *always failed* when the nature of the class session tended toward neutrality with respect to the issues under discussion. For success the feelings of the group had to be worked up sufficiently to spark a discussion. These findings based on such a large number of subjects would suggest that the technique of role-playing should not be uncritically accepted by adult educators. Research is needed to determine what sorts of people, kinds of topics, purposes and situations lend themselves to its effective use, and to determine more precisely just what are the significant or effective factors in role-playing.

The place of theory. There has been some discussion as to the amount of attention that should be paid to theoretical considerations of the various subjects in adult education teaching. There are some who claim that adults "will not stand for much theory." This issue has been all but ignored in adult education research. Again the Army supplies the most definitive data we possess on this point. It conducted several experiments, dividing contingents of inductees into two paired

[10]L. Wilson, "Training Young Adult Leaders in Public Affairs," *Adult Leadership,* February 1958. See also, I. L. Janis and B. T. King, "The Influence of Role Playing on Opinion Change," in Maccoby, Newcomb, Hartley, (eds.), *Readings in Social Psychology,* Third editon, New York: Henry Holt and Co., 1958—the factors in role-playing found most significant for opinion change were "amount of improvisation" and "degree of satisfaction with own performance."
[11]Alvin Zander, "Role-Playing," *Sociatry,* June 1947.

groups. One was taught basic skills and the theory behind them. The other was instructed in the skill only. Those that had had the theory showed an 18 per cent gain in the mastery of the skill over those who had not.[12]

In summary. In summary of this part of the discussion, it must be pointed out that the methods, techniques and materials of adult education should be developed especially with their use with adults in mind. High school procedures and materials were found inappropriate again and again by both the Army and Navy. To teach adults successfully methods and techniques understandingly adapted to their needs and their maturity must be employed. Some major topics dealing with research in methods and techniques will be dealt with in following chapters. The remainder of this chapter will be given to two topics which do not require complete chapter treatment.

READABILITY

It is obvious that printed materials used in adult education must conform at least roughly to the reading ability of the users. No one would pick a text in nuclear physics for an elementary class in teaching English to foreigners. The first systematic research on the problem of readability was by Gray and Leary at Chicago.[13] They attempted to discover what it was in writing that caused difficulties. The expected results emerged: long, involved sentences, unusual polysyllabic words and other faults tending to produce a heavy style made things difficult for all readers and discouraged some. In other words, clarity and smoothness of style made a written work more readable and more enjoyable. But unexpectedly these authors found that difficult writing did not necessarily prevent their subjects from reading such work. Interest and strong motivation could overcome such handicaps.

An unpublished study by Mrs. Elizabeth Morriss and Dr. Dorothy Holverson made at Teachers College in the middle 1930s added another element to this result. Working with adult education groups in several New York City schools, they found that if written material dealt with familiar concepts, subjects or scenes, the students read and enjoyed writing of a more difficult level than they would otherwise finish. In other words, cultural conditioning influenced the acceptability of writing even for what tests showed was a somewhat below-

---

[12]C. Houle and others, *The Armed Services and Adult Education*, Washington, D. C.: American Council on Education, 1947. Houle and his colleagues take this data from No. 16 of the series of pamphlets entitled "What the Soldier Thinks," and issued by the Army.

[13]W. S. Gray and B. Leary, *What Makes a Book Readable*, Chicago: University of Chicago Press, 1935.

average educational status group. People not only tend to read what they already know about, a reflection of their interests, but because of their interest, the meaning they give the text grows out of their own background of experience and knowledge.[14] The relation of interests to reading is discussed in Chapter V.

Using the Thorndike word count based on some ten million words and relating it to educational status, the Readability Laboratory at Teachers College, Columbia University, under Professor Lyman Bryson, produced twelve "popularly" written volumes, such as: *Getting and Spending: The ABC of Economics*, by Mildred Adams, and *The Picture of Health*, by James Clark. Well and simply written and brief in scope, these were inexpensive volumes commercially published. For most of them, however, the total distribution was disappointing. Whether this was because of faulty promotion or for other reasons, such as the unfavorable image persons of 7th or 8th grade educational status had of book reading, was never determined. The experiment was conducted before the days of paperbacks and the discovery of the means to secure a mass market for the printed word. It is possible that today such a project would be more successful from the point of view of distribution.

Readability formulae. In the meantime several persons developed formulae as an aid to readable writing. Extensive use was made of these in some quarters. Clearly, however, formulae can not be slavishly followed,[15] and indeed there appear to be some materials they can not handle at all. Bentel showed this in hand picking passages from Erskine Caldwell, James Joyce and Gertrude Stein. Both the Flesch and Dale-Chall formulae rated Stein as easiest and Joyce and Caldwell as fairly easy.[16] Such formulae take no account of the meanings expressed by the words to which they are applied, the relationships among the words of a passage or of variations in the education or abilities of readers. Nor do any formulae take account of the special vocabulary of an occupation. A study of economic terms and concepts in farm magazines disclosed the use of 385 concepts, only 43 of which were on the Dale list. These terms concerned the farmers' own busi-

[14]Irving Lorge, "How People Read and Implications for Writer and Editor," in *Report of the Central States Publications Workshop*, Manhattan: Kansas State College of Agriculture, 1947.

[15]E. Dale and J. S. Chall, "A Formula for Predicting Readability," *Educational Research Bulletin*, January and February 1948; R. Flesch, *Marks of Readable Style*, Ph.D. dissertation, Teachers College, Columbia University, 1943; I. Lorge, "Readability Formulae— An Evaluation," *Elementary English*, February 1949.

[16]D. Bentel, "Readability Formulas Given a Working Over," *Editor and Publisher*, October 17, 1953.

ness and those applying to agriculture but not to other major divisions of the economy. An unusual number of terms were concerned with the role of government in the farm economy.

For some years the Extension Service of the United States Department of Agriculture analyzed their prospective publications for readability. While no study has ever been made of these various rural experiments, the testimony of those responsible in the Department of Agriculture is clear at several points. Farmers preferred lucid writing to turgid, as who does not, but they objected to the writing down, often perforce in more words than necessary, of technical terms and processes with which they were professionally familiar.

Several farm papers ran articles covering identical subject matter at two levels of readability and checked a sample of their readers as to their impressions and recall of the material. In one such series of experiments, *Wallace's Farmer and Iowa Homestead* used more simply written articles for half of their subscribers, and a more difficult version for the other half. The reader interest score ranged from 45 to 66 per cent higher for the simpler versions. Interestingly enough, age was more significant than years of schooling in determining the score. Though most of the readers interviewed were at least high school graduates, many older readers had stopped at the eighth grade. Yet these persons were willing "to stand for harder reading than the younger folks."[17]

In terms of rural audiences, at least, content appears to count most. An elaborate comparison of the acceptance of a 64-page booklet and a 4-page leaflet on the same subject, and of preferences between them, was made in Wisconsin with about 200 farmers as the subjects. The booklet was preferred by 47.2 per cent and the leaflet by 36 per cent; 16.8 per cent were undecided. The effort to relate choices to economic, tenure and educational status and to age, produced no very significant results. For instance, as expected, those who were high school graduates or better preferred the booklet, but so did those with less than high school experience, whereas those with some high school education favored the leaflet.[18]

It is possible that prestige factors influenced the replies of the less well educated. It is also possible that each respondent preferred what

[17]D. R. Murphy, "How Plain Talk Increases Readership," *Printer's Ink*, September 19, 1947.

[18]W. L. Carpenter, *The Effect of Length and Detail on Farmer Acceptance of Agricultural College Publications*, Madison, College of Agriculture, University of Wisconsin, 1955, mimeographed. Cf. also, L. Crile, *Findings from Studies of Bulletins, News Stories and Circular Letters*, Washington: U.S. Department of Agriculture Extension Service Circular 488, 1953, mimeographed.

best met his needs as he defined them without regard to length or format.

The problem of adequate and objective criteria to determine read-ability is still not completely solved. Lorge, basing his work on that of Gray and Leary and Morriss and Holverson, attempted to predict grade level of reading. The predictors he used were the number of different words, per cent of uncommon words, relative number of personal pronouns and prepositional phrases, average sentence length and a weighted vocabulary score based on Thorndike's word count. He found that the vocabulary score or load and sentence structure were the best predictors and that some measure of both was necessary. The various aspects of vocabulary load were intercorrelated and any one of them could be used. The various measures of sentence structure were also virtually interchangeable. Reading comprehension is the interaction between reading ability, which depends on intelligence, education, interest and purpose, and the readability of the text, which involves ideas, vocabulary, style and format. Lorge's own formula uses uncommon words, average sentence length and number of prepo-sitional phrases. The readability score is based on comprehension, judged by correct answers to questions on details and appreciation of the text. The formula slightly overestimates reading primarily for appreciation and underestimates reading mainly for detail, but it offers a fairly good overall estimate of readability.[19]

"Cloze" procedure. Recently a new technique, known as the "cloze" procedure, has been developed which may offer suggestions to those preparing adult education materials. The investigator systematically deletes words from a chosen selection, replacing each deleted word with an arbitrary 10-letter blank, regardless of the length of the deleted word. The subject is instructed to guess the missing word. His "cloze score" is the proportion of missing words correctly filled in. In comparing written passages, the one that scores the largest total of correct "fill-ins" is judged most readable for the population any given test group represents. The value of this device as an indication of comprehension, learning ability and intelligence appeared to be dem-onstrated by the use of the correlation technique in a study involving about 150 trainees at Sampson Air Base.[20]

[19] I. Lorge, "Predicting Readability," *Teachers College Record*, March 1944.

[20] W. I. Taylor, " 'Cloze Procedure': A New Tool in Measuring Readability," *Journalism Quarterly*, Fall 1953; *The Cloze Procedure: How It Predicts Comprehension and Intelligence of Military Personnel*, Urbana: University of Illinois, Division of Communications, 1953; and *Application of 'Cloze' and Entropy Measures to the Study of Contextual Constraint in Samples of Continuous Writing*, Unpublished Ph.D. thesis, University of Illinois, 1954.

Part of the problem of getting adults to read is the slow reading speed many have as a result of faulty reading habits. Remedial reading techniques are now quite well developed and effective. Among a number of studies that lend encouragement to adult educators facing this problem is a recent one in Alberta. Here 64 adults in a 15-hour noncredit course in silent reading skills increased their reading speed from the 30th to the 60th percentile compared with college seniors. On the Harvard Film Transfer Test they more than doubled their speed to an average of 370.1 words per minute. Comprehension also improved, but vocabulary did so only slightly.[21]

Today with a measurement of the educational status of the American people available by counties and most cities in the decennial Census of Population, adult educators have a general guide both to reading ability and to intelligence, as noted in Chapter II. Good writing is always more readable, more understandable, and more productive of learning than poor. However, as indicated, psychological and cultural factors turn out to be quite influential. Any routine application of a rigorous formula is not likely to warrant the cost in time, in view of the rising educational level of the American people.

AUDIO-VISUAL AIDS

Probably no area of research in adult education is as obviously allied with and limited by technological change as is the area of audio-visual aids. Teachers have utilized visual aids in the form of blackboard drawings, charts, diagrams, and models for many centuries. However, during the present century we have seen the development and use of radio, recordings and motion pictures and telecasts within the educational context. Research with regard to these educational means has hardly had a chance as yet to become established, and our technology has already presented us with television as a new means which is receiving widespread use. In spite of the problems which rapid technological changes have presented to researchers, significant steps have been taken in the direction of accumulating knowledge with regard to each mode of audio-visual education.

Graphic and Pictorial Techniques. Research to discover the utility of graphic and pictorial techniques was undertaken during the 1920's. Washburne[22] compared the effectiveness of graphic and narrative

---

[21]D. Lampard, "Reading Abilities of Adults," *The Alberta Journal of Educational Research*, March 1955.

[22]J. N. Washburne, "An Experimental Study of Various Graphs, Tabular and Textual Methods of Presenting Quantitative Materials," *Journal of Educational Psychology*, XVIII, 1927.

presentations of the same data in 1927. At approximately the same time Eels,[23] Craxton and Stryker,[24] and van Huhm[25] studied the relative merits of specific forms of graphic data. These studies made it clear that various forms of pictorial and graphic presentation of data were more easily comprehended and retained than when such data were presented by narration or simple numbers.

During recent years, research in this area has received new impetus because the military has been concerned with finding the most effective means of conveying information to trainees.[26] Vernon[27] made a comprehensive review of research in the field in 1952 and pointed out four conditions under which graphic and pictorial aids are effective: (1) Readers require special training to allow them to understand most graphic material properly; (2) Diagrams do not always insure better understanding or retention than do tables of figures; (3) Different sorts of data and relationships may require different kinds of figures; and (4) Pictorial and graphic presentation is usually understood better when supplemented with verbal explanation. These generalizations tend to be substantiated by the more recent research.

It should be noted that the use of pictorial and graphic aids in these studies has been confined for the most part to quasi-mathematical material. It is doubtful that an artist or a biologist would seriously consider confining his discourse on paintings or cellular structure to written or spoken words, and various forms of nonmathematical pictorial representations have been a part of these fields for centuries. Everyone "knows" that pictorial devices are virtually indispensable in presenting certain kinds of material. Research questions have tended to arise only when there has been a problem of presenting the same material to large numbers of students without benefit of the give-and-take and questions and answers which are characteristic of the classroom situation.

Films, radio and television. With the introduction of films, radio and television, it has become possible for one adult to teach millions of others and yet teach only once and never see a student. The "Brave New World" of adult education is technically possible today; but all

[23]W. C. Eels, "The Relative Merits of Circles and Bars for Representing Component Parts," *Journal of American Statistical Association*, XXI, 1926.

[24]F. E. Craxton and R. E. Stryker, "Bar Charts Versus Circle Diagrams," *Journal of American Statistical Association*, XXIII, 1927.

[25]R. van Huhm, "Further Studies in the Graphic Circles and Bars," *Journal of American Statistical Association*, XXII, 1927.

[26]See in particular, "How Pictures and Graphs Aid Learning from Print," *Technical Memorandum No. 4*, to Human Resources Institute, Urbana: University of Illinois, 1952.

[27]M. D. Vernon, "Presenting Information in Diagrams," *Audio-Visual Communication Review*, I, 1953.

adults in the United States are not receiving a "canned" college education, and the scores of adult educators and other educators are not
among the technologically unemployed. Why such possibilities have
not become realities suggests many interesting research questions.

However, researchers have been understandably more conservative
in studying this area and have sensibly asked initially whether or not
the newer audio-visual aids are effective means of educating adults.
The answer is sought, usually, by comparing the effectiveness of one
technique with another; the question is not only whether material
can be taught by audio-visual aids, but also whether or not it can be
taught better by one means than another.

Films, slides, filmstrips. Systematic research on the effectiveness of
films as educational devices with adults was carried out during World
War II by Hovland *et al.*[28] in conjunction with imparting information
to Army trainees about the background which led to the war. These
studies clearly established the fact that adults could glean and retain
information from films. This research was conducted in terms of
learning theory, which should make it of interest to educators.

One of the interesting findings from the Army studies with respect
to the use of films was that a one-sided communication produced
positive changes in the direction intended whether or not the subjects' initial opinions on the issue agreed with the film's message.

However a communication giving both sides of an issue produced
more change in the intended direction. It became quite clear that a
man was more likely to accept a new point of view, opposed to his initial opinion if the film made what he considered a fair presentation of
the grounds for that opinion. This finding had not been anticipated.
It had been assumed those whose opinion differed from the message
of the film would already know the arguments for "their" side. But a
"one-sided" film was immediately judged biased propaganda. The
opinions originally held and the changes in them correlated with the
educational level of the subjects. It was also found that the greater
the critical ability of the subjects, the less likely they were, given the
facts, to accept an unsound interpretation from the film.[29]

VanderMeer[30] was successful in teaching high school science by film,

[28]C. Hovland, I. L. Janis and H. H. Kelley, *Communication and Persuasion*, New
Haven: Yale University Press, 1953.
[29]C. I. Hovland, A. A. Lumsdaine and F. D. Sheffield, *Experiments on Mass Communi-
cations*, vol. IV of *Studies in Social Psychology in World War II;* Princeton: Princeton
University Press, 1949.
[30]S. W. VanderMeer, *Relative Effectiveness of Instruction by: Films Exclusively, Films
Plus Study Guides, and Standard Lecture Methods,* Technical Report, SDC 269-7-13,
Instructional Film Research Program, Pennsylvania State College, Special Devices Center,
July 1950.

but he had greater success when he supplemented the films with study guides. As Allen[31] and others note, there is no *a priori* reason for expecting better results from films on all subject matter, and films are generally used in conjunction with other teaching techniques in the classroom situation. Sometimes slides or filmstrips can be used with more success than can films, especially when they are accompanied by lecture or discussion; which of these is best seems to depend upon an assortment of variables which include content, audience and situational factors. The utilization of extensive film libraries throughout the United States is testimony to the fact that educators find film useful, but whole courses are seldom taught in this manner.

One warning, however, is necessary, especially in terms of the effort to use films as a stimulus for adult education discussion groups. Since nontheatrical, documentary films are not made with a view to this particular use, their effectiveness as a stimulus for discussion is closely related to the skill of the leader in so using them as to give the discussion a focus.[32]

Radio. In a series of experiments at Harvard during the early 1930's Cantrill and Allport[33] made a pioneer attempt to isolate the relevant variables for studying the effectiveness of radio as an aid to education. They compared reactions of an audience listening to a radio broadcast, to the reactions of the same audience listening to the broadcaster in person, and they compared regular class lectures with radio lectures using the same students and instructors. Most of the differences they obtained were not particularly striking, and it became clear that education could be successfully conducted by radio.

Katz and Eisenberg[34] used the Lazarsfeld-Stanton Program Analyzer on a series of educational broadcasts to determine how these broadcasts might be improved. They found that listeners not only preferred educational material to be "entertaining" but they were likely to understand the material and retain it better when it was presented in an entertaining manner.

Harrell, Brown and Schramm[35] varied the number of items con-

[31]W. H. Allen, "Audio-Visual Materials," *Review of Educational Research*, XXVI, no. 2, 1956.

[32]H. L. Miller, "How the Film Aids Discussion," *Film Forum Review*, Fall 1948; E. Rass, "Group Discussion Through Motion Pictures," *Educational Screen*, May and June 1945.

[33]H. Cantrill and G. W. Allport, *The Psychology of Radio*, New York: Harper and Brothers, 1935.

[34]O. Katz and P. Eisenberg, "Showmanship in Radio Educational Programs," *Journal of Psychology*, 20, July 1945.

[35]T. W. Harrell, D. E. Brown and W. Schramm, "Memory in Radio News Listening," *Journal of Applied Psychology*, 33, no. 3, 1949.

tained in broadcasts of the same length and found that audiences prefer broadcasts which do not contain too many individual items even though they may retain more in absolute numbers from the broadcasts which contain more items. In more recent studies, Highlander and Silvey found that intelligibility and information gains, respectively, were highly related to interest on the part of listeners.[36] Each study has technical recommendations to make with regard to improving educational broadcasts, but suggests that interest on the part of listeners may tend to offset any technical deficiency in the programs.

Illustrative of the research seeking to determine the effectiveness of various broadcasting techniques is Goldin's study in which he measured the degrees of retention of psychological content presented by a lecture, a dialogue in interview style, and a dramatization, each of 15 minutes duration. The subjects were 141 persons, 17 to 60 years of age. The words used fell in the Thorndike 10,000-15,000 word vocabulary range. Tests of the degree of retention of the material were made at the end of each broadcast and again four weeks later. This later test was not announced in advance. The three groups used were equated on various appropriate bases.

Retention scores immediately following the broadcasts showed no significant differences among the groups. Four weeks later those who had been exposed to the talk showed sharply higher retention than either the dialogue or dramatization groups. The last group scored significantly lower than those who listened to the dialogue. There were no sex differences except that the women in the group which heard the dramatization made sharply higher scores than the men. The higher the educational attainment of the subjects, the higher were the retention scores of those who had heard the lecture. At below high school level retention was about equal from lecture and dialogue.[37]

Since the educational status of the American people is rising, this last finding suggests the hypothesis that educational techniques both in broadcasting and in other adult education situations may need to be adapted accordingly and conversely, that research findings obtained two or more decades ago should not be accepted as policy guides without retesting.

Television. Probably the earliest research concerning the teaching of adults by television was conducted by Rock *et al.* in connection with

[36]J. P. Highlander, *Audience Analysis Measurements and Informational Effects of Speaker Variables in Radio Talks,* Ph. D. dissertation, University of Wisconsin, 1954; R. Silvey, "The Intelligibility of Broadcast Talks," *Public Opinion Quarterly,* 15, 1951.
[37]F. S. Goldin, *The Effect of Program Format in Educational Broadcasts on Adult Retention,* Unpublished Ph.D. dissertation, Boston University, 1948.

training Army Reservists and Naval Air Reservists. In one study[38] it was found that television teaching was more effective than classroom instruction by local instructors for both officers and enlisted men. Another study[39] concentrated on learning and retention and found that reservists not only learned from television, but also retained most of what they learned four to six weeks later.

The Iowa State College Extension Service ran a series of programs called "Make a Dress—TV" for which more than 3,000 Iowa women registered, even though registration was not necessary.[40] A stratified random sample of enrollees revealed that 36 per cent of the women actually completed the dress, and 30 per cent of the farm women and 76 per cent of the town women had not participated in Extension prior to the series.

Husband taught a psychology course for credit at Iowa State College which adults viewed on their home television sets.[41] Millis also reports teaching a psychology course in this manner at Western Reserve University.[42] Each found that home viewers got higher grades than did on-campus classes. In another report it is stated that 1,300 students signed up for an average of two television courses from an offering of English, biology, social science, and political science offered by Chicago City Junior College.[43] Kanner et al.[44] compared television and regular instruction for 14 hours of basic training with 12,000 recruits and found that television was at least as effective as regular teaching, and was particularly effective with recruits with low Army aptitude test scores. Shimberg[45] found that home nursing could be

[38]R. T. Rock, Jr., J. S. Duva, and J. E. Murray, *The Effectiveness of Television Instruction for Training Naval Air Reservists*, Special Devices Center, ONR, Department of the Navy, Technical Report, SDC 476-02-52, Port Washington, Long Island, New York, 1951.

[39]Rock *et al.*, *A Study of Learning and Retention from Television Instruction Transmitted to Army Field Force Reservists*, Special Devices Center, Technical Report, SDC 476-02-53, Port Washington, Long Island, New York, 1951.

[40]Iowa State College of Agriculture, Agricultural Extension Service, *Make a Dress—TV*, Ames, Iowa, 1953.

[41]R. W. Husband, "Television Versus Classroom for Learning General Psychology," *American Psychologist*, 9, May 1954.

[42]J. S. Millis, "Formal Education by Television," in *A Television Policy for Education*, Newsom, C. (ed.), Washington, D.C.: American Council of Education, 1952.

[43]Anonymous, "At Exam Time—Chicago TV Classes with Honors," *National Educational Television News*, March-April 1957.

[44]J. H. Kanner, R. P. Runyan, O. Desiderata, *Television in Army Training: Evaluation of Television in Army Basic Training*, Technical Report 14, Washington, D.C.: George Washington University, Human Resources Research Office, November 1954.

[45]B. Shimberg, "Effectiveness of Television in Teaching Home Nursing: A Comparison of Television and Classroom Instruction in Teaching the Red Cross Home Nursing Course. Preliminary Report," Educational Testing Service, RB-54-19, Princeton, New Jersey, 1954.

taught as effectively by television as in the classroom. It is clear from these studies that a great variety of courses could be taught with reasonable success using television.[46]

Comparison of radio, films and television. Many of the above studies were designed so that comparison between the effectiveness of two or more audio-visual aids could be made. Such findings are summarized at this point.

According to Elliott,[47] where retention of material is concerned, television is generally superior to radio, and radio is superior to film. However, Elliott found that there were differences for sex and education groups. He cites a great deal of evidence to show that children shift from auditory to visual dominance at the time they learn to read and suggests that there is a shift back, particularly among women and the less well educated, to auditory dominance in later life.

Klapper[48] in his reports, which do not include television, found a superiority of auditory over visual methods. Goldstein[49] and Larsen and Feder[50] agree generally with these conclusions but show that the advantages of auditory devices diminish with the increasing difficulty of the material. Most authors agree that adult education can be successfully conducted using any audio-visual aid or combination of aids, and that the question of effectiveness of technique must take into consideration the habits and abilities of the potential participants with regard to each technique.

Radio, television and adult habits. With the advent of radio and television it has become possible for adult education to take place largely within the home without the need for convening at a common meeting place. Since it has been shown that adult education by radio and television is technically possible, questions regarding the listening habits of adults and the effects of one medium upon the other have become particularly meaningful.

Coffin[51] has noted that in 1955 as many families in the United States owned television sets as owned cars or had telephones. There were

[46]For an overview of classroom offerings by educational institutions on television, see Kumata, *An Inventory of Instructional Television Research*, Ann Arbor, Mich.: Educational Television and Radio Center, 1956.

[47]F. R. Elliott, "Memory for Trade Names Presented in Screen, Radio and Television Advertisements," *Journal of Applied Psychology*, 21, December 1937.

[48]J. T. Klapper, *The Effects of Mass Media*, A Report to the Director of Public Library Inquiry, New York: Bureau of Applied Social Research, Columbia University, 1949.

[49]H. Goldstein, *Reading and Listening Comprehension at Various Controlled Rates*, New York: Teachers College, Columbia University, 1940.

[50]R. P. Larsen and D. D. Feder, "Common and Differential Factors in Reading and Hearing Comprehension," *Journal of Educational Psychology*, 31, no. 4, 1940.

[51]T. E. Coffin, "Television's Impact on Society," *American Psychologist*, October, 1955.

38,700,000 television homes in the United States as of January 1957[52] which meant that about 76.2 per cent of United States households had television. It appears that sets were initially bought mostly by families which were relatively large, of high income, high occupational status and medium education.[53] There are still slight differences according to these family characteristics, and there still tends to be more concentration of sets near metropolitan areas and in the Northeast. However, each of these correlations has been diminishing during recent years as television has become almost universally owned.

A great many studies show that initial purchase of television cuts down on the amount of time spent reading books and listening to the radio. However, Crile[54] points out that there were 46 million radio homes during 1955, and Americans have been buying an average of ten million radio sets a year since television appeared in 1947. Rural owners still tend to listen to farm and county extension programs on the radio, and the dominance of television is much more pronounced in the evening.[55]

The only research which purports to be a longitudinal study of the viewing habits of adults is the intensive work that has been done in New Brunswick, New Jersey, which is known as Videotown.[56] In 1948, during the first study, only 1.4 per cent of the local families had a television set, but this figure was over 90 per cent in 1956. Perhaps the most interesting finding to come from this series of reports is that the people who bought television earliest are still the ones who view it the most. This finding has been substantiated in an independent study of the national television audience.[57] This suggests that many of the early studies of the impact of television on the lives of American adults can be applied only to the adults who bought television soon after it was put on the market.

In spite of the vast ownership and use of both television and radio, studies devoted to program content reveal that a very small proportion of time is given to educational programs on commercial sta-

[52]Anonymous, "U.S. Now Has 38.7 million T.V. Homes, B.T. Estimates," *Broadcasting and Telecasting*, January 21, 1957.

[53]Coffin, *op. cit.*

[54]L. Crile, *Some Findings from Radio Research*, United States Department of Agriculture, Extension Service Circular No. 503, November 1955.

[55]Crile, *op. cit.*, contains an excellent summary of these points. Also see, L. Crile, *Educational Televison Research Findings*, Extension Service Circular 514, United States Department of Agriculture, November 1957.

[56]See in particular, G. W. Tashner and G. R. Kanrich, *Videotown 1948-1956*, 9th annual edition, New York: Cunningham and Walsh, Inc., 1956.

[57]J. W. Seiler, "Sponsors Are Discovering TV Audiences Don't Tire," *Broadcasting, Telecasting*, September 5, 1955.

tions.[58] Carpenter[59] notes that over $25,000,000 was spent to promote educational channels from 1952 to 1955 but that "plans for and the development of research activities have been at best a very minor consideration in the rise of educational television."[60]

Viewing the entire field of mass communication, as it has come to be known, Klapper points out that researchers feel that "the formulation of any systematic description of what effects [of mass communication] are how effected" and the predictive application of principles "is a goal which becomes the more distant as it is the more vigorously pursued."[61]

This pessimism may well temper the enthusiasm of some adult educators for the utilization of mass media in their work. Klapper, however, sees some hope in the situation, as his title indicates. After an examination of scores of studies on the effects of mass communication, he advances five generalizations. While these concern the whole field, they are particularly suggestive for adult education:

1. Mass communication ordinarily does not serve as a necessary and sufficient cause of audience effects, but rather functions among and through a nexus of mediating factors and influences.

2. These mediating factors are such that they typically render mass communication a contributory agent, but not the sole cause, in a process of reinforcing the existing conditions. (Regardless of the condition in question—be it the level of public taste, the tendency of audience members toward or away from delinquent behavior, or their vote intention—and regardless of whether the effect in question be social or individual, the media are more likely to reinforce than to change.)

3. On such occasions as mass communication does function in the service of change, one or two conditions is likely to obtain. Either:
   a. the mediating factors will be found to be inoperative, and the effect of the media direct; or
   b. the mediating factors, which normally favor reinforcement, will be found to be themselves impelling toward change.

4. There are certain residual situations in which mass communica-

---

[58]Most content analyses reveal this and no single reference is adequate. However, excellent discussion of some of the problems and implications of this situation can be found in *Mass Culture*, B. Rosenberg and D. M. White, (eds.) Glencoe, Ill.: The Free Press, 1957.

[59]C. R. Carpenter, "Psychological Research Using Television," *American Psychologist*, October 1955.

[60]*Ibid*.

[61]J. T. Klapper, "What We Know About the Effects of Mass Communication: The Brink of Hope," *Public Opinion Quarterly*, vol. 21, no. 4, Winter 1957-58. Publication A-242 of the Bureau of Applied Social Research, Columbia University.

tion seems to wreak direct effects, or to directly and of itself serve certain psycho-physical functions.

5. The efficacy of mass communication, either as contributory agents or as agents of direct effect, is affected by various aspects of the media themselves or of the communication situation (including, for example, aspects of contextual organization, the availability of channels for overt action, etc.)[62]

Suggestions for further research. It is abundantly clear from the research that has already been conducted that using each of the various audio-visual aids in adult education is not only possible, but often has distinct advantages over using traditional educational techniques. However, it is also clear that only a small fraction of the time spent listening to radio and television by the average American adult has anything to do with adult education as it is usually conceived. Clearly many adult education programs in their present form would have a difficult time trying to compete with the popular network entertainment which is presented every evening. However, it is also true that some popular network programs may have more educational value than less popular ones which are officially connected with adult education.

It may distress many adult educators to hear that book reading tends to decrease with increased television ownership, but this fact does not have many implications for adult education unless we know something about both the books and the television programs that are involved. The switch from bad books to bad television is really not much of a switch, and there is no *a priori* reason to suspect that widespread adult education by radio and television should have any different effects on the population as a whole from the effects of using traditional techniques. It would be of great value to know something of the content of reading which has been suspended in favor of particular television content.

Except for the technical problems encountered in using audio-visual aids, which are not discussed in the present monograph,[63] further research in this area will probably be most useful if it follows the traditions of participation studies and comparative methods studies, which have already influenced it. This will promote the direct continuity with other areas of research which is so often lacking.

One of the most remarkably successful programs known to have relied upon the use of audio-visual devices is the Canadian Farm

[62]*Ibid.*, pp. 457-58.

[63]See in particular, *Visual Principles for Training by Television*, Special Devices Center, O.N.R., Department of the Navy, Human Engineering Report, SDC 20-TU-2, Port Washington, Long Island, New York (no date).

Radio Forum,[64] which has been active continuously since 1941. The unique character of this program is that it provides for participants' belonging to groups which discuss the programs and relay suggestions and questions to the central broadcasting office. Although farmers do represent a special interest group for which the programs had relevance, 70 per cent of the participants gave neighborliness and community spirit as reasons for affiliation. Thus mass media were utilized in a context where groups and social processes were used as part of the program. This is in direct contrast to the "passive" viewing or listening to which many such programs limit their provisions. Research concerning the comparative effectiveness of audio-visual devices would contribute information of value to adult education.

Unfortunately the direct tie-in between research in audio-visual techniques and rapid technological change may have resulted in making many of the pioneer studies "time-bound." It might be that when studies showing advantages in the use of audio-visual aids were conducted, exposure to the particular device was a rather unique and new experience for participants. Whole courses taught by film might have resulted in greatly increased attention and learning 30 years ago, but it is doubtful that students would prefer films exclusively to regular classes today.[65] It might be that there is a point of diminishing returns or a "saturation" point regarding exclusive use of audio-visual aids which can be revealed only by research over time as the novelty of the media wears off.

Klapper[66] suggests that the path for future research is

the phenomenistic approach, which seeks to account for the known occurrence and to assess the roles of the several influences which produced it, and which attempts to see the respondents not as randomly selected individuals each exchangeable for the other, but rather as persons functioning within particular social contexts. It is likewise the path of the cumulating controlled experiments in which the multifarious extra-media factors being investigated are built into the research design. These are the paths which have brought us to what seems the verge of generalization and empirically documented theory. They are the paths which have brought us to the brink of hope.

[64]J. Nicol, A. A. Shea, G. J. P. Simmins, R. A. Sim, *Canadian Farm Radio Forum*, UNESCO Paris, 1954.
[65]According to Houle, leaders in the Armed Services found that audio-visual aids were distinctly limited in their application; he came across a great deal of evidence that the men were becoming somewhat bored with their constant use in training. Houle and others, *The Armed Services and Adult Education*, Washington, D.C.: American Council on Education, 1947.
[66]Klapper, *op. cit.*, p. 471. It would be useful to study the Sunrise Semester and other telecast courses at New York University in the light of this hypothesis.

THE USE OF DISCUSSION

The value of group discussion as a technique in adult education is enthusiastically and ceaselessly proclaimed by leaders in the field. Research results clearly indicate successful outcomes from the use of this device. They also raise some questions about it, especially in situations where discussion seems to be used for its own sake because of the generally favorable attitude toward it.

Acceptance of discussion as an end in itself results in a failure both to look at its values beyond a single discussion and to measure exact results. These results are unlikely to be determined without experiments extending over a period of time and in such efforts it would be difficult to rule out other influences and variables. Not all of these considerations have been allowed for in what research has been done in the use of discussion in adult education. Such research has been largely concerned with comparing discussion with other instructional techniques and with measuring opinion change or the degree or effectiveness of consensus arrived at through discussion. One very significant exception to this statement is an as yet unpublished study of experimental discussion groups in the Los Angeles metropolitan area sponsored by the Fund for Adult Education,[1] to which several references will be made later in this chapter. About 2,000 people were

[1]Abbott Kaplan, *A Study of the Liberal Arts Discussion Program for Adults in the Metropolitan Los Angeles Area,* White Plains, New York, Fund for Adult Education, 1958, dittoed.

163

involved in the experiment. An adequate sample of participants and the leaders were interviewed and the participant observer technique was used.

Discussion defined. Discussion implies a face-to-face interacting group of persons engaged in a directed conversation about a topic of mutual interest in which they share both information and opinions or raise questions with respect to the subject under consideration. About half of the authorities who have defined the use and purposes of discussion as an adult education tool stipulate that it should be guided by a leader and there is all but unanimous agreement that it is highly desirable that this leader be a recognized member of the group. It should be noted that while by definition the use of discussion in adult education always involves a group, groups as such serve many purposes in adult education. Thus while any group illustrates social processes that inevitably develop in periodic face-to-face meetings of the same people, group discussion as considered in this section is in no sense synonymous with what some call group dynamics. Groups are discussed from these other points of view in Chapter XII and the sociological and psychological bases for adult education are there spelled out in greater detail than in this section. Comparably, there is little mention of participation in this section as Chapter VI is devoted to this topic in terms of the total field of nonvocational adult education.

LECTURE VERSUS DISCUSSION

Much of the research concerned with the utility of discussion has revolved around a comparison between it and the use of the lecture as a means not only for imparting information, but also for changing attitudes, opinions and practices.

Lewin's experiments. One of the most frequently referred to studies demonstrating the effectiveness of discussion as a teaching device is that directed by Kurt Lewin. Lewin faced a practical problem early in World War II as to how to change food habits in the direction of less popular, more easily obtainable and nutritious foods. He used groups of women from high-, medium-, and low-income levels. Half of each of these economic status groups were given a half-hour lecture by a nutritionist who then answered questions for 15 minutes. The lectures were well done. Charts were employed, mimeographed recipes were distributed and hints on methods of preparation were given. For the other half of these groups of women, discussion was employed, also for 45 minutes. The nutritionist was present as a resource person who answered technical questions. The meeting was conducted by a skilled discussion leader under whose guidance the members of the discussion groups came to regard the matter being discussed as important to them; began taking over responsibility for the flow of discussion; and after the objections to and difficulties in using the recommended foods had been aired, came to a decision. The same recipes were given to both discussion and lecture groups, but only after interest had obviously been aroused. Although the proportions varied, about ten times as many women from the discussion groups as from the lecture groups tried these foods.[2]

It should be noted that since the participants in this experiment were housewives, they came to the meetings with some knowledge. It is also important that a highly competent resource person was available to the discussion groups. In the lecture groups the lecturer led the following question and answer period and in the other groups there was a skilled discussion leader. Experience in a number of programs indicates that the presence of a competent resource person contributes to good discussion, though this observation by a number of adult educators has not, so far as this project could discover, been confirmed by research in which comparable groups discussed the same topics, some with and some without the assistance of a resource person.

It is also important to point out that the well-known Lewin experiments were not strictly a comparison of the relative usefulness of lecture and discussion as an educational tool, but rather of their effectiveness in producing a change in family menus—based, however, on the imparting of information. There is frequent confusion in adult education literature between the use of discussion as a purely educational device, as in The Great Books program, and its use to produce individual or social change. Though information that is educational in character plays a part in both situations, the objectives are quite different and strict evaluation of methods or techniques can be properly made only in terms of the objectives of the enterprise being examined.

A recent result comparable to Lewin's was secured in the health education field. Seventy-five pre-existing groups of women, 899 in all, were instructed with respect to the need for medical examinations to detect cancer and the technique for self-examination of the breasts every month. The groups were comparable to the total population

[2]Kurt Lewin, *The Relative Effectiveness of a Lecture Method and a Method of Group Discussion for Changing Food Habits,* and B. Willerman, *Group Decision and Requests as a Means of Changing Food Habits,* both Washington: National Research Council, 1942 and 1943, respectively. Also summarized in T. Newcomb, E. Hartley and G. Swanson, Eds., *Readings in Social Psychology,* New York, Henry Holt, 1952.

with respect to marital status, occupation and education, but not in age. Lectures were used with 33 groups, "discussion-decision" with 44. The latter were markedly superior in adopting the procedures advocated.[3] Here again a change in behavior was the objective.

It is unfortunate that the groups in which the lecture was used were comprised of older women. Quite possibly they were more inured to lectures. Differential motivations may also have entered into the result.

An illustration from industry. A well-designed study sought to repeat Lewin's research on eating habits under more carefully controlled conditions both with respect to the information given and in the measurement of resulting behavior changes. Answers were sought to two questions: (1) Is learning enough to lead to change in group behavior? (2) Is group decision through discussion more effective than formal lectures in changing behavior?

The subjects were a group of 29 factory foremen. The problem was to teach them to rate their 395 workers solely according to each worker's merit, avoiding any "halo effect" caused by his higher or lower job rank. All the subjects were experienced in ratings. For the purposes of the experiment they were randomly divided into three groups with 9, 9, and 11 men respectively. Group A was used as the control. Group B used discussion for one and one-half hours, seated around a table. The leader introduced the problem but did not participate in the discussion. The objective was to reach a consensus that would register in action. Group C had a lecture on the techniques and theory of rating. Previous errors were pointed out, graphs and figures were used. There was a question and answer period.

The pre-experimental ratings by the members of all three groups had shown significant biases between ratings of workers holding high and low job ranks. Post-experimental ratings can be summarized as follows:

> Group A—control—No change
> Group C—lecture—No significant differences, though the ratings for workers of high and low classification were in the direction advocated in the lecture.
> Group B—discussion—Significant change. The mean ratings of workers of high and low job ranks were equal.[4]

This result is in line with expectations, but it is possible that not all elements in the situation were fully appraised. Many experiments,

---

[3]Betty W. Bond, *The Group Discussion-Decision Approach: An Appraisal of Its Use in Health Education,* Unpublished Ph.D. dissertation, University of Minnesota, 1955.

[4]J. Levine and J. Butler, "Lecture versus Group Discussion in Changing Behavior," *Journal of Applied Psychology,* vol. XXXVI, 1952.

beginning with the famous ones at the Hawthorne plant of Westing-house, have shown that when staff are consulted on policy matters improved results are achieved. In the discussion group in this experi-ment the objective was not merely better understanding and more knowledge, but also behavior change involving policy, a change forti-fied by group processes in reaching consensus. Further, nothing is known as to the intellectual level of the lecture in relation to the edu-cational level of the men in the lecture group. In group B, once the problem was stated the discussion was in the familiar vocabulary of the foremen concerned. Using another type of population, Professor Bloom of the University of Chicago, concluded a few years ago that more actual thinking takes place under the lecture method than in discussions.[5]

Discussion and opinion change. The armed services made consider-able use of discussion in helping millions of men engaged in World War II understand why the United States was a major participant in that conflict. Objective observers have reported that the effort resulted in higher morale.[6]

Robinson is one of the investigators who have measured shifts in attitudes or opinions on social problems using 20 groups and apply-ing Thurstone Attitude Scales before and after discussion. In com-parison with control groups all discussion groups showed significant changes in attitude[7] among the college student subjects.

There is also evidence that group discussion leading toward con-sensus results in "good" decisions. Some 1,200 college students par-ticipated in one experiment in which the rightness of both individual and group decisions was studied. The evidence showed "conclusively the existence of a tendency for discussion to produce a shift toward the right, rather than the wrong answer, even when a majority influ-ence is allowed for."[8] The issues discussed in this experiment were of a character which permitted determination of right and wrong an-swers such as which of two poems or pictures was the better. The Los

[5]B. S. Bloom, "Thought-Processes in Lecture and Discussions," *The Journal of General Education,* April 1953.
[6]Jeffrey Auer, "Discussion Programs and Techniques in the Armed Forces," *Quarterly Journal of Speech,* October 1946, and Julius Schreiber, "Discussion in the Armed Forces," *Adult Education Bulletin,* February 1949.
[7]Karl F. Robinson, "An Experimental Study of the Effects of Group Discussion upon the Social Attitudes of College Students," *Speech Monographs,* 1941. Report based on a Ph.D. dissertation at Northwestern University.
[8]Robert L. Thorndike, "The Effect of Discussion upon the Correctness of Group De-cisions when the Factor of Majority Influence is Allowed for," *Journal of Social Psychology,* August 1938.

Angeles experiment alluded to above reported a change in prior opinions by about one-fourth of the group members, but perhaps more important, there was a highly significant increase in the degree of openmindedness among the participants.[9]

Some negative aspects. Other studies examined were favorable to the use of discussion in adult education. The acceptance of it by adult educators is understandable, but the available research also raises very real questions. Some accept the method almost as an end in itself. Because discussion is deemed consonant with democratic values, they fail to evaluate its outcomes and in some cases use it to the exclusion of all other methods regardless of subject matter or objectives.[10] Where discussion is conducted for its own sake, the favorable "evaluations" are of little value, since there has been no comparison with other possible methods. Moreover, some such comparisons are not favorable to discussion, as in a United States Air Force Primary Pilot Training School study among three equated groups. On the basis of pre- and post-course achievement and an Air Force standardized final examination, the lecture technique proved slightly superior to discussion and lecture-discussion. This superiority, however, was slight, reaching the .05 level of confidence only when lecture and lecture-discussion methods were compared. The author indicates that all men involved were above average in intelligence and perhaps responded better to the lecture technique because of this. Furthermore, the instructor was more familiar with lecturing than with leading discussions. The military environment being characteristically authoritarian, this may have influenced the result. On the basis of oral and written critique, the lecture-discussion method gave the greatest amount of satisfaction to the students.[11] Several other studies showed better learning results from the lecture method. The contradictory nature of the results of these studies suggests that the explanations may be not in the techniques and methods employed, but in other factors, such as the educational status and cultural backgrounds of participants, the content of the subject matter, and the facility of the leader in handling the technique.

[9]Kaplan, *op. cit.*

[10]Martin Perry Anderson in his *A Study of Discussion in Selected Wisconsin Adult Organizations and Public Agencies* (unpublished Ph.D. dissertation, University of Wisconsin, 1947) gives instances of this. This is the most detailed and thorough going study of discussion as both method and technique found in this investigation and later references will be made to it.

[11]Robert Palmer, *A Comparison of Three Techniques of Instruction Used in Teaching Aviation Physiology at a United States Air Force Primary Pilot Training School,* Unpublished M.S. Thesis, Florida State University, Tallahassee, Florida, 1958.

It has also been pointed out that those whose cultural background is that of a highly structured society with explicit and well-understood hierarchical arrangements regard group discussion as time-wasting futility. One study disclosed that many others "tolerate" democratic forms in adult education but secretly hope for definite answers to problems by someone recognized as an authority.[12] Presumably this "toleration" was a concession to a climate of opinion favorable to the use of discussion.

Even teachers who stated that they preferred discussion to other methods of instruction were found to lecture 27 per cent of the time and matched student contributions during class sessions on a one-to-one basis. In four informal classes studied by Zander, despite espousal of discussion and democratic procedures, no time was spent in student-teacher planning and about nine-tenths of the decisions to move on to new topics were made by the teachers. Moreover, almost all contributions from the classes were made by one-third of the students. Perhaps it is not surprising that in their own evaluation of these classes more than half the participants called for more content, even though a majority also said they liked meeting fellow students better than the informational content of the course. They were more critical of teaching methods than of content.[13]

Some critical considerations. The studies thus far used have been reported and criticized in their own terms. They seem to reveal at best a partial understanding of what discussion is, or of the fact that it can be employed in varying situations and for varying objectives. Possibly the enthusiasm for discussion as such, which as noted is noticeable in adult education literature, has resulted in attempting to test its effectiveness without raising questions as to its appropriateness in any specific situation. In the studies examined the appropriateness was assumed. Obviously no one would use discussion as a technique in beginning to teach English to foreigners, though it might well be employed for an advanced class. No studies were discovered in which the appropriateness of discussion in widely different adult education situations and among people of widely different experiences and abilities was evaluated. The field would, it appears, benefit from such research.

In view of the great interest in discussion, several other comments

[12]Renee Morin and Harold Potter, *Camp Laquemac—A Bilingual Adult Education Training Centre,* Toronto: Canadian Association for Adult Education, for the Fund for Adult Education, 1953.
[13]Alvin Zander, "Student Motives and Teaching Methods in Four Informal Adult Classes," *Adult Education,* October 1947.

should be added. In terms of the total research on the subject, a great majority of the studies have been in colleges and universities and have used college students, a "captive" group, for subjects. The studies by psychologists have been criticized in terms of the artificiality of the situations and their neglect of the social processes involved in discussion. Those by others are said to be weak in design and not rigorous in procedure. As with the studies by psychologists, over 90 per cent of the subjects were high school or college students. There is no guarantee that the findings, often contradictory, would be valid for non-student groups in nonstudent situations.[14]

Miller makes a more fundamental criticism to which many enthusiasts for discussion are vulnerable because of a lack of a validated theory of discussion. They have, Miller claims, simply made assumptions, not all of them well supported. Satisfaction with "beginning where the people are," justifiable as a start, becomes stultifying when, as too often happens, no effort is made to move people from where they are to deeper problems.[15]

Miller also points out that group theory, basic to discussion group procedures, relies heavily on the belief that changing behavior is the only way to change values and attitudes. This, however, involves the assumption that democracy can be defended only as a process and not as a body of social values. This contradicts another assumption of the advocates of discussion that through the intimacy of group discussion we can recapture, despite our urban society, the real democracy of rural America. If adult education remains aloof from the question of achieving democratic values and concentrates on how to achieve consensus and commitment to the goals a community happens to have, it may aid a social change it might later regret.

These and other challenges in Miller's article are, of course, unsupported by research but they are cogent philosophical considerations which might well serve as leads to fundamental research in areas of the field thus far neglected.

The participants in the Los Angeles experiment were able to identify in terms of their personal reactions both the strengths and weaknesses of discussion. The exchange of views appealed to more than half as very valuable and one-fifth noted the intellectual stimulus from this. One-fourth gained useful subject matter knowledge. Another

[14] Milton Dickens and Marguerite Heffernan, "Experimental Research in Group Discussion," *Quarterly Journal of Speech*, February 1949.
[15] Harry L. Miller, "Group Discussion—Specific or Panacea?" *Etcetera: A Review of General Semantics*, Vol. XI, Autumn, 1953.

one-fifth stressed social values. In the judgment of the interviewers many participants were intellectually starved and realized it. On the other hand, about one-third criticized the inadequacy of fellow participants, over one-fifth criticized the resource materials supplied, and the same proportion criticized the leadership. About half the members in the groups observed did most of the discussing but participation widened as the program progressed. Another value was an increase in serious reading beyond the materials supplied. On balance, the results of this carefully planned, well conducted experiment were clearly favorable.[16]

THE DISCUSSION LEADER

The leader in discussion occupies a strategic place but discussion is only one of the areas of adult education in which leaders play a prominent role. There is therefore a general section on leadership, its qualities and functions in Chapter XI of this report and the paragraphs below are limited to research which tested the mediating or neutral role of the leader of a discussion group. The general section on leadership applies to discussion as well as to other aspects of adult education and should be considered in relation to the current topic.

The leader's function. Ideally the leader simply facilitates the discussion and the process of reaching consensus. Practically, as pointed out below, this does not always happen. This problem has not been systematically attacked from a research point of view in adult education, except by Kaplan, but a study has been made with a group of 185 college women who submitted to a variety of tests, including the Social Personality Inventory and the Hartmann Social Attitudes Inventory. I.Q. scores were available, as were self-ratings on a six-item scale of dominance. A pretest on eight controversial issues was followed five days later by a small-group discussion and a recording of new judgments on the issues. There was a low but positive correlation between the grades of the group leaders and the influence they exerted on their groups measured by changes in attitudes of group members toward those of their leaders. A comparable but slightly higher correlation of $.45\pm.06$ was obtained between scholastic aptitude scores of verbal ability and influence. Quite clearly, upper-class women were much more influential than freshmen or sophomores, probably indicating a status or prestige factor. These and other results of the study are sufficient to indicate that in the training of discussion group lead-

[16]Kaplan, *op. cit.*

ers, the desirability of maintaining neutrality on issues considered should be stressed.[17]

The problems suggested by this study can be quite acute under some circumstances. Kriesburg describes a labor union whose membership was two-thirds Catholic but whose officers were admitted Communists. The result was heavy cross-pressure through various propaganda or educational devices which showed up in a study of attitudes of obvious uncertainty and serious inconsistencies.[18] The concept of the leader as a neutral agent to facilitate consensus was lacking.

Kaplan found that those with less than average education desired strong, directive leadership by the group discussion leader. The better educated resented a leader who dominated the group.[19]

Understanding function of discussion. Such data, of course, do not condemn the use of discussion as an educational technique. They do suggest that it can be imperfectly understood and employed. This point is stressed again and again by Martin Anderson.[20] Comparing the organizations and agencies in Wisconsin that utilize discussion in their educational programs, he shows the vital necessity for the leader to understand the theory and philosophy of the method and to be well trained in appropriate techniques. The success of discussion in the agencies Anderson studied was proportional to the emphasis each placed on training leaders. Five of the eight organizations he studied use the discussion as the only or the chief educational technique, yet sometimes leaders were selected because of their local prestige rather than for competence for group discussion leadership. Such persons tended to use their positions as a means of disseminating information or opinions instead of sharing them and even, with the tacit or explicit headquarter's encouragement, of insuring that any group decision arrived at the position supported by the state organization. Under good leadership, on the other hand, frankness and freedom of expression first exposed conflicts of opinion and then tended to resolve them and achieve consensus. This is truly democratic procedure. Such a process takes time, and Anderson showed that the less well-trained leader frequently failed to allow adequate time for issues to be explored or, where desired, for real agreement to be reached.

Among the eight programs examined by Anderson, only that of the

---

[17]R. H. Simpson, *A Study of Those Who Influence and of Those Who Are Influenced in Discussion*, New York: Teachers College Bureau of Publications, 1938.

[18]M. Kriesburg, "Cross-Pressures and Attitudes," *Public Opinion Quarterly*, vol. 13, no. 1, 1949.

[19]Kaplan, *op. cit.*

[20]Anderson, *op. cit.*

Extension section of the Department of Rural Sociology of the state university stressed a scientific approach to discussion, including the absolute necessity of facts on which to base discussion. Local leaders are given training in public affairs institutes, often running three days, although attendance is voluntary and local leaders, of course, are not paid. Local, state, national, and international issues are discussed. This public affairs discussion program in Wisconsin has been operating for years. The number of active groups in any one season has reached about 1,000. This would seem to be evidence that care in developing factual materials, in stating issues fairly and objectively and in training leaders pays dividends. Anderson states that most of the values claimed for the discussion method by adult educators can be demonstrated from the long continuing experience of this program.[21]

Psychological and sociological factors are involved. Psychologists indicate that the learning process can involve hearing, seeing and doing. Discussion, too, involves all three of these things, if doing is understood to mean participation, and seeing, the observations of the various speakers, not necessarily visual aids.

Sociologically the fact that it is a group which discusses means that social processes are involved. Social interaction is obviously a part of discussion and groups that continue to meet experience a degree of socialization as groups. The individual motives which stimulate participation, however, may be quite varied. Where both group loyalty and the desire to reach consensus are strong, there is cooperation and the interactive communication of member with member moves toward that goal, even though there may at times be a conflict of views. On the other hand, there may be competition for the attention of the group, whether from the yen for self-expression, from rivalry between members, or for other reasons. Thus the primary or subsidiary values in discussion some group members see for themselves are not always those stressed by adult educators.

Successful discussion is not debate. It requires an open mind—a willingness to be exposed to new facts and to different points of view. As such, discussion not only develops understanding, even if it falls short of agreement, but is also an attack on dogmatism as such. It also means making available adequate factual material, either through

[21]Wisconsin is not unique in this program. About 40 state colleges of agriculture have programs for the discussion of public affairs. Some of these programs involve hundreds of groups and the training of their discussion leaders. Others concentrate on working through existing organizations; a few do both. There has been no research looking toward an evaluation of this program.

printed materials, by the presence of a resource person or, as with the Canadian Farm Forum, by pre-discussion radio broadcasts. Certainly there is no value in pooling mutual ignorances in a discussion group, nor is there any surer method of insuring the early demise of a group.

These generalizations seem to be generally accepted by those concerned in the development of discussion as a device in adult education either as supplemental to other methods, or in terms of its own inherent values. On the basis of these, and particularly as a result of his study of the use of discussion by the agencies in Wisconsin, Anderson formulates some criteria[22] by which to judge its usefulness and evaluate its outcomes in any given situation. His formulation is briefly summarized below in terms of what *should* characterize a successful discussion experience.

Criteria for discussion. In terms of theory, discussion should be a process of sharing opinions and information about a mutual problem, purposefully proceeding in democratic fashion with full opportunity for the expression of all points of view and participation by all or most members of the group. Recognizable values should emerge from this process, though no unreasonable demands should be made on discussion as a sole method of adult education, to be used under any and all circumstances without recourse to other methods where called for. The group discussion leader should understand his function, be neutral, and make provision for a proper balance of fact and opinion and a testing of opinions by known facts.

In terms of the sociology of groups, the discussion group should conform to the characteristics and societal process of groups and contribute to the primary function of furthering both personality development and the welfare of the organization or the community of people involved. The communication process within the group should contribute to the effective use of discussion techniques, maintain a proper balance between individualization and socialization in its use, and stress the positive aspects both of cooperation and conflict in the interaction of group members.

Anderson phrases his criteria in question form and in detail. This has the advantage, for anyone who questioned whether in fact any element in the list flowed from his data, of suggesting further pertinent research to answer such a question. The discussion on the role of groups in adult education in Chapter XII bears on these points. It is clear from the research reviewed there that in naturally formed or traditional groups, or where individuals have made necessary adapta-

---

[22]Anderson, *op. cit.*, pp. 127-30.

tions to the social situation, free or democratic participation is more likely to occur than in *ad hoc* groups where there are frequently factors which inhibit meeting such criteria as Anderson has developed.

Further research desirable. There appear to be some unanswered problems with respect to the use of discussion in adult education, some of which may be indicated as suggestions for further research. Much of the investigation to date has been concerned with demonstrating the validity of the method; but discussion groups differ markedly both as to size and objectives, and therefore as to the outcomes expected from the discussion process. They are selective in their recruitment of personnel and in the conception of the role and function of both leaders and participants. They vary greatly in the use of resource persons and other techniques for introducing facts, and in the amount of prior preparation desired from group members. This suggests that discussion groups as currently utilized fall into determinable patterns and that both optimum size and procedures used need to be adapted to the particular pattern and objectives of the group. Where discussion as a method of adult education has failed, it is possible that the cause was the attempt to use techniques inappropriate for the situation, rather than a failure of the method itself. A definitive study of a large number of groups of varying purposes is called for. Does the optimum size of a group, for instance, differ according to the educational level of the participants and according to whether the objective is learning, exploration of a problem or arriving at consensus in terms of some public policy, or in terms of the program for some local agency? Is discussion desirable in adult education under all circumstances or would its use vary according to the type of subject matter and the degree of knowledge and educational status of the participants? What are the most effective ways of introducing necessary factual material in view of the obvious difficulty and expense of providing a competent resource person for every group?

In view of the reiteration in the literature of the need for trained discussion leaders, what are the qualifications for such leaders, and of what should the training consist? Are there criteria for selecting "good" topics for discussion or for avoiding certain types of topics? Would these criteria vary according to the objectives or pattern of the group and according to its educational status? Is discussion more effective when used in combination with other teaching techniques, such as films which would provide a common experience, or in an average situation can it be depended on as a sole technique?[23]

[23]On this point, cf. Glenn Burch, *Progress Report on Experimental Film Discussion Project,* White Plains, New York: The Fund for Adult Education, 1952 (mimeographed).

Does the usefulness of discussion vary according to the cultural background and expectations of the potential participants? What are the manifest and latent functions and values of discussion as seen by adult educators, group leaders and participants? Do the differences among representatives of these three categories suggest any modifications or further developments in the use of discussion in adult education? If so, what? Do the proponents of discussion in fact use it consistently? If not, under what circumstances do they use other techniques? By what criteria do they determine when to use discussion and when other techniques? Does the prestige of the group leader affect the behavior of a discussion group or, stated differently, are the "influentials" in such groups an asset or a liability in terms of the objectives of the discussion method?

The very success of the method in many situations, together with its failures in others, suggest that these unanswered questions, as well as others related to the use of discussion in adult education are worth study.

CHAPTER XI

LEADERS AND LEADERSHIP:
LAY AND PROFESSIONAL

Adult educators have long been concerned with the problems of selecting and training leaders for the many informal, usually small groups through which a great deal of adult education outside schools, colleges and other formalized agencies is carried on. Parent-Teachers associations and kindred organizations, and the discussion groups of the Great Books Foundation, each of which makes large use of volunteers in implementing its program, are illustrations, as is adult education in religion. The Agricultural and Home Economics Extension Services of the state colleges of agriculture could not operate without the more than a million persons who every year act as leaders in the groups and for the projects related to them. Research in leadership is therefore of real concern to adult educators though not much has been done by them except for studies by the Extension Service, which are largely descriptive.

In part, this gap in the research by adult educators is because group leadership is the concern of other fields than adult education, in some of which studies have been made which have applicability to adult education. Leaders, for example, are extremely important in the whole field of group work, as is noted in Chapter XII, which discusses the role of groups in adult education. Nor are the problems of leadership in adult education confined to the role of the volunteer. The field is so large and varied, and its professionalization so recent and, indeed, incomplete, that there has been mounting interest in the qualities and training needed by those who serve the adult education movement as employed leaders with professional status in the field.

Leader an illy-defined term. The terms leader and leadership have not as yet been defined with precision. One reason for this is the variety of functions performed by persons to whom the term leader is applied. In some situations the "leader" is no more than the person who performs the tasks necessary for keeping an informal group aware of its schedule of meetings and the topics for discussion. The other extreme is illustrated by Hitler's assumption of the title "leader" in Germany.

It is clear from countless observations that in any situation in which human beings associate some person or persons emerge who have more influence than any others. The term leader therefore always indicates a pattern of relationship between one so designated and those associated with him. What that relationship is will be determined by the type of group or organization and the functions assigned by common consent or formalized arrangement to the leader. Leadership, of course, is simply a term describing the function of the leader or the quality or ability he possesses.

Among the laity there is apparently considerable confusion as to the qualities necessary for leadership. An article in the June 1958 *Fortune* not only lists scores of variously defined traits corporation executives mentioned as desirable qualities for leaders, but indicates little consensus among them either as to the traits themselves, or as to what they stand for. This simply means that conceptualization and definition with respect to leadership have not advanced very far as yet. While the area of leadership has been analyzed in theoretical terms more than once with fairly elaborate classificatory systems,[1] research has by no means as yet explored or even touched upon all the elements noted in such contributions.

Fortunately for the inquirer, Murray G. Ross and Charles E. Hendry have undertaken an exhaustive survey of the research dealing with leaders and leadership. This is an invaluable contribution to group workers, social workers and adult educators dealing with informal situations.[2] In view of the recency of this volume and its comprehen-

[1]Cf., for instance, C. A. Gibb, "Leadership" in *Handbook of Social Psychology* vol. II, G. Lindzey (ed.), Cambridge, Mass.: Addison-Wesley Publishing Co., 1954.
[2]Murray G. Ross and Charles E. Hendry, *New Understandings of Leadership,* New York: Association Press, 1957.

siveness, the present section will deal, in somewhat abbreviated fashion, with the adult educator as leader. It will be concerned first with more general considerations and will then deal briefly with the volunteer workers and professional leadership so far as research is available.

Qualities needed for leadership. There is considerable agreement, backed up by research, as to the qualities a leader must have. High on the list is empathy, which may be defined as the ability to identify with the emotional needs of the group and respond to them. The leader clearly has greater awareness and sensitivity than the other members of his group.[3] In fact many have been chosen for leadership in part because of the recognition that they possessed this very quality.[4] Because of it leaders were better able than nonleaders to estimate opinions in their groups on matters of concern.[5]

Closely related to empathy is the quality of considerateness—the ability to recognize when detailed instruction is desirable, to explain actions taken when these raise doubts, and to suggest solutions or give practical help when personal problems arise.[6]

According to Cattell and Stice, enthusiasm, expressiveness, originality and kindred qualities are of "very great importance," especially if the leader is elected.[7] They subsume these qualities under the concept "surgency". Also important in leaders, according to these authors, is emotional stability. By this is meant, among other things, an integrated character or stable personality and an absence of such negative factors as anxiety and suspicion of others.

A desire to assume a leadership role and a recognition of its function are essential to a leader, since a person who is uninterested in assuming responsibility is ambivalent with respect to the role. Other desirable traits[8] involve such obvious characteristics as intelligence, competence, consistency and self-confidence, together with the ability

[3]S. Fillmore, "Leadership Identification and Acceptance," in *Groups, Leadership and Men,* H. Guetzkow, (ed.), Pittsburgh: Carnegie Press, 1951.

[4]G. Bell and H. Hall, Jr., "The Relationship between Leadership and Empathy," *Journal of Abnormal and Social Psychology,* January 1954.

[5]K. Chowdhry and T. Newcomb, "The Relative Abilities of Leaders and Non-leaders to Estimate Opinions of Their Own Groups," *Journal of Abnormal and Social Psychology,* January 1952.

[6]A. W. Halpin and B. J. Winer, *The Leadership Behavior of The Airplane Commander,* Columbus, Ohio State University Research Foundation, 1952; and D. Katz and others, *Productivity, Supervision and Morale Among Railroad Workers,* Ann Arbor: Institute for Social Research, University of Michigan Press, 1951.

[7]R. B. Cattell and G. F. Stice, *The Psychodynamics of Small Groups,* Urbana: University of Illinois, 1953.

[8]Ross and Hendry, *op. cit.*

to delegate tasks. Competence is perhaps especially important. It is defined in one important study as the ability to give help to members of the leader's group in its area of work and interest, and on a professional basis if the situation calls for it.[9]

The United States Department of Defense has been much concerned with leadership. A decade before the Ross and Hendry book appeared, Jenkins reviewed its research in this field.[10] His conclusions confirm some of the results already given and also those of a number of studies by the Extension Service. Those findings, with implications for adult education, are given and commented upon below.

1. Leadership is specific to particular situations and is a function of the situation. This relates to the matter of competence. It emphasizes that there are few generalized leaders but many recognized by their peers as superior in some one area of interest.

2. Leaders tend to exhibit certain characteristics in common with members of their groups. As Stouffer and a number of rural studies put it, the leader must be a member of his group and so recognized by others. Especially if he is appointed by an outside authority, he must identify with the group and share its objectives, maintaining friendly and helpful relations with all members and, should they exist, identifying himself with no clique.[11] In rural adult education it has been the experience of the Extension Service that leaders with subject matter competence appointed by professional agents often failed because their groups deemed them deficient in one or more of these respects. In a very recent, well-designed and methodologically sophisticated study, this same conclusion was amply confirmed, in part as determined operationally by sociometric techniques.[12]

3. Leaders usually possess some superiority in education or socioeconomic background which may facilitate their functioning as leaders. In the study just referred to, Fiedler also demonstrated that the leader "must maintain a certain amount of psychological distance from his group," rejecting co-workers who do not measure up. This "requires emotional independence and detachment." The function of maintaining this degree of distance is to prevent too great familiarity

[9]J. K. Hemphill, *Situational Factors in Leadership*, Columbus, Ohio State University, Bureau of Educational Research, 1949.

[10]W. O. Jenkins, "A Review of Leadership Studies with Particular Reference to Military Problems," *Psychological Bulletin*, vol. 44, no. 1, 1947.

[11]S. Stouffer and others, *The American Soldier*, vol. I, Princeton, New Jersey: Princeton University Press, 1949.

[12]Fred E. Fiedler, *Leader Attitudes and Group Effectiveness*, Urbana: University of Illinois, 1958.

or friendship which might lead to favoritism and impair the necessary acceptability of the leader to the whole group. If both acceptability and proper psychological distance are not maintained, communication can become inadequate and the group's effectiveness cannot be predicted.

The discussion thus far has been concerned with the qualities of leadership in general terms. Leadership, however, is always exerted in specific agencies, institutions or communities. The role of leadership in particular situations appears to vary from community to community and among institutions. Thus in one rural study covering four localities a positive relationship was found between formal leadership, defined as office holding, and participation in making community decisions. Informal leaders also were influential in this respect though less so.[13] In an Iowa study, on the other hand, leadership seemed to be largely independent of formal associations.[14] It is quite possible that these differences were due in part to different definitions of leadership, the different methods employed in the studies and to the variations in cultural attitudes and communication systems among the communities. The last factor especially, would make for very real differences in the leadership structure. The contrasts between these two studies at the least are important in alerting adult educators to the fact that some universal concept of leadership everywhere applicable may be an assumption contrary to fact. As with so many other aspects of adult education operations or any type of social organization, the degree to which any given situation is unique or deviates from the norm needs to be studied.

Leadership and the power structure. Two detailed and extensive studies of the power structure of urban communities utilized sociometric measures to identify informal power structure of the community and relate it to leadership. Hunter, in a large Southern urban community, "Regional City" and Gettel in a city of 60,000 population in a North Central state each identified a small informal power group and a somewhat larger group of sub-leaders. In "Regional City" Hunter found:

> Some of the top leaders hold board positions within associational groupings to lend prestige to the organization, but such members are noted more for their absence than for their attendance at meetings of

[13]C. Freeman and S. C. Mayo, "Decision Makers in Rural Community Action," *Social Forces*, XXV, May 1957.
[14]B. Ryan, *Social and Ecological Patterns of Farm Leadership of Four Iowa Townships*, Research Bulletin 306, Ames: Iowa State College Agricultural Experiment Station, 1942.

the respective boards. They can be called upon in an emergency and at such times they may function decisively.

The younger leaders may be pushed to take some of the top assignments. They take such duties, they say, with reluctance. . . . The less powerful under-structure associational personnel may scramble (in a dignified way, of course) for top positions in these groupings.[15]

This reluctance to serve on the part of top leaders is explained by the subordinate role of associations in decision making.

None of the men interviewed considered any of the associational groupings crucial to policy determination. Their role, like that of the organized institutional groupings, is one of following rather than leading. They may provide a forum for discussion and studying community issues, needs, and policies; but when decision is called for, another structure must come into play before action becomes the order of the day.

It is significant that two of the most influential associations were ones which were not widely known.

In the implementing stage in "Regional City" associational leaders begin to play a major role. It is significant that no relation could be found between the power group and cultural associations. Hunter charts the lines of interaction from top leaders, through subordinate leaders, to associations and institutions thus showing that the associational structure does play a major role in the chain of communication between the power group and the community at large.[16]

Gettel's findings in Denton closely parallel those of Hunter in "Regional City." The power group was not active in associations, but:

Sub-leaders are the backbone of the membership of most of the civic groups in the community . . . These groups serve as areas where minor decisions are made after basic policy has been drawn by the men in power.

Very few laymen were found to hold membership in any of the organizations in which sub-leaders or men of power held membership except in fraternal, religious, and veterans groups.[17]

In Denton, associations play a major role in the "legitimation" of decisions. The creation of a formal structure, a municipal improvement corporation, was engineered by the power group to provide a

[15]F. G. Hunter, *Community Power Structure*, Chapel Hill: University of North Carolina Press, 1953, pp. 84-86.

[16]*Ibid.*, pp. 70-112.

[17]G. F. Gettel, *A Study of Power in a North Central States Community*, Unpublished Ph.D. dissertation, Michigan State University, 1956.

means of initiating and facilitating necessary changes without permitting the process of change to get beyond their control.

The use of associations for training community leaders and the very subordinate role played by professional personnel follow Hunter's findings closely. The function of civic associations in training leaders in "Regional City" and in Denton was also evident in Thomasville, Georgia.[18] But there the role of professional personnel appeared to be quite significant, judging by the number of executive officers in key organizations and inter-organizational agencies held by professionals. This again indicates the variety of situations which may be found and suggests that the stereotype of a "power elite" cannot be assumed to apply everywhere and in identical fashion.

Not only does the leadership structure vary as between communities but it also operates on different levels. This frequent but too infrequently recognized fact is illustrated by a study of Merton's which delineated community leaders empirically.[19] He identified two distinct types of "influentials" in an Eastern seaboard community of 11,000 on the basis of orientation to the community. "The *localite* confines his interest to the community. . . . He is preoccupied with local problems to the virtual exclusion of the national or international scene." While the "*cosmopolitan* maintains a minimum of relations within the community . . . but is oriented significantly to the world outside."

Although both types are more active than the general public in formal associations, *localites* participated chiefly in secret societies, fraternal organizations, and local civic clubs, less to further the normal objectives of their organizations than to use them as "contact centers." *Cosmopolitans* tended to belong to organizations in which they could exercise special skills (professional societies, hobby groups, civil defense) more to further the objectives of these organizations than to establish personal ties.

This typology appears to have broad applicability for adult educators in that it suggests that there are types of leadership which roughly correspond to the varying types of participation in adult education programs described in Chapter VI. Promotion of adult education therefore can be facilitated by the identification of persons on these different leadership levels and working through them.

[18]John S. Newberry, Jr., *A Descriptive Study of Certain Aspects of the Membership of Formal Associations in a Southern Town,* Unpublished Ph.D. dissertation, Florida State University, 1959.
[19]R. K. Merton, "Patterns of Influence: A Study of Interpersonal Influence and Communication Behavior in a Local Community," in *Communications Research, 1948-49,* P. F. Lazarsfeld and F. N. Stanton, (eds.), New York: Harper and Bros. 1949.

Leadership training. Leaders may be born, but it is clear that they can also be made, or rather developed, through training, given the necessary, though perhaps latent, capacities and abilities. This generalization is warranted by the experience of the voluntary and informal agencies mentioned in the first paragraph of this chapter, especially the Extension Service. This rural adult education agency has utilized volunteer leaders from its very inception in 1914. These leaders can be trained in subject matter of both vocational and non-vocational character, and in techniques of presentation, as well as in administrative, organizational or program-building activities, different qualities being needed in these broad areas. The fact that the system has worked, despite many individual failures; that in the aggregate tens of thousands of rural dwellers annually participate in educational groups under volunteer leaders, numbering over a million a year for at least the last two decades, is impressive evidence of the success and practicality of using volunteer leadership in adult education.

Unfortunately, however, little research other than of a descriptive nature has been done with respect to leadership by the Extension Service. Leaders have broader interests, participate in more organized activities, are somewhat better educated than followers, as Fiedler's study, noted above, demonstrated for nonrural situations. Presumably the findings of studies already mentioned would apply in the rural field.

There is, however, evidence in some studies to support the conclusion that volunteer leaders can be developed in adult education. In one, 80 groups of four persons each were used. Forty-four of these groups were exposed to eight hours of training in the use of discussion as an adult education tool for arriving at an understanding of, and consensus about, certain changes in organizational procedure. Role-playing was one technique used. The other 36 groups were given no training except a half-hour lecture. All subjects in these groups were industrial personnel of first line or intermediate management status. At the end of the period both trained and untrained groups were allowed a half-hour discussion during which the subjects played leadership roles requiring group decision.

The results showed that resistance to change was sharply reduced in the cases where the leaders had received the eight hours of training. The primary difference between the trained and untrained leaders' conference procedures was that while the latter refuted objections to change and thus actually engendered hostility, the trained leader was inclined to present the situation as a problem and to listen to and explore suggestions and criticisms emanating from his group. The differences were statistically significant at the one per cent level.[20]

Another experiment explored the differential effects of leadership training on persons of different leadership statuses. One hundred and forty university women were used, 20 from each of seven sororities. They were divided into 20 groups of seven each, one from each sorority. At the beginning of the experiment, these groups participated in a leaderless group discussion under observation for the purpose of determining leadership status. The observers ranked each girl as to leadership qualities displayed in the discussion. Following this initial discussion, a half-hour training session was held for the women who ranked third and sixth in each of the 20 groups, followed by another discussion participated in by all members of all groups. The rank 3 women made considerable improvement, significant at the one per cent level. Those ranked 6 did not improve. These results "confirm the common-sense notion that persons differ in the extent to which they are amenable to leadership training." They also "support the argument that valid selection combined with valid training procedures will provide the most profitable approach to improving the calibre of leadership in an organization."[21]

Informal leaders. There are many subtle factors in leadership and many persons occupy leadership status unrecognized by professional workers because not formalized. An illustration comes from workers education. A study of a large union in an Eastern state showed that the union members tended to choose as their organization leaders those who were younger, better educated and more fully assimilated into the American culture. Meanwhile, however, they kept their own "opinion leaders." These latter were not even chosen as shop stewards. An unexpected result of this situation was that differences in age, social status and education between the elected leaders and shop stewards on the one hand, and the rank and file and their opinion leaders on the other, accentuated weak participation in union decisions by the membership and made for centralization of decision and action. These differences showed also in the written educational materials prepared by the leaders, which were above the reading ability of these largely foreign-born or foreign-stock workers with, on the average, less than seven years of school.[22] Saul Alinsky also discovered

---

[20]N. Maier, "An Experimental Test of the Effect of Training on Discussion Leadership," *Human Relations,* May 1953.

[21]S. Klubeck and Bernard M. Bass, "Differential Effects of Training on Persons of Different Leadership Status," *Human Relations,* February 1954.

[22]Per Stensland, *Education and Action in an American Labor Union,* Teachers College, Columbia University, Unpublished Ph.D. dissertation, 1950.

and emphasized the importance of these powerful but wholly informally recognized group leaders.[23]

Leaders and innovators. A somewhat similiar phenomenon has been found in rural areas where researchers have distinguished between innovators and leaders. The first are willing to experiment with any new practice or idea that seems reasonable. If it is successful the leaders will follow the innovator but will not risk their position of leadership by moving too quickly. However, in a highly homogeneous, conservative community the innovators are few or nonexistent. The rank and file follow the leaders but changes in attitudes and practices come more slowly.[24] One generalization from these studies points to the importance for adult educators of seeking out the influentials or innovators as well as the leaders in a community. Local influentials multiply their influence in a meeting whether they speak or remain silent. It must also be remembered that not all eager participants are considered either as influentials or leaders by the local population who, of course, know them best.

Professional leadership. Literally hundreds of organizations have what they consider educational programs focused on adults, and many have educational directors or similar officers. In many cases the content of the program is the point of view which the organization wishes to promote, or the program is concerned with the specific problems it meets. Thus, prominent in the educational activities conducted by the cooperative movement is teaching about the organization, administration, and operational philosophy of local cooperatives.

Comparably, though its program has considerably broadened over the years, workers education still naturally includes such subjects as labor union organization and history, the role of shop stewards and comparable topics vital to building the strength of the labor movement. Extension Service personnel were initially concerned with imparting information on the technical aspects of agriculture and home economics and their principal qualification was mastery of the subject matter content they were to teach. All such workers and others were

[23]Saul Alinsky, *Reveille for Radicals,* Chicago, University of Chicago Press, 1945.
[24]E. Wilkening, "Informal Leaders and Innovators in Farm Practices," *Rural Sociology,* September 1952; H. Lionberger, "Some Characteristics of Farm Operators Sought as Sources of Information in a Missouri Community," *Rural Sociology,* December 1953, and *Social Structure and Diffusion of Farm Information,* Columbia: University of Missouri Agricultural Experiment Station, 1957; B. W. Kreitlow and James A. Duncan, *The Acceptance of Educational Programs in Rural Wisconsin,* Madison: University of Wisconsin Agricultural Experiment Station, 1956; Everett M. Rogers and George M. Beal, *Reference Group Influence in the Adoption of Agriculture Technology,* Ames, Iowa: State College Agricultural Experiment Station, 1958.

expected to develop their own methods. The realization dawned slowly that there were common problems in teaching adults, that methods in one field might be useful to others. This came about in part because adult education is always education with reference to some specific subject matter which appears as the central focus of teaching, and the content of the many possible fields obviously varies.

The slow development of adult education as a methodological discipline in its own right, and as one needing to pay attention in all its aspects to adult psychology and to the implications of such social sciences as sociology and anthropology, is shown by the small number of universities which include training in this field in their curricula. As of this writing there are less than a score with programs in adult education, the first of which is less than 35 years old.

But the fact that there are such programs is in itself evidence that the situation is changing and with the change has come the beginning of research in the problems of developing professional leadership for the adult education movement.

It is interesting to note that when persons selected to function as teachers or leaders in the educational program of the Armed Services of the United States in World War II faced their responsibilities, they quickly began to request training in the methods and techniques of adult education, even where they were fully competent with respect to the subject matter they were to handle. Moreover, it was soon evident that the teaching ability of these instructors of young adults improved markedly through training in methods of instructing mature persons. Conversely, the students considered the quality of the instructor one of the most effective factors in the success of a class.[25]

Practical experience is influential. It is also evident that practical experience in adult education, at least when it is on a full-time basis, enlarges the conception of the professional leadership as to the preparation they should have. Agents of the Extension Service attached more importance to training in the social sciences than to any other area. In terms of graduate work, nine-tenths of the administrative and supervisory staffs urged that advanced training for this rural adult education group should include courses in sociology, psychology and adult education methods.[26] Even in 1938 the need for social science

---

[25]Cyril Houle *et al., Armed Services and Adult Education,* Washington: American Council on Education, 1947.

[26]J. L. Matthews, *A Method for Determining Training Needs of County Agents as a Basis for Planning Training Programs,* Washington: Extension Service, USDA, 1950; B. Cook, *A Comparative Analysis of the Training Needs for County Agents,* Ph.D. dissertation, University of Wisconsin, 1957.

training stood high on the list of desirable courses for Extension personnel as determined by an administrative questionnaire survey, to which over 7,000 responded, conducted by M. C. Wilson for the Department of Agriculture.

This emphasis probably arose because the duties of these workers involve community organization, interorganizational relations and group work. To some extent this would apply to most full-time adult educators. It was noticeable in the studies mentioned above that the minority who disagreed with these emphases in leadership training reflected a different philosophy of adult education.

There has been some research which has explored the application of the role theory—though this is admittedly "in its infancy"—to the operations of professional adult educators in the Extension Service, both with respect to the interacting roles of supervisors and field staff[27] and between the county agents and their local clientele.[28]

Wilkening found that the ratings of the importance of various program activities by the agents agreed more highly with what they felt farm people wanted than with what these agents felt they needed. The agents were strongly influenced by local interests even when these were not compatible with the individual's "ideal definition" of his role. Some agents complained of certain elements in their activities, but their time accounting showed little effort was being put into changing the expectations of the local people. Wilkening concludes that for professional leaders "it appears easier to change goals than the means of carrying them out."

This research appears to have significant implications for adult education. It raises the perennial problem of adult educators as to whether to offer what is needed or what is wanted by the clientele. It raises, but does not explore questions as to the practicability of effective professional leadership by indirection to lead participants toward what they need. Apparently few conceived this to be an important part of their role. Additional studies along these lines in all the principal areas of adult education would be most useful.

Public school adult educators and leadership. There is one considerable group of adult educators that speakers at conventions often imply has considerable leadership potential, namely the teachers in and administrators of public school adult education programs. Unfortunately, however, the influence of this group, especially the teachers,

[27]Arthur E. Durfee, *Expectations Held Toward the Extension Supervisor's Role*, Ithaca, New York: College of Agriculture, Cornell University, 1956, mimeographed.
[28]Eugene A. Wilkening, *The County Extension Agent in Wisconsin: Perceptions of Role Definitions*, Madison Agricultural Experiment Station, University of Wisconsin, 1957.

appears to be negligible outside their classrooms. Clark's study makes the reasons for this quite clear.[29] Typically the teachers are part-time workers with their major responsibilities in the dayschool or in other occupations. They therefore are characterized by a weak career pattern in adult education. The great majority of them have no tenure. Typically they are paid on an hourly basis. The salary and other employment standards advocated by teachers associations do not provide for adult education situations. In some states there are no standardized requirements for acceptance as a teacher of adults in public schools. Most such teachers, even in a large program in a city such as Los Angeles, have little contact with other teachers of adults and hence have a weak identification with adult education in either its institutional or professional aspects.

Among administrators of the program, especially in communities large enough to employ full-time personnel for administration and supervision, the situation is somewhat better. In their promotion of adult education in their communities administrators deal with many diverse groups and agencies and come to be recognized as exerting some influence and leadership. However, as Chapter VII points out, they are handicapped by a variety of conditions, largely inherent in the relatively insecure place of adult education in the public school system. In California, at least, this has resulted in "defeatism and pessimism," according to a 1953 survey by Science Research Associates.[30] Real administrative leadership, however, consists to a large degree in working out the necessary adaptations and adjustments between the environmental pressures and problems affecting a staff and its program and the organization responsible for the program. There is no comparable research to determine if the Los Angeles situation is exceptional or typical. On the basis of scattered testimony there would appear to be both similar and better situations. Since adult education has certainly won a foothold among the public school systems of the country there is clearly an opportunity for further development. Research that might assist the leadership in charting the course for such expansion would seem to be appropriate.

Other needed research. Of value also would be research that would replicate some of the studies already available among different groups and in different situations. Occupation, age, educational status, cultural backgrounds are among the variables that may influence the image of the leader's role and thus his approach to fulfilling that role.

[29]B. R. Clark, *Adult Education in Transition*, Berkeley and Los Angeles; University of California Press, 1956.
[30]Quoted by Clark, *ibid.*, p. 108.

Conversely, these same variables may also influence the acceptability of the leader to the group.[31]

It would also be useful to discover if there are opinion leaders or influentials in various areas of adult education. Who influences whom with respect to the values attached to education and the actual choices of educational activities by adults? Are there recognizable key persons performing such functions? If so, are they really members of a power elite, as some assume, or does their influence or leadership inhere in recognized competence?

Do different subject matter and different organizational auspices require different leadership qualities? Can a state director of agriculture and home economics extension, for instance, depend on the same set of qualities which research may suggest is essential for the adult education director of a library or of a public school system?

Apart from these and similar questions, many could be asked with respect to the leadership training activities for both volunteer and professional leaders sponsored by numerous agencies. These have often been subjectively evaluated by the participants, but definite outcomes as shown by the participants' subsequent behavior have rarely if ever been studied, despite the huge amount of effort put into in-service training.[32]

[31]A small study by a student of the senior author indicated that Extension groups in home economics, undifferentiated as to age, would accept younger, better educated women leaders in such newer subjects as interior decoration, art or public affairs, but that older women rebelled against having younger leaders in vocational subjects such as baking and dressmaking, in which they had had long experience.

[32]Since the completion of this report an excellent study of leadership in various types of informal adult education programs has appeared. It is based on a study of actual operating programs of varied objectives and conducted by 14 different organizations from such fields as business, labor, religion, mental health, parent education, public affairs and home economics extension. Cf. A. A. Liveright, *Strategies of Leadership in Conducting Adult Education Programs,* N.Y., Harper & Bros., 1959.

CHAPTER XII

GROUP RESEARCH AND
ADULT EDUCATION*

During the last 20 years the fields of social psychology and sociology have expanded greatly. Regardless of the many differences between the fields, each is concerned with the study of more than one person at a time. Within each field, the generic term "group" has been used to refer to the general phenomenon of "more than one person" as well as to special classes of "more than one person" phenomena which must meet specified criteria. Directions of small group research and group dynamics have emerged somewhat independently of the traditions of public opinion research, community studies, and other more "large group" or sociological studies and often without apparent regard for the ways in which the groups studied are alike or different and whether or not these differences affect results. Thus any conscientious review of group research, whether in terms of adult education or other fields, must come face to face with the problem of classification of groups and what research tells us about the various types. Only then can the relevance of group research for adult education be dealt with systematically.

Unfortunately there is no existing classification of groups which

*This chapter was written by David E. Wilder.

191

would be satisfactory to all adult educators or which would provide an adequate framework for reporting and relating the findings from the hundreds of studies of groups in the literature.[1] Merton has noted that most of the writers who have dealt with this problem

> . . . are agreed on the fundamental logical requirement that an effective classification will be not merely descriptive of observed 'types' but will derive from combinations of values of designated group properties. The decisive problem is, of course, that of identifying the theoretically strategic group properties which will serve systematically to discriminate the operation of each resultant type of group from the others.[2]

Groups defined. In the following analysis the term "group" will refer only to those more-than-one-person situations where there is interaction between members. The degree or type of interaction may vary a great deal and is, of course, an important variable. It is necessary to place this restriction upon the material because the discussion of an infinite variety of combinations of individuals selected on the basis of individual attributes would make the task at hand virtually impossible. One need only take a glance at the many attributes of individuals that have been considered relevant in the Participation chapter to appreciate this. However, what is more important is that groups will be considered as something quite different from *aggregates* of individuals since it is the *emergent* characteristics of groups which make them significant subjects for adult education research.

MAJOR AREAS OF GROUP RESEARCH

In order to survey small group research with an eye toward its implications for adult education, the present discussion centers on three areas of concern: individuals and groups compared; the internal dynamics of groups; and groups as they relate to one another and the environment. This classification is empirical because it reflects real differences in what researchers are trying to find out; however, there are many studies that do not fall neatly into one classification. The last section of the chapter attempts to put together some of the findings from the three areas and make suggestions for further research with special relevance to adult education situations.

---

[1]There are many classifications of group attributes or properties, and there will be occasion to refer to some of these. However, none of these purports to be a comprehensive classification of groups, even though all groups might be described or analyzed in terms of the designated attributes or properties.

[2]Robert K. Merton, *Social Theory and Social Structure*, (rev. ed.), Glencoe, Illinois: The Free Press, 1957.

Individuals and groups compared. Probably the oldest tradition of research about small groups is that which contrasts groups and individuals with regard to various sorts of performance. Allport and Burtt did pioneer studies in this area as far back as 1920.[3] The emphasis in these studies was to determine whether individuals are more efficient or productive with regard to specified tasks and problems than are groups. This work has obvious implications for industry and the military. However, educators are often concerned with broader goals than efficiency or production *per se* and findings from this area would have to be exceptionally clear-cut to have direct relevance to adult education.

Two excellent reviews from the research in this area have been made in recent years.[4,5] Both record a great many specific studies,[6] many of which are excellently conceived and executed. Nonetheless, the results often are not complementary and sometimes contradict one another. Therefore, there is a paucity of strong generalizations for adult education that can be made from them. This has been due partly to the fact that groups and tasks differ greatly from study to study. This difficulty becomes obvious when one examines the attempts at generalizations and summary statements made by the following authors.

Kelley and Thibaut summarize the early part of their article by stating:

> . . . as compared with working alone, working before a passive audience or with other persons at the same task seems to have the following effects:
> (a) Greater quantity of work where physical output is involved, suggesting increased motivation to perform the task.
> (b) Lesser quantity or quality of work where intellectual processes or concentration are involved, suggesting the social stimuli are able to compete successfully with the task stimuli.
> (c) Inhibitions of response and qualitative changes in the work which suggest that the person somehow 'takes account of' the others

---

[3]F. Allport, "The Influence of the Group upon Association and Thought," *Journal of Experimental Psychology,* III, No. 3, June 1920. H. E. Burtt, "Sex Differences in the Effect of Discrimination," *Journal of Experimental Psychology,* III, No. 3, 1920.

[4]H. H. Kelley and J. W. Thibaut, "Experimental Studies of Group Problem Solving and Process," in G. Lindzey (ed.) *Handbook of Social Psychology,* Vol. 2, Cambridge, Mass.: Addison-Wesley Publishing Company, Inc., 1954.

[5]I. Lorge and M. Brenner, *A Survey of Studies Contrasting the Quality of Group Performance and Individual Performance,* Technical Report No. 1, New York: Bureau of Applied Social Research, Columbia University, October 15, 1957.

[6]The bibliographies of the two reviews contain 160 and 74 items respectively, most of which are research reports; and each of the reviews is longer than this chapter.

as he goes about his work, e.g., he has fewer idiosyncratic thoughts, exercises moderation in judgment, and gives more 'popular' or common associations.

(d) Greater variations through time in his output, indicating the presence of periodic distractions and/or the effects of working under greater tension.

(e) There is some evidence that these effects wear off as the person adapts to the social situation.[7]

The first four generalizations have rather clear-cut implications for adult education. They suggest that people do not do their best, particularly with regard to the intellectual tasks which are the chief concern of liberal adult education when they work on such tasks together. Perhaps even more serious is the implication that the mere presence of other people tends to inhibit thought or expression which might occur in the "alone" situation. To the extent that this is true, getting adults together to discuss important issues might result in their showing greater consensus by paying mere lip service to a more popular or narrower range of opinions than would be the case if they felt they could express themselves freely. This possibility is consistent with the traditional distinction public opinion experts have made between "public" and "private" opinions.[8] The attempt to give anonymity to respondents on questionnaires is a conscious attempt on the part of researchers to minimize this problem. Teachers and discussion leaders are quite familiar with the problem of inducing shy individuals to participate in discussion, but it appears that even those who do participate a great deal may not be expressing themselves fully.

Generalization "e" indicates that, over time, the individual adapts to the social situation. This suggests that negative effects may be reversed and that free expression and a high level of intellectual activity may be reached. This qualification of the first four generalizations also suggests that group life might have different effects on different individuals, a possibility which a great deal of the group work literature fails to take into account. However, this can be determined only by further research.[9]

[7]Kelley and Thibaut, *op. cit.*, p. 750.

[8]It is also consistent with the Sherif and Asch findings discussed on pg. 198ff.

[9]A recent study of the experimental discussion group program in the Los Angeles area lends some support to this hypothesis in that during the program the *ad hoc* groups tended to become more like traditional social groups as acquaintance in some cases ripened into friendship and mutual confidence grew. This aspect of the experiment was not, however, specifically studied.

A. A. Kaplan, *A Study of the Liberal Arts Discussion Program for Adults in the Metropolitan Los Angeles Area*, White Plains, N.Y.: The Fund for Adult Education, 1958 (dittoed).

An additional comment should be made. Whether in a cloistered cell or in a group, a person learns as an individual and only so. Such generalizations as are given in (a) to (e) above suffer because it is obviously impossible to determine from them how well any individual will learn the same content alone as contrasted to how well he will learn it in a group. A possible hypothesis in this area would be that under the stimulation of an environmental situation certain types of people learn more efficiently in group situations than working alone. The testing of such an hypothesis would require repeated observations in which people equated for intelligence and educational status attempted to master the same content working alone and in groups. Such a situation, however, would be very difficult to achieve in adult education.

Investigators in this area have used three major types of groups which differ with regard to the relationships among members. Some investigators have combined individual results to construct artificially a "statisticized" group. Others have employed groups brought together for the first time during the investigation, i.e. *ad hoc* groups. The third type of group is that which exists before the investigation, and is usually called a "traditioned" group.

Lorge and Brenner point out that *ad hoc* groups are often used as microscopic models of "traditioned" groups, and generalizations from studies of the former are incorrectly applied to the latter in spite of the fact that one tends to act differently with strangers from the way he acts in the presence of those he knows rather well. They also note that there are variations in the amount of interaction in the various experimental groups, and that the group product may vary as a function of the sorts of mathematics used in computing it. Thus they find it necessary to employ a classification of six different types of groups in order to review the studies but recognize that their classification is far from exhaustive with regard to variables which might affect results and precludes generalizing the results of any one study.

The following excerpts reveal the sorts of generalizations that Lorge and Brenner feel free to make on the basis of the studies they review:

> What generalizations can be made about group and individual judgments? . . . At best, group judgment equals the best individual judgment, but it usually is somewhat inferior to the best individual.[10]
> Contrasting the results by groups and individuals in learning suggests quite amorphous generalizations. . . . These amorphous results suggest several explanations, the most likely of which is that

---

[10]Lorge and Brenner, *op. cit.*, p. 18.

these experiments were conducted under such varying conditions that seemingly diametrically opposed results are understandable. For example, a group's size can be expected to have a profound effect upon results. It is known that as the group size increases, individual involvement decreases, and inhibition increases. Large discussion groups, therefore, might be expected to produce less learning than smaller groups. Other factors such as announced goals, subject matter, methods of measuring improvement, etc., can be expected to have profound effects on the results. This indicates a serious need for additional experimentation which can control important conditions.[11]

Research contrasting group and individual performance in "learning" suffered from a lack of experimental controls; research with problem solving suffered from a lack of reality, etc.; problems or tasks are far removed from the genuine and real. The problems, in general, have been puzzles, riddles, or information-test questions. Results from such tasks were not sufficiently conclusive to allow an unambiguous generalization about the superiority of groups over individuals with more realistic problems.[12]

The single generalization derived from these studies is that in conformity with other studies reported in this review, evidence of the existence of both a depressing and an accelerating effect from group participation is evident. These experiments do not aid in identifying or quantifying these effects.[13]

From this limited number of studies certain tentative generalizations can be made. As indicated by South greater production on "abstract" problems can be expected from smaller groups than larger ones, and greater production on "concrete" problems from larger groups than from smaller ones. Bales *et al.*, Gibb, Carter *et al.* indicated the possibility that groups of increasing size will increase production at a negatively accelerating rate for problems of certain types. When comparing production of groups of varying size and individuals these generalizations should be kept in mind. Considerable additional research is needed to confirm or refute these expectations.[14]

[11] *Ibid.*, p. 22.
[12] *Ibid.*, p. 31.
[13] *Ibid.*, p. 32.
[14] *Ibid.*, p. 34. The studies discussed are: South, "Some Psychological Aspects of Committee Work," *Journal of Applied Psychology*, 1927, 11; R. F. Bales, F. M. Strodtbeck, T. M. Mills, and Mary E. Roseborough, "Channels of Communication in Small Groups," *American Sociological Review*, 1951, 16; J. R. Gibb, "The Effects of Group Size and of Threat Reduction Upon Creativity in a Problem Solving Situation," *American Psychologist*, 1951, 6 (abstract); L. Carter, W. Haythorn, B. Marrowitz and J. Lanzetta, "The Relation of Categorizations and Ratings on the Observation of Group Behavior," *Human Relations*, 1948, vol. 1.

It is evident from the above that Lorge and Brenner do not feel any more free to make unqualified generalizations comparing performance of individuals and groups than do Kelley and Thibaut. It would be very convenient if one could specify the tasks which individuals perform better than groups and vice versa, but these specifications would have to reflect serious differences to have "practical" implications for adult education. Both reviews make it clear that there is no justification from research findings for advocating that education should always take place in groups or with individuals exclusively. It has become evident that there are different groups, different individuals and different tasks and learning situations. Comparing "the" individual and "the" group with regard to "problem solving", "performance", or "learning" will not produce generalizations of an unambigous sort for adult education. Nevertheless, it may be possible in the not too distant future by improved research techniques to make clear generalizations comparing *certain kinds* of individuals to *certain kinds* of groups with regard to *certain kinds* of learning, performances, and problem solving.

Clearly adult education will take place in groups almost exclusively. This is true for financial reasons if for no other. Consequently, comparisons between individuals and groups are far less relevant to adult education than the question of whether there are identifiable group characteristics which are conducive or not to the educational process.

The modern emphasis upon working with groups developed first of all in the social welfare field, especially in settlement houses and in voluntary agencies such as the Y.W.C.A. Considerable enthusiasm developed for working with natural groupings of people. Many adult educators seem to have accepted this technique uncritically. What research there is indicates that groups may be more effective in achieving social objectives than strictly educational ones.

As the next section further shows, the pressures of a group may even set up handicaps to learning or to independent thinking. Since human beings are gregarious and tend to form groups and operate through them, research is clearly needed to show how groups may be used most effectively in adult education; how the obstacles to learning in group situations may be reduced; and conversely, how the processes that facilitate learning may be accelerated. At the least, research to date has shown that there are problems in this area of which adult educators should be cognizant.

Intra-group phenomena. As we have seen in the previous section, there are different kinds of groups as well as different kinds of individuals. The lack of definitive generalizations which could be derived from the studies just reviewed has been seen to be partly a result of the fact that we have been unable to specify the important ways in which groups differ. The following section will also suffer from this limitation to some extent though it is an attempt to point out some of the important ways in which groups are alike and to derive generalizations about groups which will hold true regardless of differences.

In 1936 Sherif[15] demonstrated, through a series of experiments which are now social science classics, that groups have certain emergent characteristics that make it necessary to regard them as something more than mere collections of individuals. It has been known for a long time that individuals placed in a darkened room where there is a point of stationary light will perceive the light as moving. This is known as the "autokinetic effect." Estimates of the distance the light moves vary from individual to individual, but each individual will strike upon a rather narrow range within which most of his estimates will fall. Sherif found that individuals, when in group situations, will take into account the estimates of others so that eventually a range of estimates characteristic of each group will emerge. If an individual's estimate of the distance the light moves is too much at variance with that of other members of the group, he will tend to adjust his estimate in the direction of the estimates of others. Individuals who have first been exposed to the group situation and later tested alone will tend to continue to make estimates which would be acceptable to the group.

Since the original studies on the formation of group norms were conducted by Sherif, many others have followed similar lines. Perhaps the most notable are those of Asch who, sensing the implicit tyranny of groups contained in the Sherif work, attempted to find out just how and how much of our behavior tended to be influenced by others.

Asch[16] asked subjects to judge the length of lines in relation to one another in a series of experiments in which he systematically varied the size of the majority and the number of people disagreeing with the majority by the use of stooges. Incorrect judgments were made by a number of stooges in the presence of a naive subject whose behavior was then systematically observed and recorded. Asch found that subjects were influenced significantly by the wrong judgments of others as long as the discrepancies between the correct lines and those chosen by the others were not too large.

[15]Muzafer Sherif, *The Psychology of Social Norms*, 1936.
[16]S. E. Asch, "Effects of Group Pressures Upon the Modification and Distortion of Judgments," in *Readings in Social Psychology*, Swanson, Newcomb and Hartley (eds.), New York: Henry Holt, 1952.

The tendency for individuals to shift in the direction of the majority decreased a great deal when the discrepancy between the correct lines and those chosen by the majority was very large. Nevertheless, a significant minority would still shift in the direction of the majority, and most subjects experienced very unpleasant feelings in this situation regardless of their behavior. With only one person giving wrong judgments, there was no noticeable majority effect; with two, effects became noticeable; and with three, the effect was as large as in the situations where more than three gave incorrect responses. In cases where the individual was given support for his correct judgments by a stooge, the effect of the majority was reduced a great deal.

Both the Asch and Sherif experiments show that people tend to influence one another in group situations, that there is a tendency to conform which seems to be related to a dislike of being different but which might take place unconsciously, and that the behavior of individuals alone may differ from their behavior in groups. In addition, the Sherif experiments demonstrate that individual behavior learned in the group context will tend to persist in the individual situation. These are all statements which should be familiar to adult educators and make sense to them in the light of educational experiences. However, here, too, exceptions can be found, which naturally lead to additional questions of the sort which ask, "Under what conditions will the statement hold true, and under what conditions will it be refuted?" This is a crucial query with regard to the findings of most research about groups, and it will not be adequately answered until one is able to identify all the relevant variables and control them systematically.

"*Field theory.*" Probably no man has had more influence on small group research than Kurt Lewin. In some of his empirical research he attempted to make use of group processes in changing individual attitudes and behavior. His work was done during World War II in connection with the war effort, and was successful in changing consumer food habits.[17] However, his influence has been felt the most with regard to the conceptualization and theory of small group research. In his "field theory"[18] it is pointed out that groups should be regarded as dynamic wholes with interdependent parts; this approach has been characteristic of social psychology ever since. There has, however, been a notable lack of agreement as to what parts of variables should

[17]K. Lewin, *The Relative Effectiveness of a Lecture Method and a Method of Group Discussion for Changing Food Habits,* Washington: N.R.C., 1942. Also see Chapter X of the present report.
[18]K. Lewin, *Field Theory in Social Science,* New York: Harper, 1951.

be taken into consideration in studying this dynamic whole; and where there is agreement about the variables, there is often disagreement as to how they are related.

Impressions versus observational categories. The gap between the general way in which many people talk about groups and the generalizations which can accurately be made about them on the basis of empirical research is implicit in the following statement of Lazarsfeld:

> When we deal with the characteristics of individuals, some distinctions are habitual: between an attitude, a personality trait, a biological characteristic such as height, an economic characteristic such as income, etc. When it comes to group characteristics, however, their logical structure is more obscure. If an author discusses the transition from feudal to industrial society, he implicitly claims that if he were presented with a large number of societies he could order them according to their degree of 'feudalism'. How would he proceed?[19]

Cattell[20] feels that there are three kinds of observations that can be made about groups: (a) population variables (characteristics of the component individuals) ; (b) structural variables (patterns of interaction within the group) ; and (c) syntality variables (performance of the group as a whole—as personality is to the individual). The methodological implications of such a conceptualization are very complex, and indeed, Cattell, as his main methodological contribution, used a factor analysis of forty-one variables.[21]

Carter[22] and Steinzer[23] have also proposed rather complex schemes, but the best-known and most widely used methods are those of Hemphill and Westie[24] and Bales.[25] The first of these uses scales with respect to 14 group dimensions, and the Bales system, with its emphasis on action, uses 12 categories.[26] The latter two are probably the best sys-

---

[19]P. F. Lazarsfeld and M. Rosenberg, (eds.) *The Language of Social Research: A Reader in the Methodology of Social Research*, Glencoe, Ill.: The Free Press, 1955, p. 287.

[20]R. B. Cattell, "New Concepts for Measuring Leadership, in Terms of Syntality in Small Groups," *Group Dynamics: Research and Theory*, Cartwright and Zander (eds.) Evanston, Ill.: Row, Peterson and Company, 1953.

[21]R. B. Cattell and Lauren G. Wispe, "The Dimensions of Syntality in Small Groups," *Journal of Social Psychology*, 1949, 28.

[22]L. Carter, W. Haythorn, B. Shriver and L. Shriver, "The Behavior of Leaders and Other Group Members," *Journal of Abnormal and Social Psychology*, 1951, 46.

[23]B. Steinzer, "The Development and Evaluation of a Measure of Social Interaction, Part One. The Development and Reliability," *Human Relations*, 1949, 2.

[24]J. K. Hemphill and C. M. Westie, "The Measurement of Group Dimensions," in Lazarsfeld and Rosenberg, *op. cit.*

[25]R. F. Bales, *Interaction Process Analysis: A Method for the Study of Small Groups*, Cambridge, Mass.: Addison-Wesley, 1950.

[26]There are, however, many more than twelve variables which must be taken into account in the Bales system.

tems we have at the present time, but they require highly skilled workers and can be used only under very special conditions. Neither method has been widely used in adult education situations, for practical reasons, if no other.

Some of the tentative generalizations that have been made from studies using these various methods are as follows: Pressures to conform increase as (1) the group is more attractive or cohesive;[27] (2) the individual deviates farther from the group norm;[28] (3) the leader is group-centered rather than leader-centered;[29] (4) the instructions to the group maximize the need for unanimity;[30] and (5) the individual feels more committed to the group.[31]

Similarly, when the pressures become great: (1) the number of deviates increases;[32] (2) publicly expressed and privately held opinions will diverge;[33] and (3) issues tend to become misunderstood.[34]

Each of the above statements can be seen to lend specificity to the "people tend to conform" generalization that was made from the original Sherif study. However, they are all "tends to" statements which are hardly causal. Each helps to confirm Lewin's major point by demonstrating relationships of parts, and each advances in the direction of specifying under what conditions original generalizations will hold true. Nevertheless, the research is hardly cumulative at this point, and each of the above statements should be regarded as highly tentative. The research does suggest, however, that an adult educator might well look, especially at any problem groups, from the point of view of these tentative generalizations as a first step in gaining clues as to the functioning or lack of functioning of any group with which he may be concerned.

"Group dynamics." The area of intragroup relations has come to be

[27]H. H. Kelley and E. H. Volkart, "The Resistance to Change of Group-Anchored Attitudes," *American Sociological Review*, 1952, 17; Also see G. C. Homans, *The Human Group*, New York: Harcourt Brace, 1950, and L. Festinger, S. Schacter, and K. Back, *Social Pressures in Informal Groups*, New York: Harper, 1950.
[28]S. Schacter, "Deviation, Rejection and Communication," *Journal of Abnormal and Social Psychology*, 1951, 46; Festinger, Schacter and Back, *op. cit.*
[29]E. W. Bovard, Jr., "Group Structure and Perception" in Cartwright and Zander, *op. cit.*
[30]L. Festinger and J. Thibaut, "Interpersonal Communication in Small Groups," *Journal of Abnormal and Social Psychology*, 1950, 45.
[31]K. Lewin, "Group Decision and Social Change," in Swanson, Newcomb and Hartley, *op. cit.*
[32]Festinger, Schacter and Back, *op. cit.*
[33]R. L. Gordon, "Interaction Between Attitude and the Definition of the Situation in the Expression of Opinion," in Cartwright and Zander, *op. cit.*
[34]Kelley and Volkart, *op. cit.*

known as group dynamics. While the term is new, the phenomena associated with the concept and their recognition are not. Among others, Cooley drew attention to their importance half a century ago.[35] The dynamics of groups are an important area for research and such research has, and hopefully will continue to have, important contributions to make to adult education and many other fields. Some confusion in the use and application of the concept has unfortunately arisen because some people have used the term group dynamics as if it connoted a method of operation rather than a field for research which has implications for method. This confusion may be partly attributable to the fact that the most famous study by Lewin, the recognized founder of the discipline, involved an action orientation.[36]

Rather than search out further tentative and qualified generalizations from the vast literature that already exists in the field in an attempt to extrapolate implications for adult education, it seems more profitable to offer more primitive generalizations which seem to be fairly well established. The following is a list of four generalizations:

1. Groups have, in addition to the individuals who comprise them, emergent characteristics which come about through interaction and which, in this sense, make them more than the sum of their parts.
2. Among the important characteristics of groups are the system of statuses and roles which the members occupy and play, respectively, as well as the norms which apply to them.[37]
3. Groups may change and undergo processes through time.[38]
4. Important group characteristics such as cohesion, size, atmosphere, flexibility, homogeneity, etc. tend to be related to one another in such a way that changes in one will mean changes in others.[39]

[35]C. H. Cooley, *Social Organization*, New York: Charles Scribners' Sons, 1909.

[36]K. Lewin, *op. cit.*

[37]Status is generally used to refer to the positions that individuals occupy in groups and roles usually refers to the behavior associated with the statuses. This is the sort of structural approach which can be found with minor variations throughout the literature. See T. R. Sarbin, "Role Theory," in Lindzey, *op. cit.*; M. Sherif and C. Sherif, *An Introduction to Social Psychology*, New York: Harper and Brothers, 1957.

[38]Anyone who has been connected with a class of students knows that it usually changes through time, but just how changes take place and which variables are most relevant constitute a major problem area. In the "Community" chapter of the present report, Chapter XIII, it is noted that informal groups may become formal groups over time. Doddy refers to "habit" groups and how they often become "purpose" groups. H. H. Doddy, *An Inquiry Into Informal Groupings in a Metropolitan Area*, Unpublished Ed.D. dissertation, New York: Teachers College, Columbia University, 1952.

Four stages through which groups go are designated in *Action Research in Three Towns in Connecticut, Massachusetts and New Hampshire*, New England Pilot Project Editorial Committee, Amherst, Mass.: University of Massachusetts, Agricultural Ext. Service, 1956.

[39]This can be seen by examining the studies which are concerned with these variables in Cartwright and Zander, *op. cit.*, e.g. cohesion is an independent variable in some studies and a dependable variable in others. Results are obtained either way.

The above generalizations cannot serve as an unvarying practical guide to adult educators who are trying to find out what is known about groups that would be of use in the adult education field. The specifics of how these findings from group research will apply to adult education situations and which variables will be the most relevant can be determined only by conducting such research within the adult education context.

It should be noted that although leadership has traditionally been a separate area of study from that of groups *per se,* it has become increasingly clear during recent years that it is difficult, and sometimes pointless, to study groups without studying the leadership at the same time. Indeed, a great deal of what has been learned about leadership and groups has emerged only as the two have been studied together. In such studies leadership is often treated as an emergent group characteristic which can be thought of as a status involving roles and norms. This aspect of group research has been treated in the preceding chapter.

INTERGROUP PHENOMENA

Sociological approach to groups. The sociological study of groups differs from the social-psychological studies we have already mentioned in three major ways: (a) it has concentrated on "real" groups in their natural setting, behaving in the ways they naturally behave; (b) it has been concerned with the fact that there are many groups in most settings that may have important relationships with one another; and (c) it has considered the fact that individuals may belong to more than one group as being of central importance.

The sociologist has identified social classes, organizations, voluntary associations, cliques and other collective associations which have been combined in some way to make up a larger social system. He wants to know what goes on in each of these groups, but he also wants to know how the many groups are able to exist side by side, whether they cooperate or compete with one another, or what other variable adjustments they make. Many of the groups studied are far too large for the purposes of this chapter, or are collections of individuals statistically construed as groups according to common attributes of individuals, which do not necessarily imply interaction between them. However, sociologists have encountered small groups which fit the criteria of this chapter in almost every conceivable social setting. This can be seen by examining three rather different traditions of sociological research that seem to converge at this point.

Rural sociology. Within the tradition of rural sociology there has existed for many years the concept of neighborhood. This originally referred to fairly autonomous units in rural areas and small communities which were geographically identifiable and within which there tended to be intimate face-to-face interactions as well as economic unity. This tradition can be traced directly to Toennies' concepts of *gemeinschaft* and *geselschaft*[40] (by which he differentiated the intimate ties of rural living from the more contractual and commercial bonds of the city) and Cooley's theory of primary groups.[41] Kolb used these concepts in doing empirical research as early as 1921[42] and they have been a part of rural sociology ever since.

Community studies. We will see in Chapter XIII, adult education and the community, that small, informal groups are also important units in larger communities than the ones with which rural sociologists are usually concerned. The Lynds found them in Middletown,[43] Warner and Lunt[44] encountered them in Yankee City, Davis and Gardner[45] in the Old City, the Nortons were a clique in Street Corner Society,[46] and Doddy[47] found them in a supposedly disorganized section of New York City, to mention but a few illustrations.

Organization studies. The studies in this area during the past twenty-five years have been marked by the fact that small informal groups with intimate face-to-face relations tend to emerge within the context of even the most formal organizations. This applies to large factories, government bureaucracy, stores, the military, and even patients in mental hospitals.[48]

---

[40]C. P. Loomis, *Fundamental Concepts of Sociology*, New York: American Book Company, 1940.

[41]C. H. Cooley, *op. cit.*

[42]J. H. Kolb, *Rural Primary Groups*, University of Wisconsin Agricultural Experiment Station, Madison, Wisconsin, 1921.

[43]R. S. Lynd and Helen M. Lynd, *Middletown*, New York: Harcourt Brace, 1929.

[44]W. L. Warner and P. S. Lunt, *The Social Life of a Modern Community*, Vol I, Yankee City Series, New Haven, Conn.: Yale University Press, 1941.

[45]A. Davis and B. B. Gardner, *Deep South*, Chicago, Ill.: University of Chicago Press, 1941.

[46]W. F. Whyte, *Street Corner Society*, Chicago, Ill.: University of Chicago Press, 1943. Also, "Corner Boys: A Study of Clique Behavior," *American Journal of Sociology*, XLVI.

[47]H. H. Doddy, *op. cit.;* also, *Autonomous Groups Bulletin*, Vol. VI, no. 4, 1951.

[48]F. J. Roethlisberger and W. J. Dickson, *Management and the Worker*, Cambridge, Mass.: Harvard University Press, 1939 (factory); P. Selznick, *TVA and the Grass Roots*, University of California Press, 1949 (government bureaucracy); W. F. Whyte, *Human Relations in the Restaurant Industry*, New York: McGraw-Hill Book Co., 1948; E. S. Shils, "Primary Groups in the American Army," in Merton and Lazarsfeld (eds.), *Studies in the Scope and Method of "The American Soldier"*, Glencoe, Ill.: The Free Press, 1950; and A. H. Stanton and M. S. Schwartz, *The Mental Hospital*, New York: Basic Books, 1954.

It appears that in addition to the fact that people tend to form small groups in every setting, those formed in rural America are no longer as different from the ones found in the city as they once were. Rural sociologists have recently had difficulty in finding traditional neighborhoods in some situations,[49] and there is evidence that cliques are often formed outside of the traditional geographical limitations of neighborhoods.[50] Brunner, after examining all the rural sociological research on this point states that "locality is not the only basis for neighboring";[51] and Loomis and Beegle note this trend also in their recent study and utilize the concept of clique rather than neighborhood.[52]

An examination of the growing amount of sociological research on factors influencing the dissemination of information through the rural adult education programs of the Extension Service justifies the conclusion that this has been most effective when the agents have fitted their approach either to special interest groups or to total neighborhoods as the situation demanded. There may also be sex differences. While special interest groups are by no means rare among women, it appears that they are relatively more frequent among men whereas women organize and operate more frequently on a neighborhood or community basis in many rural areas.

Primary groups rediscovered as basic. As Katz and Lazarsfeld have documented so well,[53] the "rediscovery" of the primary group in empirical research has in most cases revealed a pattern wherein the research was "called to a halt" at some point so that primary groups could be taken into consideration. This was usually necessitated by the fact that without taking small groups into consideration, the model of atomistic individuals left too much unexplained. It was generally known that these groups existed, but the fact that they were *relevant* to so many areas of behavior was not realized. Katz and Lazarsfeld document this thesis with illustrations from industry,[54] the

[49]See F. D. Alexander, "The Problem of Locality-Group Classification," *Rural Sociology*, 17, no. 3, 1952.

[50]See H. F. Lionberger and E. Hassinger, "Neighborhoods as a Factor in the Diffusion of Farm Information in a Northwest Missouri Farming Community," *Rural Sociology*, 19, no. 3.

[51]Edmund deS. Brunner, *The Growth of a Science*, New York: Harper and Brothers, 1957, p. 31.

[52]C. P. Loomis and J. A. Beegle, *Rural Social Systems*, New York: Prentice-Hall, Inc., 1950. Also, *Autonomous Groups Bulletin*, Vol. VI, no. 2, 1950-51.

[53]E. Katz and P. F. Lazarsfeld, *Personal Influence*, Glencoe, Ill.: The Free Press, 1955.

[54]Roethlisberger and Dickson, *op. cit.*

military,[55] and a community study.[56] In the first example, the experimenters used varying working conditions to find their possible effects on production by a group of girls. Much to the surprise of the experimenters, production by the group increased whether the conditions were improved or made worse. However, in another group, production was depressed regardless of how working conditions were varied. The researchers were eventually led to conclude that the variables relevant to production rates were to be found in the social processes, and that the groups of workers had norms with regard to production which were more important than any of the conditions which management might vary.

In the second example it was found that combat motivation or willingness to fight was associated with informal group relations in the Army during World War II. Subjects consistently gave reasons associated with primary group expectations as more important to their willingness to enter battle than motives related to national or military sources.

In the third example, the authors note that "the discovery of the clique and the determination of its great significance as a social and structural mechanism came rather late in our field investigation. . . . We eventually became convinced that the cliques were next in importance to the family in placing people socially."[57] In this way it became clear that "mobility" was not simply a matter of moving from one class or stratum to another; but could be characterized as moving from one informal group to another; the informal groups being located in different strata. Katz and Lazarsfeld also point out that it was the subjects themselves who brought the researchers' attention to the importance of small groups.

As Merton had noted,[58] the "rediscovery" of primary groups has been mainly with regard to their latent functions. It has been known for some time that people seem to like to have lasting intimate relations with one another, but the groups they form do more than provide such relations.

Katz and Lazarsfeld show that individuals in such small groups (a) receive benefits from conforming to them, and (b) are provided "social reality" by virtue of membership.[59]

---

[55]Shils, *op. cit.*
[56]Warner and Lunt, *op. cit.*
[57]*Ibid.*, p. 10.
[58]R. K. Merton, *op. cit.*, pp. 60ff.
[59]Katz and Lazarsfeld, *op. cit.*, Chapter II.

Wayland and Lennard[60] point out that there have been four essentially different approaches with regard to the function of small groups in the larger social system:

a. Its role as a basic unit in the status system of a larger social system.
b. Its role as a basic mediating unit within which the societal forces and influences are interpreted and reacted to in terms of the values of the group members.
c. Patterns of responses (structural and operational) of different kinds of small groups to social change in the larger social system.
d. Impact of small groups of various kinds on the structure and dynamics of a larger social system.[61]

Homans has attempted to deal with intra-group and inter-group phenomena simultaneously in *The Human Group*,[62] but this represents the only extensive and systematic attempt in the literature at the present time. Nevertheless, many small group studies are now conceptualized in such a way that both sorts of variables are taken into consideration. These studies suggest the following generalizations:

1. Conformity to one group may preclude conformity to another when norms are different.[63]

2. Extra-group statuses of members may affect intra-group statuses, behavior and decisions.[64]

3. Individuals are often aware of the fact that norms differ from group to group and status to status and behave accordingly.[65]

Despite the tentativeness of many of the research findings on group research, especially as related to adult education, one statement may be made which grows out of a comparison of nonresearch adult education literature with such findings as exist. Adult educators place considerable emphasis upon the role of interests in the participation of persons in their programs. It is a cardinal principle in adult education philos-

[60]S. Wayland and H. Lennard, "Current Conceptual Trends in Small Group Study: Sociology," *Autonomous Groups Bulletin*, VIII, no. 2.

[61]*Ibid.*, p. 4.

[62]Homans, *op. cit.*

[63]See R. K. Merton, *loc. cit.*, "Social Structure and Anomie"; and A. C. Cohen, *Delinquent Boys*, Glencoe, Ill.: The Free Press, 1955.

[64]See M. Sherif, J. B. White and O. J. Harvey, "Status in Experimentally Produced Groups," *American Journal of Sociology*, LX, no. 4; F. L. Strodtbeck, R. M. James and C. Hawkins, "Social Status in Jury Deliberations," *American Sociological Review*, Vol. 22, no. 6.

[65]This would be true for group members by definition if one defined norms as "mutually held expectation." However, norms vary within groups also, and the degree to which they are "mutually held" can best be treated as problematic. See S. A. Stouffer, "An Analysis of Conflicting Social Norms," *American Sociological Review*, XIV, No. 6.

ophy that participants should be offered what they want. When a program fails to hold its enrollees or achieves but indifferent success, the tendency is to assume that the methods and techniques used have been at fault or that the leader-teacher has been ineffective. Just as the research reviewed in the chapter on Motivation indicates that many adult education participants have noneducational motives and may drop out if these are not satisfied, this chapter suggests that some difficulties may result from the group situation. If this is so, it indicates that the current explanations of lack of success may be too limited in their scope, and that evaluation is a more complicated process than the small amount of research on this topic, reviewed in the last chapter of this report, has taken into account.

Suggestions for further research. A number of extremely interesting problems are generated by combining the sorts of things that are known about the internal dynamics of small groups with the fact of a multiple group society in which individuals tend to belong to a multiplicity of groups.

Given the fact that groups have norms, and that there are pressures on individuals to conform to these norms, what happens to the individual who belongs to groups which have conflicting norms? With regard to attitude items this situation is similar to what is usually called "cross-pressures." However, behavior is also a normative item. In the case of the adolescent, for example, it is quite common that uncomfortable situations arise wherein the same behavior which would give him high status or make him acceptable to his peer group would be frowned upon or result in punishment by his family. Situations which are analytically similar but different in content would seem to have direct relevance to adult education.

The chapter on Participation indicated that adult education programs do a rather consistent job of getting participation from only certain segments of the population, which might be loosely designated as middle-class. Agencies have cooperated to a large extent with formal organizations and voluntary associations throughout the community, but these tend to have members who are also primarily middle-class. This has been a source of embarrassment and something of an enigma with regard to the democratic orientation of the adult education movement, and it has been variously explained or rationalized. However, considering the fact that there are small groups which persist over time within all the social strata, many of which are not reached by adult education to any appreciable extent, many interesting questions for research emerge.

Why indeed should members of these groups participate in programs where other participants differ from them in many ways? Participation on the part of a given individual might mean that he would be a deviant in the eyes of the other members of his group and a violator of important norms. It would mean being unavailable to participate in important activities with his group and being exposed to norms and values which run counter to those which he has already learned. It is also likely that he will be identified according to his membership in other groups and that he will not know how to play appropriate roles in the unfamiliar one. What rewards are there for participation which would offset the possible risks involved for individuals who are well integrated in traditioned groups whose other members do not participate? It seems highly probable that group processes are operating to prevent participation on the part of many individuals, and this is a question with which adult education should be directly concerned.

It has been shown earlier in comparing individuals and groups that *ad hoc* groups often do not present the sort of atmosphere which is conducive to free expression of ideas and a high level of intellectual attainment. This, combined with the fact that group pressures might prevent individuals from participating, would seem to provide good reason for adult educators to study and work with traditioned groups whenever possible rather than to attempt to get individuals to form *ad hoc* groups within the movement. This suggestion has been made by such authors as Doddy, Alinsky and Hallenbeck[66] who feel that adult educators should make the forces that operate on the members of such groups work for adult education. This would undoubtedly mean that where group norms and values run counter to those of adult education, a great deal of initial group resistance could be expected. Overcoming this resistance, becoming accepted by such groups, and carrying out programs with them would be very similar in principle to the sorts of things that social workers do with informal groups. Many individuals are extremely skillful at this work, but unfortunately there has never really been any systematic research carried out in this area with regard to nonvocational adult education.

It would appear from the above that the research about small groups which would answer both the theoretical and practical questions of direct concern to adult educators has yet to be conducted. However, the more general research that has been carried on to date

---

[66]Doddy, *op. cit.*; Alinsky, *Reveille for Radicals*, Chicago: University of Chicago Press, 1946; W. C. Hallenbeck, "New Needs in Adult Education," *Teachers College Record*, May 1947, vol. 48, no. 8.

would seem to be useful to adult education in at least three ways.[67] First of all, by showing that man is a "small group" animal throughout the social structure, it has suggested that programs be directed at existing groups rather than at isolated individuals. Secondly, it provides a conceptual framework within which researchable questions about groups in relation to adult education can be raised. And thirdly, it has been developing the techniques and general methodology with which further research can be carried out. In addition to the suggestions for further study already made, some of the research questions about small groups in adult education growing out of the above discussion follow.

Under what circumstances do the forces which make for group cohesion inhibit active participation in adult education programs? Does the impact of these forces vary with the type of group or the educational status of the members? How may these forces or types of groups and individuals be identified? Are there situations in which groups as groups are resistant to adult education programs? How do these differ from effective, adult education groups in their composition, characteristics and relations to the larger social structure? Under what circumstances do *ad hoc* adult education groups persist over time and become traditioned groups? Does this process dilute the adult education interests of the group or its individual members?

[67]Probably the Agricultural Extension Service of the United States Department of Agriculture has more experience working with as well as doing research about informal groups throughout the United States than any other single organization. Unfortunately from the standpoint of nonvocational adult education, the central focus of this research has been the diffusion of new farming techniques. Hoffer's study, in particular, suggests that there are clear advantages in trying to coordinate programs with groups that already exist in the community rather than trying to form new groups. C. Hoffer, *Social Organization in Relation to Extension Services in Eaton County, Michigan,* East Lansing, Michigan State University, 1941.

Similarly, a study by Duncan and Kreitlow suggests that groups which are homogenous with regard to religious and ethnic composition will offer more resistance to new ideas than groups which are heterogeneous in these respects. Such studies might well serve as models for future research in nonvocational adult education. J. Duncan and B. Kreitlow, "Selected Cultural Characteristics and the Acceptance of Educational Practices and Programs," *Rural Sociology,* December 1954.

THE COMMUNITY
AND ITS INSTITUTIONS
IN ADULT EDUCATION*

The groups which the previous chapter discussed exist for the most part within communities. Within communities also there are many agencies and institutions formally organized for the achievement of social purposes or to give expression to the varied interests of like-minded people. Some of these are of such importance that society has accorded them legal status and sanction. The school is an illustration of such an institution. Others are purely voluntary in character, such as the churches. Some are purely local in scope. Others have affiliations of greater or lesser strength with state or national bodies. Adult education is one of the interests which has found organized expression. Moreover, many of the existing agencies and institutions, though organized for other purposes, engage in educational activities, as was pointed out in Chapter I.

Until recently each agency entering the field, often in response to public pressure, operated its own particular program with only casual reference to the activities of other institutions. Evidence mounted of lack of effective communication among agencies operating within the

*The first draft of this chapter was written by John S. Newberry, Jr.

same areas, resulting in duplication, competition, and waste. Recognition of the need for coordination among the many agencies developed slowly both in the adult education field and in general, but efforts toward meeting this need have been made with increasing frequency, especially since the end of World War I.

Two basic approaches. Among the efforts to provide coordination and direction to adult education at the level of the local community, discounting the unilateral "public relations" approach which conceives of organization in terms of a single institution, two basic approaches may be identified: community organization and community development. The two are by no means mutually exclusive; the difference is primarily a matter of emphasis.

The emphasis in community organization is upon the coordination of the resources of the community *for* adult education, *for* social welfare, *for* recreation, etc. The approach is administrative. Any educational value in the process is secondary. A rationale for the community organization is provided by Howard McClusky:

> A comprehensive program of adult education should serve the interests of the entire community . . . potentially it must be accepted by all groups and must be as universal as possible in its appeal. Adult education, therefore, is too large for any one agency. It requires the combined planning of all organizations and the coordinating service of some group . . . continually investigating, planning and acting in the interests of the community as a whole.[1]

Community development, on the other hand,

> refers to programs, whatever their names or sponsorship, which stress the citizens' participation in the improvement of their physical and social environment.[2]

The community development approach stresses process rather than content. "Changed attitudes of people are more important than the material achievement of community projects."[3] The scope of community development is more inclusive than adult education but as a process of improving the common life of the community it is necessarily educational.

[1]H. Y. McClusky, "Mobilizing the Community for Adult Education" as quoted by P. H. Sheats, C. D. Jayne and R. B. Spence (eds.) *Adult Education: The Community Approach*, New York: Dryden Press, 1953, p. 295.
[2]"The Role of Adult Education in Community Development, A Symposium," *Adult Education*, VI, Autumn 1955, p. 3.
[3]A. B. Dunham, *Adult Education*, VI, Autumn, 1955, p. 19.

Whether approached from the standpoint of community organization or that of community development, the problem of providing comprehensive programs of adult education and community self-improvement must necessarily involve the existing social organization of the community, a vital part of which is the complex network of formal organizations. Knowledge of how these operate, what functions they perform for their members and for the community, is essential if there is to be an effective, integrated adult education program for any community. Indeed, the more complete the knowledge of the community is, the more effective any agency, be it educational, religious or social, will be. It is now axiomatic that what a community is influences markedly the organizational structure and conditions to some degree the program and conduct of its institutions and agencies. To take a single illustration from two contrasting communities in one state, making parent education central in adult programs in a city where the median age of the population is close to 50 years would invite failure, whereas in another where the median age is less than 21 years it might be the most effective approach to a broad adult education program.

Organizations do not exist in isolation; there are in every community certain activities which depend upon cooperative effort involving two or more organizational structures. Adult educators must utilize existing channels of interorganizational and even informal communication. Ignorance of the kinds of cooperation and communication which may exist may lead to waste, excessive and useless formal structuring and bureaucracy, and even lead to antagonism and competitive programs.

Community research and adult education. The evaluation of research relating to community organization for adult education presents certain special difficulties. There are comparatively few studies which deal directly with community organization for adult education, and still fewer treating directly the process of community development. Most "studies" are accounts of particular programs or sequences of events of a very low order of methodological sophistication. Some few attempts at comparison of a number of such reports have drawn "conclusions" which are really no more than tentative hypotheses.

There are, however, a large number of studies drawn from a number of research approaches and disciplines which relate to community adult education and to the processes of community organization and community development. Many of these may appear to have only slight or tangential application to adult education. Certain of their findings, however, when related to those of studies from other approaches, become significant. Pertinent findings are related through application to a consistent theoretical structure.[4] Therefore, because of the nature of the material upon which this chapter is based, more space will be given to some of the content of the studies reviewed than has been the practice in other chapters of this report. Before considering any of this research, however, it is important to indicate how the term community is defined in this report.

Defining the community. The term community in popular as well as sociological usage embodies several meanings which, while they overlap to some extent, are distinguishable. Without entering into a discussion of the various sociological approaches to the definition of a community, it is clear that as the concept of community is applied to adult education, the following elements are implied:

1. A contiguous geographic area and the people and resources contained therein.

2. A social and economic unit possessed of basic service institutions to provide for the common and recognized needs of its residents.

3. A social unit exhibiting certain definite cultural characteristics and patterns of behavior which tend to persist despite changes in the persons making up the community.

4. A group of people sharing a number of common interests and participating in a "common life."

5. A "consciousness of kind" among the sharers of this common life. An awareness of the community and a degree of identification with it on the part of the members.

Community, then, implies more than a geographic area or an aggregate of people. Limits of community are not established by artificial political or jurisdictional boundaries. Community is rather a natural social unit delimited by the behavior patterns of people.

In a complex, technologically advanced society, such as our own, community is a relative term. A community is an aggregate of people tied together by relatively frequent contact and interaction. Communities are more interdependent than independent. The modern metropolitan area is a constellation of specialized communities, a "community of communities."

Most service agencies, including those with a major orientation

---

[4]The number of such studies is legion. Sociologists, anthropologists and social psychologists have made the study of communities a major element in their research. Rural sociologists alone are responsible for several hundred such studies. It is obviously impossible to consider more than a few in this discussion. The criterion for selection has been the degree of pertinence of the findings for adult education. The summary at the end of the chapter, however, is based on a far larger number of studies than have been cited in the text.

toward adult education, are organized to serve a definite area or population or a definite segment within the population of an area. This is their *functional community*.[5] Differences in area of jurisdiction and the lack of a common functional community among highly specialized agencies working in the same general area, pose a formidable obstacle to community reorganization. A major assumption of this report is that the natural community, bounded by patterns of behavior, not by legalistic limits of authority, is the logical unit for the reintegration of "common life" and for the development of opportunities for continuing adult education for its residents.

NATIONAL STUDIES OF ADULT EDUCATION

Among the more useful studies in terms of the whole country three may be noted because they are national in scope. The National Education Association and the American Library Association have each studied, on the basis of mailed questionnaires, the adult education programs of schools and libraries respectively, and the Adult Education Association has similarly studied the problems of financing adult education through a small number of Councils. Each of these is descriptive, deals with urban situations, and is limited because each represents the viewpoint of a single agency and offers no information as to the interaction of the agencies studied with others in their communities.[6]

A more comprehensive investigation has attempted to show the interaction of a large number of institutions and agencies in rural nonvocational adult education. It used a representative sample of 263 counties and a variety of techniques.[7] Unique in this study is its delineation of cooperative interaction among the various institutions and organizations through a form of sociometric measurement based upon groups named by informants in the various programs studied.

[5]M. G. Ross, *Community Organization, Theory and Principles,* New York: Harper and Bros., 1955.

[6]National Education Association, Division of Adult Education Service, *A Study of Urban Public School Adult Education Programs of the United States,* Washington, D.C.: the Association, 1954; E. B. Olds, *Financing Adult Education in America's Public Schools and Community,* Commission on Adult Education Finance, Washington, D.C.: Adult Education Association of the USA, 1954.

A serious limitation of the N.E.A. study is the likelihood of considerable variation in interpretation of the questions by respondents. The meaning of "community council on adult education," for example, appears to include everything from an advisory committee to the public school program to a genuine community-wide council with broad representation.

[7]C. P. Loomis *et al., Rural Social Systems and Adult Education,* East Lansing: Michigan State College Press, 1953.

The basic patterns of interaction are thus presented graphically. Further mention will be made of these studies later in this chapter.

COMMUNITY STUDIES

In the area of community studies Burton Clark's *Adult Education in Transition*[8] is mentioned first because it concerns the entire public school adult education program in the Los Angeles community. It was cited a number of times in earlier chapters. In terms of the interests of this chapter, its value is in the detailed analysis of the cooperation, and lack of it, of the adult schools with other organizations and groups in the city. This cooperation was in part sought and in part impeded by the marginal status of adult education and adult educators in the public school system. The study is useful in documenting difficulties arising from the present stage of adult education in which many institutions and agencies have educational programs deemed necessary for furthering their major objectives but which, in the nature of the case, are merely contributory to this objective. The marginality of adult education is clearly not confined to the public school. The study pinpoints problems which, as such, seem to have had but little attention from adult educators.

On a broader community-wide level is one study describing the pattern of life in a "dormitory" suburb with its welter of organizations, its divided loyalties and preoccupation with the "consumption of leisure." This is of interest because in some suburban communities, judging by news reports, adult education is relatively successful and thus contributes to the process of adjustment.[9] One development in the dynamic movement into the commuting areas of large cities may have real significance for adult education. Recent unpublished surveys of several Connecticut communities by groups of citizens indicate that the services both attracted and demanded by the influx of population have resulted in commuters' families becoming a declining proportion of the population. The indigenous group may have different

---

[8]B. R. Clark, *Adult Education in Transition: A Study of Institutional Insecurity*, Berkeley and Los Angeles: University of California Press, 1956.

[9]J. R. Seeley, R. A. Sim, and E. W. Loosley, *Crestwood Heights: A Study of the Culture of Suburban Life*, New York: Basic Books, Inc., 1955. Other studies of suburbanization and suburban life include N. L. Whetten and others, *Studies in Suburbanization*, five bulletins, Storrs: University of Connecticut Agricultural Experiment Station, 1936 ff.; E. L. Koos and E. deS. Brunner, *Suburbanization in Webster, New York*, Rochester: University of Rochester, Department of Sociology, 1945. One early study of the use of leisure in "suburbia" has special relevance for adult education: G. A. Lundberg, M. Komarovsky, and M. A. McInery, *Leisure, A Suburban Study*, New York: Columbia University Press, 1934.

educational needs and interests from commuters, just as it certainly has different hours.

Another finding of significance to adult education emerges from a number of community studies. This relates to the demonstration that there exist status or prestige groups informal in structure but recognized by the citizens.[10] The boundaries between these groups are not inflexible and too rigorous an interpretation is sometimes read into the concept social stratification used to describe the phenomenon.[11] Nonetheless, in small communities especially, the upper population limits of which have not been determined by research, but which certainly extend to places of 20,000, the phenomenon must be reckoned with by adult education planners and other social servants.

The lines of division in some communities often follow ethnic or ecological lines as A. A. Kaplan's study in Springfield, Massachusetts, described in Chapter VI, showed. This study of diverse participation trends in the ecological areas of the city became the basis for a reorganized public school adult education program and thus shows the practical value of such research.

The present status of research relating to community organization and the process of community action may be summarized in the following generalizations.

1. A large number of studies have been made of existing community social organization in communities of all sizes and of widely differing characteristics. The vast majority of these studies are either descriptive or analytical only to limited aspects of community organization.

2. The study of existing community organization, particularly with respect to patterns of interaction, has, however, progressed rapidly in recent years with considerable refinement of research techniques and more rigorous conceptualization.

3. Even at the purely descriptive level the studies reviewed relating to the organization of adult education provide a totally inadequate view of the patterns of organization for adult education which have developed in American communities, possibly because of the marginal position of adult education alluded to above. Except in such rural studies as deal with the Extension Service, adult education may have seemed unimportant to the researchers.

[10] W. L. Warner and others, *The Social Life of a Modern Community, I, The Yankee City Series*, New Haven: Yale University Press, 1941, and *Democracy in Jonesville*, New York: Harper and Bros., 1949. Cf. also, H. Kaufman, *Prestige Classes in a New York Rural Community*, Ithaca: Cornell University Agricultural Experiment Station, 1944; and J. West, *Plainville, U.S.A.*, New York: Columbia University Press, 1945.

[11] R. M. Williams, Jr., *American Society*, New York: Alfred A. Knopf, 1951; O. D. Duncan and J. Artis, "Some Problems of Stratification Research," *Rural Sociology*, March 1951.

4. The study of the process of community action has been confined almost wholly to descriptive accounts and "action research." Some recent studies indicate a trend toward refinement and standardization of case study methods and more careful conceptualization.

5. The full development of adult education in any community, whether approached from the standpoint of community organization or community action, depends upon the effective utilization of the existing social structure of the community. The discovery of this structure is a task for research.

TYPES OF ORGANIZATION

In projecting such research there are three significant forms of organization, recognized both by social theorists and students of community structure, which have contributions to make to adult education: (1) *community institutions*—schools, churches, social welfare agencies, businesses and the like—which perform certain well-defined functions recognized as necessary and desirable by the community; (2) *formal associations*—the multiplicity of clubs, lodges, church societies, fraternities, professional associations and labor unions (also referred to as voluntary associations) —which are so ubiquitous a feature of American social organization, and (3) the complex, unstable and infinitely varying pattern of *informal groups* and patterns of social interaction which underlie the formal organizational structure of the community.[12]

Community institutions, because of their fixed areas of responsibility, bureaucratic organization, and established patterns of operation, are slow to adjust to changing conditions. They often take on new areas of responsibility only when these are forced upon them by public demand.[13] Informal groups, on the other hand, are difficult to

[12]Attention may be called to the growing concern for developing a more adequate conceptual framework for research in the processes of community action. Cf. Kaufman, "Toward Delineation of Community Research with Special Implications for Community Dynamics and with Reference to the South," *Community Series*, no. 4, State College: Mississippi State College, 1954 (multigraph); G. W. Blackwell, "A Theoretical Framework for Sociological Research in Community Organization," *Social Forces*, XXXIII, March 1958.

Sanders, using the term community development, points out that this may be viewed as a process with emphasis on what happens to people socially and psychologically; as a method, with emphasis upon some end; as a program with emphasis on activities; and as a movement stressing an idea promoted and interpreted by its devotees. In each case, Sanders allows for the differing role of education. I. T. Sanders, "Theories of Community Development," *Rural Sociology*, XXIII, March 1958, p. 24.

[13]A specific example of the role of public demand in the expansion of institutional adult education is provided by a significant conclusion of the N.E.A. study of Public Junior Colleges. "Adult education as a major activity of the junior college has grown up in a haphazard manner, largely in response to direct pressures from the public." N.E.A., *op. cit.*, p. 158.

identify and, because of their lack of well-defined structure and purpose, extremely difficult to involve in organized community activities.[14]

Formal associations have been found by students of community organization to have sufficient structure and definition of function to be able to meet new needs as they become recognized if they are sufficiently flexible and their purposes are broad enough to permit active commitment to community action in many areas.[15] Leaders who can marshall the resources of groups which involve a significant segment of the population of the community are easily identified. Recent studies have shown, furthermore, that the formal associational structure of the community overlaps and interacts with the institutional structure and the social sub-structure of informal groups so that the associations can be used to involve institutions and informal groups in the processes of adult education and community action.[16] Formal associations are of vital concern to the adult educator also because usually they are themselves actively engaged in adult education.

Purposes and activities of formal associations. Generally it has been found that associations in rural areas, particularly those relatively unaffected by factors associated with urbanization, tend to have more undifferentiated purposes, but as urbanization increases, purposes becomes more specific and activities tend to be more diversified and specific. This was the case in four Kentucky counties selected to represent four positions on a rural-urban continuum. In the more rural counties there was a proportionately greater emphasis upon educational objectives although educational objectives were important in all areas.

The rural-urban differences in *activities* appeared to be less marked than for objectives, particularly with respect to recreation, indicating that "the inclusion of a new need in the list met by special-interest

[14]Both these difficulties are illustrated by a study of informal groups in an economically and socially "deteriorated" urban neighborhood. H. Doddy, *Informal Groups and the Community*, New York: Teachers College Bureau of Publications, Columbia University, 1952.

[15]W. W. Bauder, *Objectives and Activities of Special Interest Organizations in Kentucky*, Bulletin 639, Lexington: University of Kentucky Agricultural Experiment Station, 1956; J. S. Newberry, Jr., *A Descriptive Study of Certain Aspects of the Ecology of Formal Organizations in a Southern Town*, Tallahassee; Florida State University, unpublished Ph.D. dissertation, 1958; R. O. Buckman, *Interaction Between Women's Clubs and Institutions in Greater Lafayette, Indiana*, Unpublished Ph.D. dissertation, University of Chicago, 1952. Also an earlier study of rural associations bears on this question: J. H. Kolb and A. F. Wiledon, *Special Interest Groups in Rural Society*, Research Bulletin 84, Madison: University of Wisconsin Agricultural Experiment Station, 1927.

[16]Buckman, *op. cit.;* Newberry, *op. cit.* Cf also E. deS. Brunner, *Growth of a Science*, New York: Harper and Bros., 1957, pp. 105-106 and footnote 12, Chapter 2.

associations takes place first, more or less informally, by inclusion in the list of activities and only later is formalized by inclusion in the list of professed objectives.[17]

Kolb and Wileden in their 1927 study of special interest groups in five Wisconsin counties—presumably toward the rural end of the rural-urban continuum—found that:

> Most of the organizations have more than one purpose. . . . The (interest) class that has the fewest purposes is 'better business' and the one that seems to have the most is 'health and welfare.'[18]

Even though social activities were an important purpose in all classes except "better business", when activities were compared with purpose:

> In every functional class the social functions went higher than the stated purpose had indicated and were most frequently reported by 'all organizations.' In four of the seven functional classes the social accomplishments outranked the characteristics which determined the class, such as 'home conditions improved' for 'home improvement.'[19]

Studies of purposes and activities of formal associations in urban areas indicate, however, that statements of purpose frequently do not reflect the increasing specificity which might be anticipated on the basis of Bauder's hypothesis.[20]

Buckman found that certain characteristic features of women's clubs appeared to be related to the social atmosphere in a group of "semi-strangers"; " (1) The club seldom flourished without a 'social hour', (2) It needs to plan its program in advance, and (3) It usually engages in 'good works'."[21] Devices such as "the serving of food, games, entertainment, talks, demonstrations and ritual" are necessary to overcome the awkwardness of a situation involving "semi-strangers."[22] As most groups assembled for adult education also involve semi-strangers, the need for overcoming awkwardness may justify the use of devices which are not inherently educational.

[17]Bauder, *op. cit.*

[18]Kolb and Wileden, *op. cit.*

[19]*Ibid.*, p. 41.

[20]"Despite a certain measure of individuality as between one statement of purpose and another, all of them possess enough sameness of sentiment to make variations insignificant. [They are for the most part] merely an expression of the values emphasized by American culture." Buckman, *op. cit.* This conclusion is supported by a study of formal associations in Thomasville, Georgia, Newberry, *op. cit.*

[21]Buckman, *op. cit.*

[22]*Ibid.*

A rather neglected aspect of the activities of formal associations concerns to whom the activities are directed. The Thomasville study found that among the 105 associations studied only four directed their programs, activities and services exclusively toward members or their families. None directed *all* their activities outside the membership, and 18 were predominantly oriented toward others in the community. The remaining 76 associations combined in-group and out-group activities in various proportions. In-group activities tended to be proportionately more important in associations with less than 20 members and also among those with 100 or more members while associations with 20 to 100 members tended to stress proportionately more out-group activities.[23]

Societal functions of formal associations. The propensity of associations to perform certain functions for the society in which they operate which are incidental (or accidental) with respect to their recognized purposes has been frequently noticed and documented by observers of the American social scene for well over a century.

These societal functions have been variously defined, but in general may be said to include the categories listed below:

1. Adjustment to social change— (a) the *interstitial* function: Formal associations provide a means of continuous adjustment to social change. The increase in the number of associations, their greater specificity of function, increasing participation, and the multiplication of activities and services which appear to accompany urbanization suggest that new needs resulting from change are frequently met by the expansion of the activities and structure of community associations. As Bauder suggested in the case of the four Kentucky counties:

> Although the general institutional pattern for education is the same in these counties as for the society as a whole, the social organization for its accomplishment is not the same and is likely to prove inadequate under conditions of rapid change. Some cultural lag is likely to occur. These data indicate that special interest organizations play an important role in correcting this lag and thus function as mechanisms of adjustment in the institutional structure of society.[24]

In Lafayette, Indiana, Buckman found that "clubs are frequently able to mobilize the latent community resources of money and talent to relieve emergency situations in which the institution is hampered or completely paralyzed."[25] The capacity of associations to meet needs

[23]Newberry, *op. cit.*
[24]Bauder, *op. cit.*
[25]Buckman, *op. cit.*

which institutions are unable or unwilling to meet provides a flexibility which can be "harnessed" to assist in the process of community development.

(b) The *adhesive* function: A major function of associations which has received less general recognition than has their role in social change, is that which Buckman has called "the adhesive function"—the role of associations in harmonizing and adjusting the relations of community institutions with the community at large. She showed that institutions used their systems of satellite clubs to supplement, augment, and support their programs.[26]

Buckman also noted that satellites operate as "pseudo-primary groups" to "humanize" the institutions to the "strangers within the gates."[27] Similarly, Warner and Lunt state:

> All churches and many economic organizations in Yankee City surround themselves with associations which act as implements in organizing and dissolving their antagonisms toward the larger community. Such associations play a subordinate role in the structure to which they are affiliated.[28]

The satellites, however, are not completely the creature of the sponsoring institutions. They are, as Buckman points out, quite capable of independent action. They can exert a measure of influence upon institutional operations and policy and thereby act as agents for change.

The utilization of formal associations of various kinds by institutions engaged in adult education appears to be quite general. The Cooperative Extension Services rely heavily upon clubs and formal associations in planning and carrying out programs of vocational and nonvocational adult education. Many of these, such as the Home Demonstration Clubs, are directly sponsored organizations. In some areas, particularly in the South, County Councils are organized with the cooperation of "bankers' associations, chambers of commerce, and other merchants' associations."[29] In Mississippi, 33 per cent of the 164 community improvement organizations identified in 1952 were reported to have been organized by county extension agents.[30]

---

[26]*Ibid.*
[27]*Ibid.*
[28]Warner and Lunt, *op. cit.,* p. 302.
[29]E. deS. Brunner and E. H. Yang, *Rural America and the Extension Service,* New York: Teachers College Bureau of Publications, Columbia University, 1949.
[30]R. Payne and A. A. Fanelli, *Community Organization in Mississippi,* State College: Mississippi State College Agricultural Experiment Station, 1953.

2. Communication function—The significant role of associations as channels of communication in an urban area has been described by Hunter in "Regional City" where associations function in the chain of authority between top community leadership and the community at large.[31]

It is evident from Hunter's study and from Gettel's analysis of power in a city of 60,000 that only certain associations play a major part in this chain of communication. Cultural, religious and veterans organizations appear to be involved only slightly while civic clubs and business and professional groups are in the chain of communication.[32]

There are other chains of communication, however, which do involve all groups and which have great potential significance for adult education. As Clark points out, when an institution co-sponsors an activity within an association it uses the association as a link to its membership.[33] The increased use of such associational networks would seem to be an effective means of establishing two-way communications with significant segments of the community.

It should be noted, however, that such "networks" are only as effective in reaching people as the associations involved are in eliciting and sustaining participation. The evidence concerning participation, presented in Chapter VI, indicates that associational networks are more likely to be effective in reaching large segments of the population in urban than in rural areas and in smaller rather than larger urban communities. Finally, it seems evident that in any community there is likely to be a segment of the population not reached by any formal association or institution.

3. Adult education as a function of formal associations—Few if any formal associations recognize adult education *per se* as a primary function. Many local associations stress *education* as an absolute good, but, for the most part, they define education as schooling for children (the P.T.A.), or as college or university education (the American Association of University Women, alumni associations) and direct their activities toward the improvement of education at these levels. For these organizations adult education is a means to that end.

The degree to which any association recognizes adult education as a legitimate sphere of activity depends upon realization of its necessity for implementing organizational objectives. Because they do not con-

---

[31]F. G. Hunter, *Community Power Structure*, Chapel Hill: University of North Carolina Press, 1953.

[32]G. F. Gettel, *A Study of Power in a North Central States Community*, unpublished Ph.D. dissertation, Michigan State University, 1956; Hunter, *op. cit.*

[33]Clark, *op. cit.*

sider their function as educational many associations fail to recognize the educational nature of their activities.[34]

The increasing recognition of adult education as an important instrument by associational personnel is shown by the membership in 1957 of 74 national associations having local branches in the Council of National Organizations of the Adult Education Association.[35] A 1956 study of the members of the Adult Education Association of the United States of America found that 29.3 per cent of members responding were workers in formal associations, but 63.6 per cent of volunteer workers responding were from formal associations (civic organizations; clubs; fraternal organizations; Parent Teachers Associations; professional associations; religious organizations; rural organizations; veterans organizations; youth serving organizations.) [36]

Community associations vary considerably in the degree to which their educational activities are oriented toward members or directed toward the community at large. Longmore and Nall attempted to rank certain national civic, professional and service organizations along a continuum from "in-group recreative" to "out-group educative."[37] The scope of the adult education activities of formal associations also varied greatly. Some confine themselves to a very narrow interest range, while others cover virtually every aspect of community life.[38]

[34]C. Corbin, *A Comparative Study of Adult Education Activities of Women's Business and Professional Groups in New York City,* Unpublished Ph.D. dissertation, New York University, 1956.

[35]*The 1957 Council,* Circular 264, Council of National Organizations, Adult Education Association, 1957.

[36]From unpublished data obtained in a 1956 mailed questionnaire study of the membership of AEA by its membership department. Summary of findings: "Who We Are," *Adult Leadership,* V, September 1956.

The League of Women Voters recognizes the need for continuing educational activities to achieve its objective of an informed and politically active electorate. Farmers' organizations, on the other hand, engage in adult education as a means of improving the social and economic condition of farmers and the enrichment of rural life. W. C. Rohrer, *Structure and Value Orientation of Farm Organizations and their Relation to Nonvocational Adult Education,* Ph.D. dissertation, Michigan State University, 1955. Civic associations are oriented to community action, not for its educative value, but in order to achieve specific and limited local improvements. Newberry, *op. cit.*

[37]The most "out-group educative" association was the NAACP; business and professional associations fell toward the center of the continuum, while civic "luncheon" clubs fell nearest the "in-group recreative" end of the continuum. Longmore and Nall, "Service, Professional and Other Civic Clubs," in Loomis, *op. cit.*

[38]In Thomasville, Georgia, programs of heritage preserving associations tended to cover a narrow range and were concerned with the single aspect of community improvement. Two civic clubs, on the other hand, conducted, sponsored or participated in a wide variety of activities and programs in many fields. There was also considerable variation in the scope of activities within functional type categories of associations. The greatest variation was among social-fraternal organizations and the narrowest range was among business and professional associations. Newberry, *op. cit.*

In general, the adult education activities of formal associations fall in one of the categories listed below:

1. *Directed toward the community.*

a. Cultural events, programs, and facilities: Concerts, theatricals, public lectures, forums, exhibits, libraries, museums, are among the many services and facilities provided for the community by formal associations. While the quality of these facilities and services is decidedly uneven, in many smaller communities these projects and programs of formal associations provide cultural and educational experiences available from no other source.[39]

b. Preservation of the cultural heritage and the promotion of its appreciation: Patriotic societies, historical societies, and other associations perform a valuable educational service by preserving and exhibiting the record and the relics of the local past and by sponsoring activities to promote the appreciation of local tradition.[40]

c. Programs directed toward particular groups outside the membership: Historically, at least, such activities have played a significant role in the development of adult education.[41]

d. Organizations such as the National Association for the Advancement of Colored People exist to support causes which may be unpopular. The League of Women Voters performs a similar function by supporting causes which "may not have widespread community approval and which service clubs (and community institutions) cannot espouse because of their controversial nature."[42]

e. Community action programs frequently involve civic clubs and service associations specifically oriented toward community improvement. General purpose organizations with a dominantly social function also frequently assume "improvement" projects.[43] Action programs with goals related to organizational interests and objectives are also quite characteristic of associations with more specialized purposes

[39] The historical contribution of formal associations to the development of adult education must be recognized. The lyceum movement was wholly a voluntary association for the purposes of adult education.

[40] Newberry, *op. cit.;* A. T. Oliva, *The D.A.R. as a Pressure Group in the United States: A Study with Special Reference to its Educational Activities,* unpublished Ph.D. dissertation, Teachers College, Columbia University, 1952.

[41] The Americanization programs of the Colonial Dames, Sons of the American Revolution, YMCA and other groups served as a stimulus to the development of public school adult education for the foreign-born which—according to one historian of the movement— thus provided the basis for establishing adult education as a legitimate function of the public schools. C. H. Grattan, *In Quest of Knowledge,* New York: Association Press, 1955.

[42] Longmore and Nall, *loc. cit.*

[43] Buckman, *op. cit.*

such as business and professional associations and, upon occasion, special member interest organizations.[44]

2. *Improving membership-community relations.*

a. Business and professional associations quite frequently carry on educational programs to familiarize the public with the services provided by their members. Health education activities of medical societies, and similar public service education activities· of business groups are a distinct form of adult education.[45]

b. Formal associations, particularly business and professional groups, provide valuable public services through educational activities for their members to establish ethical practices and to improve service to the public.[46] There are those, however, who feel that such activities lie more in the realm of public relations than of adult education.

3. *Directed toward the membership.*

a. Vocational and related programs of professional, business, and labor organizations serve to keep members abreast of recent developments in their fields and to provide for continuing vocational education.[47]

b. Formal associations provide members with training and practical experience in leadership and participation. The experience of practical application of democratic processes and procedures on a limited scale and applied to a special member interest represents an effective form of education for democracy. While there is abundant evidence that this experience is limited to a fraction of the membership,[48] and that certain types of associations are not organized or operated democratically,[49] the value of associations as areas for the development of community leadership has been extensively documented.

As the need for effective leadership and broad participation is common to all associations, this appears to be one area where institutionalized adult education can provide valuable service to community associations and at the same time make effective use of the community organizational network.

c. Formal associations conduct a wide variety of programs and activities intended to broaden the general cultural experience and knowl-

[44]Newberry, *op. cit.*

[45]Corbin, *op. cit.;* Newberry, *op. cit.*

[46]*Ibid.;* Corbin, *op. cit.*

[47]*Ibid.*

[48]See Chapter VI, Participation.

[49]D. L. Sills, *The Volunteers, Means and Ends in a National Organization,* Glencoe, Ill.: The Free Press, 1957. Significantly, in the case of the local chapters of the National Infantile Paralysis Foundation, it is not so much the actual structure but the perception of structure held by the members which determines the democratic operation of the local.

edge of members. "Cultural" activities of associations have been frequently criticized as "passive", "diffuse", and "superficial."[50] Association headquarters have attempted to provide "focus" through an annual "theme" and to improve content and method by providing materials, consultative assistance, and some training through conventions and institutes. Nevertheless, cultural activities of associations for their members continue to be of extremely uneven quality.[51]

d. Formal associations, particularly those oriented toward a common avocational or recreational interest of members, provide information and training in specialized skills for the personal development of their members.[52]

Many shortcomings of the educational activities of formal associations appear to stem from failure to recognize that these activities are indeed educational.[53] Lack of clear-cut objectives[54] and failure to change objectives[55] are contributing factors to the stereotyping of educational programs and methods into patterns which persist from year to year. The need for adequate time, materials and training is not, therefore, generally recognized.[56]

Some generalizations for adult education. The extreme variation in the activities of associations and the lack of specific research addressed to this problem makes it difficult to predict the scope, direction, or effectiveness of adult education activities of a particular association in a given community and emphasizes the absolute necessity for close study of local associational programs. From the few studies available, however, certain generalizations appear to be justified.

1. The scope, direction, and objectives of adult education activities of associations tend to reflect the dominant value systems of their leadership, both national and local, and the interests and concerns of members.[57]

2. Methods, content, and organization of programs are limited by patterns of organization and resources, both physical and human, of headquarters and particularly of the local organization.[58]

---

[50]R. S. Lynd and H. L. Lynd, *Middletown*, New York: Harcourt Brace, 1929; Lundberg *et al., op. cit.;* F. E. Hill, *Man Made Culture,* New York: American Association for Adult Education, 1940.
[51]Corbin, *op. cit.;* Longmore and Nall, *op. cit.*
[52]Newberry, *op. cit.*
[53]Corbin, *op. cit.*
[54]Buckman, *op. cit.*
[55]Corbin, *op. cit.*
[56]*Ibid.*
[57]Rohrer, *op. cit.;* Longmore and Nall, *op. cit.*
[58]Rohrer, *op. cit.;* Longmore and Nall, *op. cit.*

3. The dead hand of tradition is often a far more significant limiting factor than those imposed by either physical or ideological restrictions.

The role of the leadership of formal associations in making and implementing community decisions appears to vary widely from community to community. Where there are relatively low rates of participation, associations may play a less vital part in decision making than where the reverse is true. It would appear from the studies reviewed that the role of associations in making and implementing community decisions differs with the size of the community and with the complexity of the organizational structure, though the lack of uniformity suggests that other factors are also involved.

COOPERATION AMONG COMMUNITY ASSOCIATIONS

Patterns of cooperation among formal associations have considerable meaning for community organization. This appears to be an area of research which has been largely overlooked. The studies reviewed provide comparatively little data relative to cooperation in formal organizations.

Of the 100 associations studied in Thomasville, Georgia, 26 reported cooperating within the previous year with other associations with which they had no formal connection. For 12 of these, cooperation was regular and routine. Fifteen associations reported participation in an annual festival program sponsored jointly by the Chamber of Commerce and a number of civic and special interest associations. Associations structurally linked to local institutions were less apt to cooperate with nonconnected associations. Civic clubs and service associations were most frequently reported to cooperate with two or more local nonconnected associations while only three of 30 church-connected groups reported cooperating with nonconnected associations. There was a marked tendency for patterns of mutual cooperation to follow interest lines. With few exceptions cooperation between nonconnected associations was confined to a single activity or type of activity.[59]

Bauder, in his study of special interest organizations in four Kentucky counties, found that fewer organizations reported cooperating with other local than with nonlocal organizations (48 per cent as compared with 56 per cent). Local cooperation was most frequently reported on "major projects" such as contests and building memorials.[60]

[59]Newberry, *op. cit.*
[60]Bauder, *op. cit.*

Cooperation between associations and institutions with major orientation toward adult education. Burton R. Clark's detailed study of the forces impinging upon the administration of the public adult schools in Los Angeles, California, found a conspicuous lack of coordination and cooperation between the public adult schools and the junior colleges, although both operate under the Division of Extension and Higher Education of the Los Angeles school system. "Conflicts were developing between adult schools and the colleges in regard to overlapping subject matter and clientele"—conflicts which remained unsolved by higher administrative decision and were forcing the adult schools to assume an "extreme service position" to compensate for the better competitive situation of the colleges.[61]

Curiously enough, lack of cooperation with the colleges forced the adult schools to emphasize co-sponsorship of classes by businesses, governmental agencies, and formal associations of all kinds. Co-sponsorship, Clark found, had the following advantages for the adult schools:

1. Access—"nearly all the sponsoring agencies have their own channels of communication to internal membership and their clientele." Thus, publicity and communication are greatly simplified.

2. Prestige—the prestige of the co-sponsor increases the drawing power of a class or course and "is reflected in a small segment of the school program, with the possibility that this prestige may be generalized . . . to the entire program."

3. Personnel and content—particularly in the more specialized or technical classes content or instructor, or both, may be supplied by the co-sponsoring agency.

4. Recruitment and enrollment—the co-sponsor frequently recruits students. This was particularly true of P.T.A. co-sponsored classes which constituted approximately 20 per cent of those reported.

5. Evaluation—co-sponsors participated in evaluating classes, students and teachers, but, except for the simpler vocational and driver-training classes, no systematic objective techniques were available and "informal assessment must be backed by student enrollment."[62]

Clark noted the following weaknesses in co-sponsorship: 1. Most of the co-sponsored classes were a marginal activity of the co-sponsoring associations. 2. Co-sponsorship is often temporary because job-training possibilities are soon exhausted. The program is not pinned down by a long-term commitment to particular groups, with the important exception of the P.T.A.

[61]Clark, *op. cit.*
[62]*Ibid.* pp. 113-116.

Over the long run, co-sponsorship means that an adult school can establish a service relationship to most of the organized groups in its district. This is done directly through co-sponsored classes. It is accomplished indirectly and symbolically by establishing the idea in the community that the adult program is a community program, potentially available for service to any organization.[63]

It should be noted that this type of cooperation was initiated by one institution for its own benefit and was successful because it also offered advantages to the institutions and agencies it approached. The procedure was unilateral; no adult education council played any role.

The "web of cooperation" in rural adult education was analyzed in the comprehensive study directed by C. P. Loomis.[64]

A different patterning of organizational interrelationships prevails among men's organizations than among women's organizations. All associations interact with the schools and with other civic and service type organizations, and most of them work with churches. However, it is exclusively the women's organizations and the P.T.A. (predominantly a women's organization) which work with libraries, welfare councils, women's clubs, UNESCO, community councils, and parent's organizations. The women's organizations also outnumbered the men's three-to-two in cooperation with colleges and universities. On the other hand, Kiwanis, Rotary, and the Chamber of Commerce indicate farm organizations as the type worked with by at least 25 per cent of the local units.[65]

Organizations vary in the frequency and intensity with which they work together in obtaining their objectives or meeting their respective needs. . . . 'Farm organizations' was mentioned most frequently as cooperating by nine organizations, 'schools' by five organizations and 'churches and religious organizations' by four. Those three organizations were mentioned second most frequently by a total of ten organizations. Thus, the importance of these three organizations in the adult educational network in rural areas is crucial. In addition, frequent mention was made of the Cooperative Extension Service, and civic and service clubs. . . . The 'Big Five' organizational categories mentioned above received eight out of every ten 'most frquent' mentions whereas the remaining categories received only two out of ten of the mentions of leaders requested to indicate names of three organizations with which you work most. Some of the less frequently mentioned organizations, such as labor unions, are not prevalent in rural areas; whereas the church, for example, is everywhere.[66]

[63]*Ibid*. pp. 110 ff.
[64]Loomis, *op. cit.*
[65]Longmore and Nall, *op. cit.*
[66]Loomis, *op. cit.*

This specific conclusion with respect to rural adult education is confirmed in general terms by a study of one of the authors of this report which reviewed the product of rural community research and especially a series of elaborate and well-designed studies made under the direction of Dr. Carl C. Taylor by the United States Department of Agriculture. One of the findings was:

> There are overlapping memberships among the organizations, and while there are some community councils for coordination, there is a surprising degree of interagency cooperation despite competition and overlapping. Thus while the organizational pattern is complex, substantial adjustment and accommodation among organizations has produced a functioning structure.[67]

Community councils. The community council approach to community organization has a long history and has achieved such wide acceptance in the United States, particularly in the area of social welfare, that a "council" is often regarded as the *sine qua non* of community organization. In 1955 there were no less than 1,858 communities supporting *Community Chest* or *United Fund* campaigns in the United States and Canada. In the same year some 434 *community* or *social welfare* councils were reported.[68]

The conspicuous success of the council of welfare agencies is attributable to two factors: (1) the councils are usually supported, at least in part, by "chest" funds, and (2) the agencies represented share a view of social welfare as a primary function of their agency.

The number of community councils which recognize adult education as an important area of concern or which take as their responsibility the improvement of broad areas of community life extending beyond the confines of "social welfare" is not shown by the studies reviewed. There are, however, indications that the "general council" approach to community organization, in some sections of the country at least, has received considerable acceptance.

The large number of cities (350) reporting that there were "community councils of adult education" to the N.E.A. survey (32.3 per cent of those returning questionnaires) unquestionably included many cities with "general" councils which recognized at least some responsibility for adult education. The figures also included, no doubt, a number of advisory bodies functioning primarily in relation to public

[67]Quoted from E. deS. Brunner, *The Growth of a Science, A Half-Century of Rural Sociological Research in the United States,* New York: Harper and Bros. 1957.

[68]Community Chest and Councils, Inc. *Directory of Community Chests and Councils of Social Agencies,* New York: Community Chests and Councils of America, Inc., 1955.

school adult programs bearing the name of "adult education council."[69]

The A.L.A. survey of public library adult education activities found
that 372 libraries, 21.0 per cent of those returning questionnaires, reported serving "community councils or interagency councils." This, of
course, does not mean that all the councils reported served, recognized
an adult education function.

In Michigan, where the "general community council approach" appears to have enjoyed a particularly long and productive development
it would seem that such bodies have tended to be short-lived.

> Over 120 community councils were organized in Michigan in a
> 10-year period from 1936 to 1946. The mortality rate was high, with
> an average life span of three years. Recent listings indicate that
> about 50 to 60 community councils are in operation in any given
> year. About 10 councils have existed continuously for 15 years. Sev-
> eral which died have been revived. The greater number of councils
> take root in towns under 5,000 population, places having no Council
> of Social Agencies or specialized interest councils.[70]

Thomasville, Georgia, has a "general" community council which includes rather impressive representation from many formal associations
of all types and from practically every major institution in the community. Participation in council affairs, however, was reported to involve professional representatives of institutions and agencies, some
few representatives of "prestige" associations, and a scattering of interested citizens. Few other representatives attended meetings.[71]

This would appear to be one of the most neglected areas of research
relating to community organizations.

Adult education councils. Following the organization of the first
adult education council in Cleveland in 1925 the Adult Education
Council movement was actively supported and promoted by the American Association for Adult Education. The rapid growth of adult education since World War II does not, however, appear to have resulted
in the formation of many new adult education councils. In 1954 there
were reported to be 28 cities in the United States which had adult
education councils, one for every eighth city with 50,000 or more
population. Twelve of the 28 councils were in cities participating in

[69]N.E.A., *op. cit.;* Olds, *op. cit.*
[70]C. M. Jones, "A Report on Community Councils in Michigan," *Adult Leadership,* IV,
May 1955.
[71]Newberry, *op. cit.*

the "Test Cities" project. These twelve councils received financial support from the Fund for Adult Education.

> Of the remaining 16 councils, only six had budgets of $5000 or more per year. Highest budget in a non-Test City council was $26,713 in New York.
>
> While there is no one clear pattern evident in the financing of adult education councils there are several trends reported. . . . Income from dues and gifts was most common but in none of the councils was major or chief support derived from this source (New York, 45 per cent, was highest). . . . Another trend is toward major or minor support from Community Chests.
>
> The ideal pattern, toward which some communities are heading, would seem to be major support by the public school system, the local college or university, and the public library system with some support coming from community councils in recognition of services rendered to member agencies, and membership dues paid by private individuals. Denver appears to be coming close to this pattern and each council illustrates it to some degree.[72]

Planning and conducting coordination meetings was an important function of all councils reporting. Otherwise there was wide variation in distribution of effort among various councils. Chicago devoted 25 per cent of staff effort to "general administration of the council"; in St. Louis 35 per cent of staff effort was given to "provide information to individual inquirers concerning specific kinds of educational opporunities." St. Louis devoted 25 per cent of its volunteer effort to planning and conducting classes, forums, lectures, etc., while in New York 25 per cent of volunteer effort was devoted to conducting and participating in surveys of adult education needs and programs.[73]

Despite the fact that six councils operated on budgets of $100 or less it appeared from questionnaires returned by these councils with limited budgets that:

> A certain amount of seemingly worthwhile activity can develop without a large budget or even a staff. What is not known, however, is whether some agency is not really assuming the burden of supplying staff services, office facilities, etc.[74]

Cologne reported that coordination became effective where the problem requiring joint action was clearly defined, broad enough in scope

[72]Olds, op. cit., pp. 70-73.
[73]Ibid., Table 8, p. 75.
[74]Ibid., p. 77.

to suggest the need for cooperation and where the associated groups both already knew something of each other and understood the requirements of cooperation. Finally, she suggested that successful coordination must be regarded as a means for achieving an agreed upon objective, not as an end in itself.[75]

A comparative analysis of adult education in two Colorado cities, Denver and Pueblo,[76] the former with an adult education council active since 1930, the latter with no council, found that the two communities showed similar needs and trends. Denver interviewees indicated slightly higher rates of participation in adult education classes and more of them were active readers of magazines and books, or were users of library services than was the case with a corresponding sample of Pueblo residents. Differences, for the most part, were small and could not be attributed to the influence of a council.

Despite the continuous operation of the Denver council for 25 years the general public and even members of organizations represented on it were largely unaware of its services and activities. Even though nearly half of the organizations interviewed were members of the Adult Education Council, few of their executives interviewed seemed cognizant of this affiliation. Nevertheless, Denver organizations placed greater emphasis upon educational activities and greater use of all methods than did Pueblo organizations. There was more widespread knowledge of services available in Denver than in Pueblo.

The comparatively few surviving adult education councils and the reports available of council operations appear to indicate two chronic weaknesses in the specialized adult education council: (1) a lack of any obvious or consistent basis for adequate financial support; and (2) a persistent failure to involve and sustain the cooperation and support of groups which engage in adult education only as a secondary or marginal function.

Failure to obtain support from community agencies forces councils to engage in money raising activities which may have but slight relation to their primary function. Failure to function effectively as a coordinative agency may force a council to undertake directly sponsored adult education activities, potentially at least in competition with the agencies which should form the main support of the council.

[75]R. Cologne, *Coordinating Resources for the Development of a Community Program in Family Life Education,* New York: Teachers College, Columbia University, unpublished Ed.D. dissertation, 1947.
[76]R. B. Minnis, *The Adult Education Council of Denver, An Evaluative Study Based on Case Studies in Two Cities,* Denver, Colorado: The University of Denver, 1955.

As adult education councils also are subject to the same difficulties encountered by any interagency coordinative body it would seem likely that this specialized council approach would be inappropriate except in areas served by several large institutions and many associations with major commitment to adult education and where less formal means of coordination would not provide the necessary liaison. This would appear to eliminate all but larger cities or area councils serving a considerable population, except under unusual circumstances.

Necessary coordinative functions for community adult education. From the studies reviewed it is evident that local communities have a wealth of organizational resources and have developed many patterns of interorganizational communication. It would appear that the particular type of coordinative effort adopted in any given community should be related to the existing organizational structure and supplement rather than replace existing patterns of communication. There are certain coordinative functions which appear to be necessary for the development of community-wide adult education. Examination of the activities reported for coordinative structures indicates that those activities which are really *coordinative* may be classified under one of the following categories:

1. Study of community and citizen needs.

2. Survey of existing programs and resources.

3. Dissemination of information about needs, programs and resources: (a) publication, (b) publicity, (c) public relations, (d) referral services.

4. Exchange of information and views among agencies, institutions, and groups.

5. Improving existing programs through: (a) training personnel, (b) exchange or pooling of facilities and equipment, (c) pooling of "talent."

6. Securing out-of-community resources.

7. Joint planning including: (a) establishment of long-term goals and short-term objectives, (b) development of programs in terms of goals and objectives.

8. Evaluation in terms of goals and objectives.

Whether these tasks are entrusted to a single specialized agency, to an overall "general community council," carried out by existing agencies or institutions, or through some combination of these approaches, should be determined locally in response to recognized needs and with consideration of available organizational resources and patterns of communication.

The need for formal and specialized structure is related to the size and heterogeneity of the population to be served, and to the number of agencies and institutions engaged in some form of adult education. The high mortality rate of coordinative bodies suggests that no more formal structure should be developed than is necessary to meet recognized needs for cooperative and coordinative effort. In rural areas with relatively homogeneous populations the general approach would appear to provide the greater opportunity for success. In towns and cities of less than 50,000 population with a wealth of relatively flexible organizations and adequate communication, improvement of existing communication and greater use of informal cooperation may suffice. In large, complex metropolitan areas there is acute need for social invention in the development of comprehensive coordination at many levels from the local neighborhood to the over-all area.

Particularly in areas lacking in adequate resources or organizational structure, or suffering from depressed or retarded economic conditions the community development approach would appear to offer a more dynamic and direct method of community organization. The coordinative and developmental functions are complementary. They may well involve use of the same organizational structures and can become, in reality, one process.

A somewhat different formulation dealing with recent trends in community education in action, stated to be based on case studies, was issued a decade ago by a committee on community organization. The trends noted are the consideration of the "wholeness of life" in the community and conscious extension of democratic educational processes. Educational methods involved securing and publicizing facts, mustering community action based on the facts and involving all members in informal participation based on education. Failures of programs were traced to fuzzy, outworn objectives, conflicts among groups, and failure to locate and utilize local resources.[77]

Summary and conclusion. The findings of the studies necessarily present an incomplete picture of community organization. As in all generalizations developed from social research, they must be qualified by the assumption that other factors are constant. In any given community the presence of other factors or a combination of factors, known or unknown, could produce conditions contrary to the trends noted. Hence the necessity for the adult educator to know the community in which he functions.

[77]Committee on Community Organization, Robert Luke, Chairman, *Community Education in Action,* New York: Teachers College Bureau of Publications, Columbia University, 1948.

The studies reviewed indicate that communities are possessed of extensive and extremely varied organizational structure. The types of structure found, the extent of formal organizations, and the relative significance of the various types of structure appear to be associated with certain characteristics of the community or of its population.

The number of formal organizational structures tends to increase with urbanization or urban influence more rapidly than population increase would explain. The proportion of the population reached by formal organizations also tends to increase up to a point. The functions and activities of associations tend to become increasingly specialized, diversified, and specific as urbanization increases.

These changes appear to be related more to the diversity of the population than to sheer gain in number of inhabitants. As the population becomes progressively more heterogeneous with respect to race, cultural background, ethnic division, socio-economic and educational status, the number and relative importance of organizations representing special interests tend to increase.

Other factors which appear to be related to the development and significance of associations include degree of contact with out-of-community forces and structures, and basic value orientations which emphasize formal associational participation rather than informal social relationships.

The findings appear to support the hypothesis that formal associations constitute a distinct sub-system of social organization which is linked both to the institutional structure and to the social sub-structure of informal groups or cliques. A wide variety of patterns of linkage among associations and between associations and institutions, channels of communication among community associations, and patterns of linkage with out-of-community organizational hierarchies have developed in the communities studied. The more persistent and consistent patterns of formal and informal communication among associations tend to develop along lines of primary interest.

Formal associations are flexible in structure and in purpose so that they can and do act to meet the needs of the community and of its citizens as these develop and are recognized. Associations act as agents of social change and are, in turn, affected by change. Because they are essentially autonomous, formal associations are capable of acting independently of agencies with which they are linked structurally. They exert influence upon and in turn are influenced by their sponsoring institutions.

The findings indicate that formal associations can play a significant role in community action because: (1) their basic value orientation and the dominant social atmosphere of a group of semi-strangers incline them toward "good works"; (2) associations have a role in implementing (if not in making community decisions.)

The relative significance of any association in the making of major community decisions is related to the degree to which that organization involves those in the community who make the decisions. The role of an association in implementing decisions is related to the degree to which it acts as a channel of communication between community leadership and the community at large.

Formal associations are extremely active in various fields of adult education. Few associations, however, regard adult education as a primary function. Associations and institutions alike tend to approach adult education from the basic value orientation of the members in general and of the leaders in particular. The content, methodology, and even the meaning of "adult education" reflect the basic structure and value orientation of the organization.

The studies of adult education programs and institutions suggest that there has been a singular lack of effective coordination of adult education at the level of the local community. Patterns of cooperative action have developed, but these seldom appear to lead to joint participation in long-range planning. Coordinative structures such as adult education councils have tended to be short-lived or have persisted as sponsors of activities rather than as coordinators. Three basic patterns of coordination have emerged:

1. Primary responsibility for coordination is vested in a specialized adult education council made up of representatives of the agencies and associations involved and of interested citizens. This approach seems to be best adapted for large urban communities where the need for such an agency is recognized. Even under such conditions, however, the adult education council has seldom been fully successful.

2. Primary responsibility for coordination is vested in a general community council responsible for over-all community improvement. This approach appears to be suited to smaller communities or to those where adult education has received only limited recognition.

3. Coordinative functions are assumed by existing agencies and institutions. This pattern, unsatisfactory as it often is, appears to have achieved the widest measure of acceptance.

The studies reviewed suggest that the failure to achieve more effective coordination of community programs and activities stems from the following factors:

1. The marginal status of adult education—and particularly nonvocational adult education—in the great majority of agencies, institu-

tions and associations active in the field has tended to obscure the need for coordination. Adult education is seldom regarded as an end in itself, even among agencies valuing "education" as an absolute good. Programs of adult education have tended to develop in response to demand without adequate planning to meet recognized community needs. Institutions are prone to evaluate their adult education activities solely in terms of participation and to assume that a policy of "service" constitutes adequate planning. This lack of definition has led to needless and wasteful competition.

2. Agencies and institutions are generally unwilling to support coordinative structures for which they recognize no real need or even view as a threat to their own prestige. Except where foundations have provided support, coordinative agencies have had to operate on minute budgets or devote much time and energy to fund raising.

3. Failure of coordinative bodies to involve the real decision makers within the agencies and within the communities has made them unable to achieve sufficient concensus to permit long range planning or implementation of council recommendations.[78]

Some implications for the development of more effective coordination of adult education. The comparative lack of success of attempts to provide coordination for existing programs of adult education in the community gives strong impetus to the more dynamic community development approach which seeks to achieve coordination through action to improve broad aspects of community life. From the findings of the studies reviewed this approach would appear to be sound. Adult education is viewed by most institutions as a process. In community development associations and institutions can find common ground through the process of adult education.

The wealth of organizational resources in all but the most rural communities strongly suggests that the process should involve the existing organizational structure of the community. Certain "principles of organization" emerge from the review.

1. No new structure should be created until a need for it has become evident.

2. No coordinative structure will continue to function unless its usefulness is recognized by those groups which it seeks to coordinate.

3. Patterns of organization should follow as closely as possible accepted lines of communication and interaction in the community.

---

[78]This last conclusion is more of an "educated guess" than one based upon clear evidence from research. The findings of Gettel, *op. cit.*, and Hunter, *op. cit.*, suggest that failure to involve the power group may contribute to the failure of adult education councils.

The extreme variation in patterns of organization would seem to indicate that there is no one ideal way to organize community action. With these reservations the following suggestions appear to be valid.

In rural communities where existing patterns of organization are deficient it may be useful to stimulate the organization of "general community clubs." In rural communities and smaller towns which are heavily over-organized the emphasis should be upon consolidating existing organizations, particularly those with similar programs and purposes.

Smaller cities with fairly homogeneous populations and reasonably extensive organizational structures may well be able to achieve coordination entirely by informal means.

As size of the community increases, as the population becomes more heterogeneous, and as the existing structure becomes more segmented and specialized, the necessity for social invention increases. Here the studies reviewed provide very little indication of how the proliferating organizational structure and the mounting problems of urban life can be accommodated without robbing the action process of its vital core, the immediacy of citizen participation.

Tentatively, however, it would seem that a system of over-all planning involving the significant sources of power and legitimacy should be tied to a series of neighborhood or subcommunity developmental problems organized in conformity with the ecological patterns of the city. There should be great flexibility and full autonomy within local programs. Where need for specialized professional councils is recognized these should be developed. If such councils already exist they may be tied into the function of the over-all structure. Such a complex structure should develop gradually in response to recognized needs but with support and encouragement from adult educators, city planners, and with consultative assistance from experts in many fields.

Finally, whether or not effective community-wide coordination is achieved institutions accepting a responsibility for adult education must seek ways of cooperating with other agencies to bring their programs into relation with the recognized needs of the community. The studies reviewed suggest that this may be accomplished by informal contacts with organizations and associations of all kinds, by extensive use of representative bodies in planning, and by a policy of service consistent with the basic objectives of the institution.

Maintenance of a flexible program and structure are vital not only to meeting the needs of the community but to the continued existence of the institution. Flexibility, however, does not mean formlessness. Clark's study suggests that long-range planning may be as essential as flexibility to the continued prosperity of institutionalized adult education.

Some avenues for the development of further research. Further study of patterns of interorganizational communication, particularly the functional interaction of formal associations, would provide many indications of how present organizational structure might be utilized to effect greater coordination of adult education at the level of the local community. Relationships of associations with institutions would seem to require more extensive study.

The study of leadership of formal associations should be extended and developed. The influence of various approaches to leadership training upon the function of associations, appears to have direct applicability to the role of adult educators in stimulating the development of more effective community organizations.

The study of existing community programs and institutions engaged in adult education. There is great need of more comprehensive descriptive and analytical study of patterns of formal and informal interaction among the various agencies involved in adult education. Case study analysis of the function of community councils, adult education councils and other coordinative bodies based upon study of records, observation, and interview could be used to identify factors associated with the success or failure of these bodies.

A series of case studies based upon a common typology and designed to gather data relative to a standardized group of hypotheses or propositions could be developed if initial exploratory and descriptive studies appeared to warrant such an approach.

Another approach would be to study a small number of pairs of communities matched for similarity except that each pair should contain one community with little adult education and one with a considerable amount. This, in both members of each pair should include interviews with participants and nonparticipants as to their reasons, motivations and satisfactions with respect to enrollment in adult education activities. Leaders and organizational officers should also be interviewed and the results related to the background data. The objective would be to discover factors conducive to the successful development of adult education.

The study of the community action process. The relatively undeveloped state of research in community action appears to stem from the very nature of the action process. Any attempt to impose a research design upon the process of action in the community is likely to alter the dynamics of the situation and affect development of the process. The variety of forces operating within the local community, furthermore, would require the participation of persons trained and experienced in a large number of scientific disciplines if the research were to progress beyond the level of description. As interdisciplinary research is obviously expensive, except in isolated and special circumstances, such an approach is likely to be more costly than the results anticipated would seem to justify. Nonetheless, arrangements to record the progress of specific programs, especially of an experimental nature, with emphasis upon the processes involved, would be of value.

In all areas of community research there is a continuing need for the refinement of methodology and the development of more precise conceptualization. If the study of the community is to contribute to the development of more effective social interaction and greater co-ordination it must progress beyond the levels of exploration and description. There is a danger that if the social sciences continue to develop in these directions the gap between research and application may be widened. There must be a continuing program of interpreting and relating the findings of basic research so that they may be used by practitioners who are not social scientists.

PROBLEMS OF
EVALUATION RESEARCH[*]

This report on adult education research opened with several chapters which dealt with the contributions of the research of psychologists and social psychologists to adult education. There followed a number of chapters concerned with studies of the methods, techniques, mechanics and operations of adult education as it is conducted in the United States. Where appropriate, and especially in the previous chapter, pertinent studies by sociologists have also been reviewed. This report has concerned itself therefore with studies undertaken with diverse objectives by members of diverse disciplines. Some of these studies proved of value to adult education only as a by-product, not always foreseen in their designing. Consequently, there is no neatly definable universe that can be labelled adult education research. This is inevitable in a field as relatively young as adult education and as heterogeneous in its interests, programs, and practices. Generalizations applicable to the entire field have been difficult to arrive at although some have emerged and have been noted.

One thing, however, is clear. Whether one prefers the highly conservative and restricted definition of the United States Census or the more inclusive and more optimistic estimates of some adult educators,[1]

*This chapter was written by David E. Wilder.
[1]Cf. Chapter I, "An Overview of Adult Education Research," pp. 2-3.

the manifold activities subsumed under the term adult education en-list the freely allotted leisure time of millions of Americans in purpose-ful educational activities. The purposes, motivations and interests which produce this major social phenomenon are varied in the extreme as the research has shown. Adult educators themselves have studied ways by which they could most effectively satisfy the yearnings represented by the adults who have flooded into class rooms operated and staffed by both public and private institutions and agencies.

The American public has placed a high value on education as such for generations. It was natural therefore that the programs of adult education were regarded as a good in themselves, a good not to be doubted. Only in recent years have questions arisen as to whether the goals, implicit and assumed for so long, were in fact as important as imagined, and more important, whether they were being measurably attained. In crass terms, was the huge investment of time and money bringing commensurate returns?

Research to attempt to answer these questions is in its infancy.[2] The term used to describe it is evaluation. This final chapter is devoted to a discussion of evaluation research in adult education. Attempts at such research have been made in most of the many areas of adult education. This chapter can do no more than describe a few representative studies, indicate the problems they met, their contributions and dif-ficulties, and in conclusion suggest those considerations which must enter into any effective evaluation study.

What is evaluation research? During 1952, the Committee on Eva-luation of the Adult Education Association published a pamphlet titled *Program Evaluation in Adult Education.* The pamphlet "sets forth some of the major concepts and principles of program evaluation in adult education as developed in Committee deliberations during . . . two years."[3] As boldly stated by the authors:

The purposes of education are growth and change—change in

[2] It is probably no accident that the first formal efforts to evaluate an adult education pro-gram were made by a public agency, the Extension Service of the U.S. Department of Agriculture, in part to justify requested appropriations. Probably no other adult education agency has so constantly subjected itself to self-study over the years. Nor is it without significance in view of the emphasis of some adult educators upon changes produced by adult education that even in its first superficial attempts to evaluate its programs the Ex-tension Service emphasized not merely attendance at its meetings and demonstrations but the number of changed practices reported on the farms, in the homes and in the commu-nities of rural America.

[3] Committee on Evaluation, AEA, *Program Evaluation in Adult Education,* Washington, D.C., 1952, p. 3.

behavior of individuals and groups. People behave differently as a result of education.

The primary purpose of evaluation in education is to find out how much growth and change have taken place as a result of educational experiences. One evaluates a total program or major parts of it to find out how much progress has been made toward program objectives.[4]

Other purposes of evaluation are seen as being program improvement, program defense, and professional growth and security. It is made clear that evaluations for the purpose of making comparisons between different programs are apt to do more harm than good and result in invidious comparisons. Rather each program must be viewed and studied with respect to its own objectives and the progress it makes toward them.

It is obvious that all the purposes of evaluation mentioned above are not the purposes of researchers, and the pamphlet was not directed at researchers.[5] Nevertheless, the general conceptual framework in the pamphlet, as quoted briefly above, is consistent with the framework that researchers use; and it is presented so that this consistency will be apparent. Evaluation research also involves trying to find out whether or not some goal is being achieved by a program. Such research either has a sponsor who declares what the goals are that he has in mind or the researcher is free to specify the goals himself. In either case the goals are made explicit, and the techniques of social science are applied to the problem. It is the application of social science which makes "research" out of an evaluation, but it is the assessment in relation to a goal or standard which makes it an evaluation. With this distinction in mind, it is clear that not all evaluations are research and vice versa. Programs may be called poor, good, or indifferent by recognized authorities for all sorts of reasons and important decisions which affect many lives are made this way every day. However, one can hardly regard such activity as research even though it may be wiser or in some sense more correct than the results obtained from social science research.

What are the goals of adult education? Judging from the contents of the books and journals in adult education, there are numberless

---

[4]*Ibid.*, p. 7.

[5]The pamphlet does address the "role of research in evaluation" briefly, e.g. "Research is a somewhat broader term. Through research one attempts to probe into the various relationships which might help to explain the changes revealed by careful evolution." (p. 23) This is probably correct, but it should be pointed out that "evaluation research" is a somewhat narrower term as used in this monograph than is either research or evaluation used alone.

goals with reference to which evaluation studies might be conducted.[6] These goals may be expressed by administrators, educators, adult students, or taken from the American creed, and in any given adult education situation there will probably be many different goals held. An adult course in French may find the administrator primarily interested in keeping attendance up, the teacher may simply want to earn enough money so that he can continue to teach children during the daytime, and the student may want to make friends or get out of an unpleasant home during the evening. There is no *a priori* reason for assuming that the goals held by any of these individuals should be or are the same,[7] and it is perfectly legitimate that research be conducted with regard to any of the goals which are present. One might not particularly approve of some of them, but this could be one of the best reasons for conducting research with regard to them. Most people probably feel that the goal of a French course is to teach French and that an evaluation study should measure achievement in learning this language before measuring anything else. This would be the traditional sort of evaluation study, and the sort with which this chapter will be chiefly concerned. However, there is a paucity of such studies in adult education. This is a fact acknowledged by Kaplan, who, in discussing the 217 studies reported in the annual "Research Review" issues of *Adult Education*, notes that:

> The majority of studies in all four issues were descriptive or surveys based on questionnaires. Undoubtedly a number were fact-finding reports rather than research studies in the true sense. Very few were experimental. . . . Similarly, only one or two examined changes in attitude or perception resulting from adult education programs.[8]

This situation seems to be partly a result of the fact that testing adults is often taboo, which is not surprising when one considers that most adult courses are not given for academic credit. It is also related to the fact that adult programs do not consist of one course in French but include all sorts of activity. In evaluating a whole program, what

---

[6]For typical lists of such goals, see *ibid.*, p. 11; G. Burch, "Evaluating Adult Education," *Adult Education Journal*, vol. 6, April 1947; P. Stensland, "Criteria of Adult Education," *Adult Education Bulletin*, vol. 8, August 1944.

[7]One study which touches this problem slightly points out that the students' motives for entering classes varied a great deal, with over two-thirds attending for reasons other than course content. See A. Zander, "Student Motives and Teaching Methods in Four Informal Adult Classes," *Adult Education*, October 1951.

[8]A. Kaplan, "Introduction to Research Review," *Adult Education*, vol. 7, no. 4, Summer 1957.

relative weights should be assigned to French as compared to, for example, basket weaving? Whole programs are usually very broad and diffuse, and they may have many discrete goals in addition to the more general ones.

There are "levels" of evaluation which correspond roughly with the goals in regard to which the research is conducted. Good organization, administration, teaching and training are all necessary to adult education, and each needs to be evaluated as objectively as possible in terms of some specified standard. Unfortunately, objective standards are difficult to come by. One of the main reasons why the present chapter discusses program evaluation almost exclusively is that this represents the area within which the most research has been done to date. However, comprehensive evaluation research with regard to any level tends at some points to have implications for other levels, and it is not too far-fetched to consider such things as administration and teaching as aspects of a whole program.

It should be obvious that certain goals may be met successfully while others are not. The French course may not teach a student enough French to buy a pack of cigarettes in Paris, much less allow him to read French classics, but it might meet other goals successfully. One of these might be improving "international understanding for peace", and who is to say that this is a less important goal than learning French? In keeping with the principles stated by the Committee on Evaluation and the tradition of evaluation research in other areas, this chapter will be chiefly concerned with goals that have to do with change. Such goals are generally "program goals" which might in some sense imply manipulating people in some way. The propriety of such manipulation raises a legitimate ethical question as far as all education is concerned, but it would seem to apply more to the compulsory education of children than to the education of adults who are volunteers. Indeed, the typical goals one finds associated with adult education (e.g., "teaching democracy" or "meeting the needs of adults") are far more in keeping with the American creed and imply less manipulation than teaching "the three R's" or "keeping the kids off the streets." Essert's words would seem to be appropriate:

> To a major extent adult education stands on its own merits. It responds to changing needs of society to whatever extent people can articulate those needs clearly in educational terms. In the final analysis there is no need for elaborate schemes of evaluation of adult education in the United States, or in any nation in which adult education responds to the eternal search by individual human beings for redeeming life from insignificance. It must add significance to the

life of the adult momentarily or permanently or it does not continue.[9]

The frame of reference. If one wishes to attribute some change to a program or determine whether or not some change happened as a result of a program, he must be very careful in conceptualizing and specifying variables. It should be realized that growth or change might well occur *in spite of* a program, but this is only one of the difficulties encountered in evaluation studies. Probably the simplest and most useful way of thinking about evaluational research is in terms of the traditional experiment. The program becomes the independent variable to which the students are exposed, and whatever growth or change is observed in the students is the dependent variable. It should be pointed out that although such an experimental model might well be impossible to achieve in some types of research on adult education programs, it is a good model to keep in mind for two reasons. First, it forces specification of just what the variables are (e.g., is the teacher a part of the program or independent variable to which the students are exposed?), and second, it helps one raise questions and employ methodology which may allow him to determine whether or not whatever change occurs is in some sense a result of the program rather than of something else.

In spite of the above reasons, thinking of evaluation studies in terms of the experimental model might seem overly restrictive to many adult educators. Nevertheless, this model can be applied to the clear recommendations of the American Library Association for evaluating its Library-Community Project:

Four basic steps of evaluation before the activity is undertaken:
1. Setting of goals—what specific outcome is expected from this activity?
2. Establishing a baseline—what is true of this situation now?
After the activity has been completed:
3. Noting and recording change—what happened as a result of this activity?
4. Considering the change in the light of the circumstances—what does it mean and what shall we do about it?[10]

A similar but more complex model for program evaluation is provided by the Federal Extension Service in 14 steps designed for "de-

[9]P. Essert, *Creative Leadership of Adult Education*, New York: Prentice-Hall, Inc., 1951, p. 161.

[10]Library-Community Project, *Guide to Activities*, American Library Association, Chicago, Illinois, August 1957, p. 16.

termining if objectives are reached: (1) Problems, (2) General objectives to be achieved, (3) Who has been reached, (4) Specific objectives or changes to be achieved, (5) Information or subject matter taught, (6) Teaching methods, techniques and devices used, (7) Calendar of work, (8) Evidence of accomplishment, (9) Measuring device, (10) Face or descriptive data, (11) Sampling of the population, (12) Collection of data, (13) Editing, tabulation and interpretation of data, (14) Presentation of data or findings."[11]

It is easy to see that the 14 steps and the four steps are not identical; and if all evaluation studies did the same thing, there would be no need to address the question of a suitable frame of reference to use in discussing them. However, every educational situation and adult education program is a *potential experiment* inasmuch as students are being exposed to various stimuli. If one wants to find out what happens to the students or what they do as a result of being exposed to the stimuli, then, clearly, thinking about such phenomena in experimental terms is appropriate.[12]

Procedure. In the following section an attempt will be made to show how studies of attendance, participation, and dropouts are related to evaluation studies and may be an integral part of them. Some evaluation studies, in several content areas of adult education will then be reviewed. No attempt will be made to report all the findings of these studies in detail since doing so would require a volume in itself and would place too much emphasis on the particular and idiosyncratic. Rather, an attempt has been made to select studies and findings that are representative and that illustrate points which can be generalized and applied to other evaluation studies. The studies so used will then be discussed and suggestions made for further research under an accounting scheme of categories of research problem areas.

Related research: attendance studies. There are many studies having to do with attendance which will be mentioned only briefly. They do not represent what has been designated as evaluation research but

[11]J. Neil Raudabaugh, "Program-Plan of Work-Program Evaluation," *Extension Service Review*, September 1955.

[12]Certainly it is possible to think of evaluation research in terms of other models and sometimes this is very useful. Miller refers to three principal methods of evaluation, (a) survey, (b) field study, and (c) field experiment, in his excellent article. (K. M. Miller, "Evaluation in Adult Education," *International Social Science Bulletin*, vol. VII, no. 3, 1956.)

On the other hand, Silberman argues that " 'Evaluation' should be used in a strictly technical sense. It deals with a field experiment *during the course of its operation.*" L. Silberman, "Problems of Evaluation Research," *Rural Sociology*, vol. 20, nos. 3 and 4, 1955, p. 229. There are good evaluations which use survey and field study methods, but the experimental model is used herein for the reasons stated above.

they sometimes pass for it and are often useful *parts* of evaluation research. These are studies that are chiefly concerned with determining whether or not arbitrary attendance goals have been met. It is essential to any program that people somehow get exposed to it regardless of the other goals which may be involved. Taking attendance is a common practice in adult education, and it is a simple matter to compare the number who actually attend with the goal one has set. This is bookkeeping, but it is necessary for the many adult schools which are dependent on public funds for support—especially when the amount of support is computed in attendance units. Thus, it is not surprising to discover that Banta found that all seven of the public junior colleges in Colorado used "growth in total enrollment" as a source of data for evaluating adult programs in their communities, and six used "record of student enrollment."[13]

Similarly, Freeman sent a questionnaire to the staffs of 54 Jewish Community Centers which asked the leaders what sort of criteria they used for determining whether or not adult programs are successful. Attendance was mentioned the most (68 times), followed by enthusiasm and interest (50 times), and the degree of participation (27 times).[14]

If the high enrollment figures presented by Professor Essert are at all accurate (see Chapter I), attendance goals are probably being met all over the country unless they are fantastically high. The question is, what good are the attendance figures by themselves in terms of evaluation research in general, and in terms of other goals of adult education? Simply to know adults attend gives no idea of who they are, why they attend, or what happens as a result of their attending. Attendance data are necessary to begin to answer these questions, but there must be other data too.

Participation studies. The studies discussed in Chapter VI, "Participants and Participation in Adult Education", may be treated as parts of evaluation studies or as evaluations themselves with regard to *participation goals.* The findings and generalizations presented from participation studies will not be repeated, but an attempt will be made to show their value for evaluation.

The virtue of most participation studies is that they tell something about the people who attend, thus making it possible to specify rela-

[13]C. O. Banta, "Sources of Data for Program Evaluation," *Adult Education*, vol. IV, no. 4, 1955.

[14]S. D. Freeman, *Adult Education in the Jewish Community Center*, Ed. D. dissertation, Teachers College, Columbia University, New York, 1953.

Center leaders sometimes mentioned criteria with reference to more than one program which accounts for the discrepancy between the N of 54 and "attendance" mentions of 68.

tionships between attendance and other variables. Most programs are aimed at a certain target population. In the case of public agencies, this target is usually felt to be all the adults in the community. Income data alone might show that only the middle stratum is being reached. Comparably, participation can be related to occupation, educational level, ethnic background, career aspiration, or any number of variables or combinations thereof. Such data are relatively easy to obtain since students are usually required to fill out forms upon registering.

When comparisons between participants and nonparticipants are desired, comparable census data for the community as a whole is often available. However, if the comparable data are not available for nonparticipants, and this will usually be the case when the relevant variables are such things as attitudes and beliefs, it is necessary to undertake a survey in order to make such comparisons. To do this adequately requires money, personnel, and at least a rudimentary knowledge of sampling technique and social science methodology. This is the point at which research becomes impractical for most adult education agencies.

In addition to being concerned with participation goals, evaluation studies should describe participants carefully. This is necessary for two reasons: (a) the participants might have characteristics which would help explain the success or failure of the program, and (b) it would make it possible to duplicate the study and know whether or not participants in various programs are similar. Examples of the first reason should be familiar since it is standard procedure to see whether people with different characteristics are affected differently by the program. The second reason is of special interest to researchers since comparisons of various programs may lead to valid generalizations.

Dropouts. The matter of dropouts was considered to be "one of the foremost problems facing adult educators" by the AEA Research Committee in 1955.[15] However, the Committee noted that:

1. There has been almost no comprehensive research on adult education dropouts.
2. There have been some related studies in other areas.
3. There have been suggestions from several adult educators regarding the handling of dropouts. Most of these, however, are not based on experimental evidence.[16]

[15]R. B. Spence and L. H. Evans, "Dropouts in Adult Education," *Adult Education,* vol. VI, no. 4, 1956.
[16]*Ibid.,* p. 224.

Probably one of the main reasons why the dropout situation has not been systematically studied is that dropouts present an initial methodological problem; dropouts are not accessible by virtue of their having discontinued the educational activity.

High dropout rates are reported by such diverse organizations as the New York City College of Business,[17] The Great Books Foundation,[18] and the United States Armed Forces Institute.[19] Unfortunately it is usually just the number of dropouts that is reported. It would be possible for most adult education agencies to find out at least if dropouts differ from students who remain simply by collecting more information about students when they enroll and then comparing those completing courses with those who do not. However, in order to find out why people dropped out, someone must locate and interview them, and this takes time and energy.

Two studies have gone to considerable trouble to do this.[20] Probably their most significant finding was that a great many adults dropped out for reasons which were personal and had nothing to do with the adequacy or inadequacy of the programs they discontinued. To the extent that this is true, treating dropouts as a reflection of things which are wrong with adult education programs is doing an injustice.

In addition, the study of USAFI dropouts[21] reports that approximately one-third of the participants in their programs claim they had not enrolled for credit and quit courses only after they had gotten what they wanted out of them. Such participants were nevertheless automatically counted as dropouts. This reveals a point at which the general philosophy and goals of adult education tend to run counter to the administrative needs and goals of adult education agencies. On the one hand, adult educators want to treat adult students as adults and allow them to determine their own needs. On the other hand, dropouts cause a great many administrative headaches, particularly in cases where school funds are allocated according to attendance units. Some dropouts are inevitable when participants are allowed to determine when their own needs have been met. The number may tell

[17]R. E. Love, "A Call for Action," *School and Society*, vol. 70, no. 1816, 1949.

[18]R. Hemenway, *Great Books Under Discussion*, The Great Books Foundation, Chicago, Illinois, 1954.

[19]K. H. Bradt, *Why Service Personnel Fail to Complete USAFI Courses*, Washington: Department of Defense, Office of Armed Forces Information and Education, 1954.

[20]Bradt, *op. cit.*, and J. T. Carey, *Why Students Drop Out*, Chicago: Center for the Study of Liberal Education for Adults, 1953. The USAFI study was done by way of a mailed questionnaire, and the Carey study used mailed questionnaires as well as both telephone and personal interviews.

[21] Bradt, *op. cit.*

an administrator what he needs to know with regard to basic attendance goals, but such a number will not provide any answer as to why participants stopped attending or whether or not other goals are being met by the program.

Evaluation studies usually report dropouts as a matter of routine when a before-and-after study design is employed because each dropout represents a loss in the experimental group. They are not always reported when effects are measured only after the program has been completed. If completing a program is in itself a program goal, then dropouts assume a great deal of importance. However, it might be that people who do not complete programs get just as much or more out of them than those who do. Whatever the effects which are being measured, it makes sense to measure them for the people who fail to complete the program as well as for those who do. This is often overlooked in evaluation research, and is unfortunate since dropouts provide an opportunity to try to find out whether subjects who are exposed to only part of a program are affected differently from those who are exposed to the whole program. Studying dropouts in this way would contribute a great deal to evaluation studies, but it would mean going out and tracing people from phone numbers and addresses which may not be up-to-date. This is often not practical, and interviewing or giving questionnaires to people who are still attending a program usually is practical.

METHODS STUDIES

Many of the better studies reported in the various chapters concerned with methods and techniques can be regarded as evaluation research. In comparing lecture with discussion methods or the use of television with the use of the traditional classroom situation, each becomes an independent variable, and the success, or lack of it, which results becomes the dependent variable. These studies are sometimes referred to as evaluations of methods. There is no necessary reason for distinguishing them from other evaluation research except for the fact that they normally utilize more than one independent variable (method) in order to make systematic comparisons of effects. Clearly, one must specify what the goals or desired results of employing any given method are in order to know whether it is successful and even to know what to measure in order to ascertain its success.

Interestingly enough, testing of adults has been done rather extensively in methods studies because the explicit goal involved was learning, and it is generally accepted that subjects must be tested in some way to find out whether learning has occurred. As will be pointed out in more detail later, most evaluation studies regard whole programs as the independent variable; and since most programs are rather complex, it is not possible to evaluate them with the rigor which characterizes the evaluation of specific methods. There are simply too many variables to take into account. Nevertheless each is essentially an attempt to ascertain whether an adult education activity has produced desired effects. Thus the sorts of categorical problems which will be alluded to later apply equally to methods studies.

Evaluation studies: parent education. An excellent summary of evaluation research in parent education has been written by Brim.[22] The participation aspect of these studies, and some studies devoted entirely to participation in parent education programs, reveal that the percentage of persons reached varies directly with the parents' socioeconomic status and sex, and the age of the parent's child. Participants tend to come from middle and upper social strata, to be women, and to have children who are of pre-school age or are just starting school. Two studies indicate that reading materials reach the greatest number of parents; nurses, pediatricians and doctors are next most effective; lectures, next; and study groups reach the least.[23] In addition, programs have varied from mass media to group procedure and counseling. The goals of parent education[24] are usually seen to be some sort

[22]Orville G. Brim, Jr., "Evaluating the Effects of Parent Education," Working Paper No. 2, *Social Science and Parent Education*, New York: Russell Sage Foundation, September 1956 (mimeographed).

[23]Michigan State Department of Mental Health, "A Report of Some Aspects of the Effectiveness of the Pierre the Pelican Mental Health Pamphlets," Lansing, Michigan, 1952, (mimeographed); White House Conference on Child Health and Protection, Section III, Education and Training, Committee on the Infant and Pre-school Child, *The Young Child in the Home: A Survey of Three Thousand American Families*, New York: D. Appleton-Century, 1936.

[24]Instruments for measuring parents' attitudes can be found in D. B. Harris, H. G. Gough, and W. E. Martin, "Children's Ethnic Attitudes: II. Relationship to Parental Beliefs Concerning Child Training," *Child Development*, 21, 1950; E. J. Shoben, Jr., "The Assessment of Parental Attitudes in Relation to Child Adjustment," *Genetic Psychological Monographs*, 39, 1949. Instruments for measuring parental overt behavior can be found in: A. L. Baldwin, J. Kalhorn, and F. H. Breese, "Patterns of Parent Behavior," *Psychological Monographs*, 58, 1945; I. E. Sigel, *et al.*, "Toward a Theory of Influence Techniques: Preliminary Report," *Merrill-Palmer Quarterly*, 1, 1954.

Instruments for measuring the child's perception can be found in: C. G. Hackett, "Use of an Opinion Polling Technique in a Study of Parent-Child Relationships," *Studies in Higher Education*, 75, 1951, Lafayette, Ind.: Purdue University, Division of Educational Reference; H. W. Lyle and E. E. Levitt, "Punitiveness, Authoritarianism and Parental Discipline of Grade School Children," *Journal of Abnormal and Social Psychology*, 51, 1955; M. J. Radke, *The Relation of Parental Authority to Children's Behavior and Attitudes*, Minneapolis: University of Minnesota Press, 1946. An instrument for measuring the child's behavior can be found in: R. R. Sears *et al.*, "Some Child-rearing Antecedents of Aggression and Dependency in Young Children," *Genetic Psychological Monographs*, 47, no. 2, 1953.

of mental health objectives regardless of the program. However, as Brim points out, it is usually the parents' motives, beliefs, or attitudes that are actually measured as the dependent variable, whereas one might also measure the parent's overt behavior, the child's perception of parent's motives or the child's behavior; and instruments have been developed to measure each of these.

Probably the most instructive studies in this area for the present purposes are three in which the programs had similar content but were presented in three different states.[25] The general program consisted of sending 12 four-page pamphlets of the "Pierre the Pelican" series to parents of young children, one pamphlet sent each month during the first 12 months of the infant's life. The pamphlets discussed child care and made suggestions as to what parents should do.

Each study used an after-only study design wherein experimental groups were exposed to the program and control groups were not. Measurements of the dependent variables were made after the exposure to the pamphlets, and it was inferred that differences found resulted from the program. The New Orleans study used a 60-item questionnaire for interviews in the subjects' homes; the North Carolina study used five key questions about feeding practices for interviews in homes; and the Michigan study used a 43-item questionnaire which was mailed to all subjects, plus interviews with a small sample from both the experimental and control groups. The North Carolina study results showed no significant differences between the experimental and control groups, while the New Orleans study revealed significant differences on 18 comparisons, and the Michigan study on 10.[26] However, as Brim points out,

> If one generalized from the findings of either the Michigan or Louisiana study, he would have been wrong on his predictions about the outcome of the other on about one-half of the items (approximately the results he would get if he had flipped a coin). . . . Whatever the source of disagreement between the studies, the results clearly should make one cautious in generalizing the results of any particular evaluation study in parent education.[27]

[25]L. W. Rowland, *A First Evaluation of the Pierre the Pelican Health Pamphlets, Louisiana Mental Health Studies,* No. 1, New Orleans: Louisiana Mental Health Society, 1948. B. G. Greenberg *et al.,* "A Method for Evaluating the Effectiveness of Health Education Literature," *American Journal of Public Health* 1953, vol. 43, (conducted in North Carolina). Michigan State Department of Mental Health, *op. cit.*

[26]The only item on which the experimental groups of both the Louisiana and Michigan studies showed significant differences from the control groups was "Asks child's permission to use his things for new baby." Brim, *op. cit.,* Table I.

[27]*Ibid.,* p. 12.

Another study in this area which has particularly interesting implications is one which was conducted by Balser *et al.*[28] The program
consisted of a series of group-centered, psychiatrically led, seminars
concerning child development and parent-child relations. The experimental group consisted of 12 parents who were exposed to the program. Two control groups of parents not exposed were used. A
before-and-after design was employed and the subjects were measured
twice with the Minnesota Multiphasic Personality Inventory, a sentence completion test, and a scale of parent attitudes. The most important finding at this point is that while the experimental group showed
improvement on the attitude scale ($<.10$), one of the control groups
showed a larger and statistically significant difference ($<.01$) on this
scale between the before and after measurements. This is probably
one of the finest demonstrations in the literature of why control groups
should be used whenever possible. When they are not used, there is
always the possibility that more change might occur in subjects who
have not been exposed to the program, and inferring that observed
change in the experimental group is a result of the program is not
warranted.

Brim concludes:

> In sum, we saw that the majority of the 23 studies reviewed here
> found positive or beneficial effects to result from parent education
> programs; this was true regardless of the educational technique in-
> volved, and regardless of how the 'effect' was conceptualized. On the
> other hand, two excellent studies among the 23 . . . in essence show
> no important results to occur.
>
> The evidence from these studies is not really cumulative because
> they vary so in conception and procedure. It is perhaps startling
> that there exists for the far-reaching and multi-million activity called
> parent education this mere handful of efforts, many of them crude
> indeed, to discover whether this activity has any effect at all.[29]

Evaluation: Race relations. Summaries of evaluation studies of race
relations programs have been written by Rose,[30] Williams,[31] and
Harding *et al.*[32] These works refer to many studies which cannot be

[28] B. H. Balser, F. Brown, M. L. Brown, E. D. Joseph, and D. K. Phillips, "Preliminary
Report of a Controlled Mental Health Workshop in a Public School System," *American
Journal of Psychiatry*, 112, 1955.

[29] Brim, *op. cit.*, p. 21.

[30] A. Rose, *Studies in Reduction of Prejudice*, Chicago: American Council on Race Relations, 1948.

[31] Robin M. Williams, Jr., *The Reduction of Intergroup Tensions*, New York: Social Science Research Council Bulletin 57, 1947.

[32] J. Harding *et al.*, "Prejudice and Ethnic Relations," in *Handbook of Social Psychology*,
Lindzey (ed.), Cambridge, Mass.: Addison-Wesley, 1952.

considered part of adult education by any stretch of the imagination; but many of them could be used as models for duplication in adult education research. In addition, the discussions of conceptualization, methodology and instruments are very comprehensive and the difficulties one encounters in doing such research are fairly well spelled out. Anyone interested in this area or in doing evaluation research about a race relations program would find these works very useful.

Franklin has done an evaluation of four human relations workshops which were conducted during the summer of 1953, in four different communities.[33] These programs differed a great deal in length and content with some participants living at the workshops and others commuting. The goals attributed to the programs were very diffuse and emphasis was on meeting the needs of the participants. The study design consisted of interviews with a sample of 34 participants six months after the workshops were ended, plus a mailed questionnaire which drew a 92 per cent response (N=190).[34] The results showed rather conclusively that the subjects liked the workshops and considered attending them a valuable experience, but they also revealed some negative criticisms of programs and facilities. Franklin takes the word of the subjects that their interracial attitudes and actions changed as a result of the program, but has no independent measure for this.

One is obviously limited in the sorts of inferences that can be made from the data that Franklin collected. The fact that people liked the programs is obviously important, but people like all sorts of things, and what relevance, if any, this might have for the various program goals is unknown. Similarly, one does not know what to make of the fact that people say their attitudes and actions changed as a result of the program. If one could demonstrate some sort of relationship between people's saying that such changes occurred and an independent measure of their change, then inferences might be made on the basis of such retrospective judgments alone. Until this is done, and done with regard to the specific content of the change, such inferences can best be treated as hypotheses for further research.

These statements are not meant to infer in any way that adults tend to be dishonest. Undoubtedly adults do change as a result of exposure

---

[33]R. C. Franklin, *An Evaluation of Workshops in Human Relations,* Ed.D. dissertation, Teachers College Columbia University, 1955.

[34]This is a fantastic response to a mailed questionnaire in comparison with responses to mailed questionnaires in general, which tend to run around 40 per cent. Unfortunately there is no way of knowing what this means in terms of unusual characteristics of participants in general, but it certainly tends to eliminate the possibility of bias introduced by virtue of respondents' differing systematically from nonrespondents on significant items.

to education programs, but one cannot demonstrate this in any systematic way simply by asking them if they have changed with regard to the complicated area of race relations. Franklin is very explicit about the assumption that one can take the word of respondents when they say their interracial attitudes or behavior have changed; but there is no way of being sure that any two respondents are talking about the same thing or comparing the amount of change, when they say they have changed. Moreover the initial attitudes of the respondents may have differed widely. This is one of the main reasons why so many scales have been developed in the area.

Furthermore, memory has a tendency to be faulty even when one knows exactly what is being asked of him—he simply cannot remember everything and there is nothing at all strange about this. Again, to say that one has not changed after exposure is in effect a negative reply. There is evidence to support the contention that some people tend to make or avoid making negative or positive replies regardless of the content of the interview items.[35] We have no way of knowing the extent to which any of these factors may be operating unless additional data are collected. The following study does this.

One of the best designed inquiries in this area was conducted by Smith[36] whose subjects were graduate students at Teachers College, Columbia University. Smith administered a test of attitudes toward Negroes to 354 students in six classes. He then obtained a sample of 46 experimental subjects from the larger group by sending them all invitations to attend a seminar which would meet during two weekends; the purpose was to acquaint people with the cultural life of Negro Harlem.

The program itself was a rather complex one, which consisted of an attempt to show the subjects many aspects of life in Harlem, including: lectures by prominent Negro writers, ministers, doctors, and community leaders of various sorts; trips to Negro homes and institutions; meals and parties at which informal discussion and behavior could take place; a concert by a famous Negro singer; and many other activities. In this way it was felt that stereotypic and prejudiced images of Negroes would tend to be subverted by meeting Negroes of all sorts, many of whom were obviously very articulate, intelligent and responsible members of the community.

[35]R. Christie et al., "Is the F Scale Irreversible?" The Journal of Abnormal and Social Psychology, vol. 56, number 2, March 1958.
[36]F. T. Smith, An Experiment in Modifying Attitudes Toward Negroes, Bureau of Publications, Teachers College, Columbia University, 1943.

A control group was established by matching individuals who did not take part in the seminar with individuals in the experimental group on the basis of initial test scores. Two hundred sixty-five of the original students were retested approximately ten days after the seminar ended. It was felt that by giving the attitude tests in an entirely different context from the seminar on both occasions, subjects would not tend to make any connection between the two events. This technique evidently worked rather well according to the testimony obtained by the author in interviews with 45 members of the experimental group two months after the seminar. In this way the probability that subjects who learned the right answers during the seminar expressed these rather than their actual attitudes on the second test would seem to be reduced. At any rate, statistically significant changes occurred in the attitudes of the experimental group as a whole and did not occur with the control groups. Changes were not, of course, uniform for all individuals, and Smith does an excellent job of analysis of various patterns of change and deviant cases, which was made possible by having both test scores and interview responses as data. Thus the fact that a person says he has changed or not can be compared to whether or not any change occurred in his scale scores.[37]

An evaluation of a program which is unique, well conceptualized, and fairly discrete, was conducted by Citron, Chein, and Harding.[38] The research is also unusual in that it consists of a series of studies in which the program and instruments were developed and tested. Only the last part of the study will be discussed here but the first parts are recommended to those who are studying race relations. The program for this study consisted of a short play presented by professional actors. The scene depicted is public, and anti-Semitic remarks are precipitated by the behavior of one individual who unintentionally offends another. The program is then varied for different groups of subjects by having another actor answer the anti-Semitic remarks in various ways.

The subjects were coopted in Times Square, New York City and downtown Newark, New Jersey, by the use of a pitchman who offered "50 cents for an hour of your time to watch a little play and give us your opinion." Each subject filled out a demographic information

---

[37]It should be noted that graduate students are not adult participants in the usual sense and may well differ from them in important ways that would affect the results of study. This, however, in no way affects the validity of the way in which Smith went about conducting his study which remains an excellent model for evaluation research.

[38]A. Citron, I. Chein and J. Harding, "Anti-Minority Remarks: A Problem for Action Research," *Journal of Abnormal and Social Psychology*, 45, 1950.

sheet before being exposed to the program and was asked to answer attitude scales before and after various parts of the program. The results of the study are rather complicated, but those of special interest here are: attitudes toward Jews as measured by the scales tended to change differentially according to (a) the type of reply that was made to the anti-Semitic remarks, (b) changes in the acting personnel, (c) charactertistics of the subjects, (d) the point in the program at which the scales were administered, and (e) the city in which the program was administered. In Newark, attitudes toward Jews become *worse* at the .05 level of significance when an attitude scale was administered just after the anti-Semitic remarks were made. Thus variations in the program itself, changes in the personnel presenting the program, differences in the subjects themselves, differential exposure to the program, and the locale or context in which the program is presented can all affect the amount of change brought by the program. In addition, it is quite possible that undesirable effects are produced at some point.

Evaluation: Cancer education. The American Cancer Society is currently conducting a series of evaluation studies in conjunction with its cancer detection program. These studies are particularly interesting because they will eventually include evaluation of almost every phase of a very broad and inclusive program. At one extreme this means that they are doing an evaluation of the effects of a movie on cytology which has been designed to show that women can do something about cancer of the cervix.[39]

This phase of the study involves a series of administrations of a true and false test to populations after they have seen the movie. Whether or not the message of the film is conveyed can be determined fairly well in this manner, but the Society has also been varying the content of the film systematically and attempting to find out whether this produces differential effects; a Horn-Solomon scale was used to measure the amount of concern the subjects showed with regard to cancer. In this way they have built in a system of possible program improvement (in terms of the content of the movie), and also attempted to find out whether certain undesirable effects (too much concern with cancer) are being produced. At the same time they have established norms for their test scores in the process of testing different individuals and populations.

The Society has also had a program in Philadelphia wherein over a

[39]D. Horn and E. S. Solomon, "Evaluation of 'Time and Two Women'" New York: American Cancer Society, Inc., Medical and Scientific Department, June 1957.

thousand doctors have cooperated in teaching women patients "breast self-examination" and distributing literature through their offices.[40] Follow-up questionnaires from nearly 500 of the physicians mailed one year later revealed that some 32,000 women had been taught self examination, 359 women had found breast cancer themselves, and 857 breast cancers had been found by the participating physicians during the first year of the program.

Both of the above studies are concerned with the same large program but neither one is an attempt to determine the effects of the program as a whole. In the first study it was necessary to develop and test very sensitive instruments in order to get at the dependent variables with any amount of precision. Such tests and scales cannot be developed without a knowledge of testing and scaling technique and how to test for reliability. However, it was the nature of the independent and dependent variables which made the development of tests and scales necessary and determined their form and content. Similar tests and scales were not used in the study concerned with "breast self-examination." Here the chief concern was with whether or not cancer detection after instruction would be carried out by the women themselves, and the only practical way of finding this out was to ask the physicians who participated in the program to keep records.

It is unfortunate that no control group of physicians was used, but this would probably be difficult to do without alerting them to the purpose of the study and thus affecting their behavior. It is possible that some women detect cancer themselves without having the benefit of instruction in breast self-examination, but there is no way of knowing this without using a control group of physicians.

Probably the most instructive thing about these two studies taken together is that they show how a very complex and far-reaching program can be evaluated systematically by taking sensible units from the whole for intensive study. The American Cancer Society could publish a great many impressive statistics about its activities, participants, and local organizations, and let these serve as an evaluation of their program as a whole. Such material is certainly a necessary part of their evaluation reports, but taken by itself it would provide little more than an excellent description of a huge undertaking. At each point the interested person would be left to his own resources to speculate about the possible effects of individual activities and combinations thereof. By asking very specific questions about parts of their program

---

[40]American Cancer Society, *A Study of the Effectiveness of Physicians in Cancer Education Through Their Offices*, Philadelphia Division, Inc., 1957.

they have come up with some researchable problems and may get answers to some practical questions of whether or not some of their activities get more or better results than others.

Evaluation: A community-wide information campaign about the United Nations. One of the most ambitious evaluation studies in adult education was an attempt to measure the effects of an educational campaign directed at the whole population of Cincinnati.[41] The program for this study was a monumental undertaking which covered six months of efforts during which time every school child was given literature to take home, radio stations broadcast facts about the U.N. (one station scheduled 150 spot announcements a week), newspapers ran special articles and advertisements; 59,588 pieces of literature were distributed; 2,800 clubs were addressed by special speakers, hundreds of documentary films were shown; and the city was bombarded with information about the U.N. from almost every conceivable source.

A before-and-after design was used on one representative sample of the population, and an after-only measure was taken on another sample. Although the primary goal of the program was to increase information about the U.N.; the researchers also asked questions about interest, general orientation, opinion, and actions so that relationships between these might be examined. Without attempting to report all of the tentative findings of the study, it should be noted that 30 per cent of the respondents had to be classified as knowing nothing about the main purpose of the U.N. in September before the campaign; the figure was 28 per cent in the following March.

On the basis of this and other informational items the authors report: "The inescapable conclusion is that in the six months the local level of information did not alter very much."[42] When the first survey revealed that women, the relatively uneducated, the elderly, and the poor tended to know the least about the U.N. an effort was made to direct the campaign at such people. However, the second survey found that these were the people reached the least by the program. It was the people who expressed interest in international topics who tended to be reached most, and these were the ones who already knew the most about the U.N. Thus what educators have "known" for a long time, that merely exposing people to information will not make them learn, was demonstrated on a rather large scale.

[41] S. A. Star and H. M. Hughes, "Report on an Educational Campaign: The Cincinnati Plan for the United Nations," *American Journal of Sociology*, vol. 55, 1949-50.
[42] *Ibid.*, p. 393.

SOME GUIDES TO FURTHER RESEARCH

It was noted at the beginning of this chapter that it is difficult to discuss evaluation research in a general way because of the diversity of the studies and the fact that results are often not comparable even when two studies are ostensibly about the same thing. Thus rather than discussing individual studies in great detail and reporting a great many unrelated findings, an attempt was made to choose studies which illustrated points which should be taken into consideration in evaluation research. In order to summarize some of these points this section will discuss the studies briefly from the standpoint of (a) conceptualization, (b) techniques and instruments, (c) design, and (d) analysis and interpretation. These are hardly mutually exclusive categories and perhaps not the best ones that might be used, but the points that have emerged do seem to fit into them fairly well.

Conceptualization. All evaluation research has been conceptualized in terms of the experimental model throughout this presentation. Independent variables and programs have been regarded as synonymous, as have dependent variables and goals or effects. This gave a frame of reference for talking about all the studies, but the task of conceptualizing any individual study can be far more complex than has been indicated. At each point in a study how the conceptualization of the various problems is done will determine what factors the researcher must take into consideration. This task may be relatively simple for the example of the French course, especially if the problem is to discover whether adults can pass a given test after taking the course. However, most of the studies have not been this simple. Conceptualization involves first of all the careful specification of the independent variables.

Independent variables or programs. Adult education programs range from relatively simple or discrete phenomena such as movies, lectures or discussions to more complex phenomena such as long courses, intensive workshops, or interracial living. As the programs become more complex, it becomes more difficult to specify just what students are exposed to. One would probably expect to get more results in changing attitudes [43] with interracial living than with a movie, but the price paid in terms of scientific rigor is that it is not nearly as difficult to specify what it is about a movie that might have changed attitudes,

---

[43]For a careful conceptualization of some of the factors which should be taken into consideration in interracial living see H. Hyman, C. Wright and T. Hopkins *Youth in Transition: An Evaluation of the Contribution of the Encampment for Citizenship to the Education of Youth,* forthcoming, Bureau of Applied Social Research, Columbia University, 1959.

whereas similar specification with regard to interracial living is probably not feasible. Furthermore, the same movie can be shown to different subjects and this makes it possible to say that the independent variable is the same for each group. One cannot make this statement when he tries to repeat more complex programs, and this is one of the main reasons why it is so difficult to generalize results from a study.

Similarly it is relatively easy to test subjects before and after a movie, use appropriate controls, and determine with a certain amount of rigor whether or not any changes occurred which can be attributed to seeing the movie. However, one cannot be as certain that similar changes noted after a more complex and long-term program are a result of the program rather than something else unless one considers the program to be *everything* that happened to the subjects over that period of time. Thus one is faced with an initial paradox inasmuch as the independent variables from which he would expect to obtain the most growth or change are those variables which it is most difficult to specify and those variables to which it is most difficult to attribute the change with scientific rigor. The re-creation or systematic variation of programs for research purposes is virtually impossible without such careful specification.

Dependent variables or goals. At one level of generalization the goal or purpose of every program is change. The problem is how to specify what change the researcher is looking for so that it can be translated into indicators which can be measured or at least identified. This is initially a similar problem to one which was encountered with independent variables. As the goals change from fairly simple ones such as learning to read a foreign language, to more complex ones such as learning to understand and live with one's problems, it becomes more and more difficult to find acceptable means of specifying and measuring progress toward the chosen goals. Usually one can designate that the desired change is in knowledge, attitude or behavior, or in some combination of them. The distinctions between these "levels" of phenomena may sometimes tend to be merely analytic, but they are sometimes empirical as well. One may improve one's knowledge with regard to races without changing one's attitudes,[44] and one may change verbal attitudes toward other races without changing his behavior toward them.[45]

[44] G. Saenger, "Effectiveness of UNESCO Pamphlet Series on Race," *International Social Science Bulletin*, vol. 3, 1954.

[45] R. La Piere, "Attitudes vs. Actions," *Social Forces*, 13, 1954; I. Chein, M. Deutsch, H., Hyman and M. Jahoda, "Consistency and Inconsistency in Inter-group Relations," *Journal of Social Issues*, vol. 3, 1949.

It is important to know whether a course in race relations is supposed to teach about races, change the amount of prejudice that is expressed in attitudes, or reduce the number of discriminatory acts. By making such specifications the research can help avoid making two sorts of errors: (a)) the logical error of inferring that a program has produced change on one level when it has been measured on another level, and (b) the procedural error of using available or familiar techniques to measure whatever they measure instead of having the specification of goals determine the techniques.

In addition to specifying the analytic level of the dependent variable, the researcher must determine whether he is interested in more than one such dependent variable and whether there are possible undesirable effects that could come about as a result of the program which it would be useful to know about. The American Cancer Society felt it was important that women who viewed the movie on cancer of the cervix did not become too worried about cancer afterwards. It is not unreasonable to assert that too much concern might offset any possible gain in knowledge and result in the movie's over-all effects being harmful.[46] It is not difficult theoretically to think of *possible* harmful effects of a great many adult education programs. The universe of such possible harmful effects is probably as vast as the universe of possible beneficial effects and the selection of the ones to be measured, both harmful and beneficial, is perhaps the most important part of any evaluation. Obviously all the possible effects cannot be assessed in any systematic way, and it is up to the sponsors and researchers to decide which are to be investigated.

The study in race relations by Citron *et al.*, had one of the most short-run or discrete independent variables which was encountered, but this study also contains one of the most complex conceptual models in the literature. It was only because the researchers realized that specific changes in the way the program was presented, in the people who present the programs, and in the setting or context in which the program was presented, *might* have an effect upon the results that they designed a study that took these factors into consideration. Similarly the most relevant characteristics of the experimental subjects might or might not be such traditional demographic variables as age, income and occupation. If one suspects that it is more important that subjects have a certain level of interest or are motivated in some way, he

---

[46] These sorts of unintended consequences of a program can probably be best thought of as latent functions. See R. K. Merton, *Social Theory and Social Structure*, Glencoe, Illinois; The Free Press, 1957, Chapter I.

must start conceptualizing what he means by these terms before they can systematically be taken into account in evaluation studies. Improvement of the evaluation studies in adult education can only come about after the various elements that enter into the studies have been more carefully conceptualized. One cannot begin to evaluate programs systematically with regard to such goals as "meeting the needs of the adults," or "helping adults become better citizens" until he has clearly formulated what is meant by these goals.

Techniques and instruments. One of the clearest statements of conceptualization and how it relates directly to the instruments and techniques used in evaluation studies in adult education has been made by Otto Klineberg:

> One of the aspects of evaluation which may appear rather obvious but which still requires some clarification, refers to the goals or aims of any particular action project. . . . In order that the social scientist may be able to give efficient help to the administrator in the development of evaluation techniques, he must have clearly before him the purposes which the administrator has in mind in setting up a particular project. If it is a project in fundamental education, for example, it is usually beyond the competence of the social science consultant to formulate the goals: without such a formulation, however, his aid will be greatly restricted, and may possibly be worthless. Something can of course occasionally be done to study the effects of a program without too much concern with goals. If one has asked merely what has happened as a consequence of introducing a new school, or a change in diet, it may be possible to give a partial answer. We might refer to this as the natural history approach to evaluation. More frequently, however, the techniques of evaluation must be adapted to the goals. That means that practitioners must be prepared to supply to their social science consultants, in the clearest and most direct form, a statement of the general principles under which they are operating, as well as the specific purposes for which the project has been launched in the particular case. Such a clear formulation has not always been forthcoming.[47]

A related statement has been made by Brim:

> We must emphasize that any *new* conceptualization of factors, whatever they may be, requires development of new measurement devices. If the research demands this development, then the reliability and validity of the new instruments must be established in the customary manner, otherwise the research in which they are utilized will be of little value.[48]

[47]Otto Klineberg, "Introduction: The Problems of Evaluation," *International Social Science Bulletin*, vol. VII, no. 3, 1954.
[48]Brim, *op. cit.*

An example of how the above might work in adult education can be found in the Kropp-Verner Scale.[49] This scale was developed in acknowledgment of the fact that the post-meeting reactions of participants are gathered in so many different ways and refer to so many different phenomena that there is no way of objectifying or comparing the attitudes they elicit. Kropp and Verner utilized the Thurstone and Chave scale construction method[50] with an adaptation devised by Remmers for measuring "attitudes in general."[51] The scale is intended for measurement of "the satisfaction of group members with an educational experience"; and the authors state explicitly that "it is not suitable as a device to evaluate content nor to diagnose particular aspects of program design or management. In the latter case, specific scales may be designed to measure the specific attitude object."[52] Kropp and Verner have thus found it necessary to develop a new scale; but in so doing, they have been very explicit about what it is designed to measure, how it is meant to be used, and the problems of establishing its reliability and validity.

The "clock hour index" devised by Kempfer[53] is another example of a specific instrument which was developed within adult education and which might be used or abused in evaluating programs. This index is another reflection of the "attendance fixation" in adult education; it is merely the ratio between total clock hours of attendance per year and the number of adults over 18 in the community. Presumably this index might be varied in certain ways and provide some idea of whether or not attendance goals are being met with regard to specific populations. However, it is difficult to see how it could be used for much more than this in its present form, particularly when it treats each class hour and student as equivalent to every other class hour and student. This appears to be another case where available data have been used ingeniously but they are unrelated to many potentially important variables and permit no analysis of specific neighborhoods of varying socio-economic or demographic characteristics within

[49]R. P. Kropp and C. Verner, "An Attitude Scale Technique for Evaluating Meetings," *Adult Education*, vol. VII, no. 4, 1957.

[50]L. L. Thurstone and E. J. Chave, *The Measurement of Attitude, A Psychophysical Method*, Chicago: University of Chicago Press, 1929.

[51]H. H. Remmers, "Generalized Attitude Scales—Studies in Social-Psychological Measurements," *Studies in Attitudes—A Contribution to Social-Psychological Research Methods, Studies in Higher Education XXVI*, Bulletin of Purdue University, 35, 1934.

[52]Kropp and Verner, *op. cit.*, p. 214.

[53]H. Kempfer, "Formula for Measuring Adult Education Programs," *Adult Education Bulletin*, 13, October 1948.

the community. Improved program evaluation requires planning ahead, developing new instruments, and collecting data which have not been available in the past.

There is a vast literature about instruments and techniques which it is beyond the scope of the present chapter to discuss in detail. Presumably, anyone doing evaluation research in adult education will familiarize himself with existing instruments and techniques that might apply to his area as Kropp and Verner have done. Unfortunately there is no single volume which comprehensively lists instruments and techniques developed in the many content areas of adult education and the social sciences. The studies discussed above have utilized instruments and techniques for measuring such diverse things as: (a) knowledge about cancer of the cervix, and about the United Nations, (b) attitudes toward Negroes, various programs, and parts of programs, (c) personality variables and concern about cancer, and (d) behavior toward children and the results of behavior with regard to breast self-examination.

Most adult educators are familiar with instruments and techniques for measuring knowledge, how they are devised, and the principles they are based upon. They may not be familiar with techniques and instruments for measuring other variables, how they are devised, and the principles they are based upon. These have been developed for the most part within the fields of psychology, social psychology, sociology and anthropology. When dependent variables or program goals consist of such things as attitudes, behavior, or personality attributes, it is quite possible that there will be available techniques and instruments in one or another of these fields that could be used. This will not only save the educator-researcher a great deal of initial trouble, but it will also mean that he may have some idea of how his participants compare with the participants in other studies. The adult educator who is not familiar with the variety of available instruments and techniques can gain some idea of the complexity of the area by reading the contents of Campbell[54] and Strauss[55] which both cover a great deal of territory in understandable terms and contain excellent bibliographies.

Design. Whether or not one is able to attribute change of any sort to a program is to a large extent dependent upon the study design that is employed. Assuming that one has carefully conceptualized and spec-

---

[54]D. T. Campbell, "The Indirect Assessment of Social Attitudes," *Psychological Bulletin*, 47, 1950.

[55]M. A. Strauss, *Direct, Indirect and Disguised Measurement in Rural Sociology*, Pullman, Wash.: Washington Agricultural Experiment Station, State College of Washington, Technical Bulletin 26, 1957.

ified the variables he is interested in and has found satisfactory techniques for locating them, there are still many designs that might be used. These may be classified as ones which measure the dependent variable only after exposure to the independent variable, and ones which take measurements both before and after exposure.

The simple after-only design is probably the most appropriate when the researchist is working with a fairly clear-cut dependent variable or is not interested in attributing results to the program with any rigor.[56] Thus if one is teaching something which he knows is new, such as the use of a new seed or drug, it is fairly easy to find out later if the drug or seed is being used, and it is known that it was not used before. However, if one is trying to get people to vote, he must do more than simply count the number who voted if he wishes to attribute voting to the program, since he knows that a great many people would probably vote even if there had been no program. Still taking the measurement at only one point in time, one might (a) ask people whether they voted before, (b) expose subjects differentially to the program, or (c) use various sorts of control groups.

With each one of these variations of the after-only design the inquirer has to make some assumptions which might be inappropriate. In the Franklin study it was necessary to assume that the retrospective opinions of people are accurate. In the Citron *et al.* and the American Cancer Society studies it was necessary to assume that subjects differentially exposed to the program were similar with regard to the dependent variable before exposure, and in the three parent education studies that used the "Pierre the Pelican" pamphlet, it was necessary to assume that the experimental and control groups were similar before the program. These assumptions may often be warranted, but this cannot be substantiated without further research. The researcher should bear in mind that his inferences are based on these assumptions; and if there is good reason to believe that the assumptions should be made, he will be on safer ground measuring the dependent variable at more than one point in time.

Even when one uses a panel or before-and-after design, any inference that the program produced the change observed will still be based on some fairly broad assumptions:

A. If one takes before-and-after measures on the experimental group

[56]Obviously, the researcher is forced to use an after-only design if he is unable to start his study until after the program is completed. This was the unfortunate situation with which Franklin was confronted. Unfortunately this occurs quite often when agencies provide money for evaluation only after they discover they do not know how to tell whether they have met various goals with a program which they have just finished presenting.

only, the change he observes might well have been caused by something other than the program. This should not be a serious problem with things such as teaching French, but it might be a serious problem with a study such as that in Cincinnati, where international events might well have affected attitudes toward the United Nations more than the program did. In that study the use of a control group would have meant, ideally, using another community which was not exposed to the program. This was not practical, but by using some standard items in the questionnaire, it was possible to compare responses in Cincinnati to those made in public opinion surveys in other parts of the country at the same time and thus have some pseudo controls.

B. This sort of problem is often met by using control groups as well as experimental groups during both measurements. The F. T. Smith study design is a good example of this. There are many more complicated designs than this in the literature,[57] and there are factors such as intervening variables and sensitization which can limit the validity of the inferences even when one goes to the trouble of having control groups and a before-and-after design. An attempt has been made to point out that at times it does not make sense to use such a complicated design or it may even be impossible to do so. However, more often the value of the research will vary directly with the complexity of the study design in the above terms.

Analysis and interpretation. By the time the inquirer gets around to analyzing and interpreting data, the extent to which either can be done has been largely determined by the work that preceded. As a result the educator-researcher must anticipate some problems of analysis and interpretation before they are actually undertaken. This, of course, is usually more easily said than done.

Analysis is potentially a process which is limited only by the number of variables which have been taken into consideration and the possible combinations thereof. Usually it is not possible to make all mathematically possible "runs" within the limits imposed by time and money. Furthermore such procedure would reduce the research to a hit-or-miss undertaking. As Jahoda, Deutsch and Cook point out,[58] one should expect a number of statistically significant relationships if he relates every variable to every other variable. Clearly, one must have some way of selecting the variables to be systematically considered. Previous research reporting significant findings combined with the special objec-

---

[57]Hyman and Wright, *op. cit.*

[58]M. Jahoda, M. Deutsch, and S. Cook, (eds.), *Research Methods in Social Relations,* New York: The Dryden Press, 1951.

tives and hypotheses of the individual study form the usual basis for such selection.

To illustrate, one usually finds that subgroups of participants are differentially affected by an adult education program. Older adults may change more than younger adults, and those with more formal education may be more or less flexible than their opposites. Such possibilities can be treated systematically in the analysis only if they are anticipated before the analysis is undertaken. However, anticipating this depends upon knowing that it was found true in a previous study or having an hypothesis which states it might be so. There are rules which can guide one through the literature of prior studies, but there are no known rules for developing fruitful hypotheses.

A special problem of analysis in evaluation research is what is the proper way to show the net change that has been brought about by the program. Most of the studies discussed have attempted to assess changes in individuals at some point and then have gone on to say that the group was changed in some way. It is possible to point out that so many individuals changed one way, so many did not change, and so many changed another way. It is also possible to say that the average (arithmetic) individual changed a certain amount. There are many such ways of showing the net effects of a program, each having its own advantages and disadvantages; but it is important that somehow all participants are taken into account in showing net effects. It is mathematically possible that the average change would be some plus figure even though more than 50 per cent of the participants showed negative change. Such a situation would oblige the researcher to express the net change in more than one way.

Statistics are usually used to show how many participants with given attributes did or did not change, with reference to the dependent variable. This phase of analysis may vary from presenting the breakdowns in terms of raw numbers or percentages to an elaborate use of tests of significance and analysis of variance. The particular device used at this point may not be nearly as important as the fact that the researcher should make it very clear what he has done. This makes replication and comparison of findings possible and also can lead to fruitful secondary analysis.[59]

Probably the most common error in interpreting the results of evaluation research occurs in trying to make the data show something they

[59]Probably the most elaborate example of secondary analysis is R. K. Merton and P. F. Lazarsfeld, *Studies in the Scope and Method of "The American Soldier,"* Glencoe, Ill.: The Free Press, 1950.

cannot show. One might use a Kropp-Verner Scale after a meeting and then assert that the meeting was or was not a success on the basis of scale scores. This is legitimate if one means by success nothing more than the general post-meeting attitudes held toward the meeting by the participants. However, if one means anything else by success, it is not legitimate. Probably the greatest danger, as far as adult education is concerned, is the negative example of this sort of interpretation. If it is shown that adults did not learn anything from a program or attitudes did not change favorably, it is then asserted that the program is unsuccessful and should be changed or discontinued. This too is legitimate as long as one is only interested in whether or not what was measured was learned or changed. Interpreting these findings as meaning that such goals as increasing international understanding for peace, strengthening of democracy, or understanding and strengthening the economy have not been met is, of course, absurd.

It is clear from the material presented in this chapter that studies evaluating adult education are a relatively recent development and that they vary greatly in their scope and in the level of methodoligical sophistication displayed. The variations in methods reflect in part varying conceptions as to the purposes of adult education and the varying objectives of the researchers. If an administrator needs only to know the enrollment and attendance of programs under his supervision in order to secure the funds needed to sustain adult education activities a careful evaluation of the outcomes of these activities is unnecessary. Others may need no more than such limited information to feel secure in their educational work with adults. The fact that people keep attending is assumed to be adequate proof of the worthwhile character of the program.

Increasingly, however, as some of the examples used in this chapter show, more fundamental questions are being raised. This is evidence that the easy assumptions of earlier years are being questioned. The Cancer Society, for example, was interested in finding the most effective way of presenting its material both out of regard for its audience and for reasons of efficiency and economy.

The rapid development of studies such as this one and several others noted is handicapped by several factors. One of these is the paucity of funds available. The very growth of adult education has absorbed all available resources, especially in institutions where adult education is considered a marginal activity. Moreover, when some adult educators take the position that "adult education stands on its own merits,"[60]

[60]Essert, *op. cit.*

the atmosphere is not favorable to research and outside sources of funds, such as foundations, may be hesitant to invest in fundamental research projects.

A more serious handicap to the development of needed research in adult education is the very heterogeneous and amorphous character of the field and especially the vagueness of its announced objectives, laudable as these objectives are. Adult education "for the solution of problems in a democratic society" or for "cultural development," especially when these phrases are declared to "include the total range of human learning"[61] is certainly desirable in our society but such objectives are so broad that it is not possible to measure with any degree of exactitude the extent to which they are successfully and meaningfully implemented. Until such objectives can be broken down into small and more precise and manageable units the existing gap between the expressed goals of many adult education programs and the phenomena with which evaluation research is concerned will not be closed or even reduced.

The closing of this gap can probably never occur. Its considerable reduction, however, is highly desirable for the sake of adult education itself since high level evaluative research can improve both content and method and more sharply define target populations and the various possibilities of more effectively reaching them. It is not necessary to attempt to evaluate what adult education does for the human spirit, the personality of the participant, in order to justify more rigorous research procedures. This is the ultimate that may never be achieved, but between that ultimate and the present stage both of evaluation research and of all adult education research there is a vast No Man's Land, the exploration or mapping of which will be of untold value to this young discipline. It is hoped that the suggestions for possible research given in every chapter of this report indicate some of the most important areas for profitable research.

[61]Quoted phrases from State of California, Department of Education, *Bulletin 20*, 1951.

INDEX

Accessibility: of education centers, 97-8, 134; of organization membership, 229; of reading matter, 76-7
Activities, 63, 64, 219-20
Adams, Mildred, 149
Administration, 143, 189
Adult Education Association, 215, 224, 244
Adult Education Councils, 232-35, 238
Advisory committees, 136
Age: and attitudes, 19, 60-1; and audio-visual education, 158; and intelligence, 10-11; and interests, 67ff, 72-3, 80, 87; and learning ability, 8-9, 12-3, 20, 21; and participation in adult education, 105-6; and reading interest, 150; and social participation, 105-6; motivations affected by, 37
Agencies, 4-5, 45-6, 122-4, 130-41
Agger, R., 103
Agricultural and Home Economics Extension Service, 5
Alinsky, Saul, 185-6, 209
Allen, W. H., 155
Allion, H., 91
Allport, F., 155, 193
Allport, Gordon, 49, 50, 155
American Association for Adult Education, 8, 232
American Cancer Society, 260ff, 265, 269, 272
American Library Association, 215
American Philosophical Society, 2
Analysis, 270-2
Anderson, John E., 22
Anderson, Martin, 172-3, 174
Anti-Semitism, 260-1
Armed Services, 17, 25, 36, 58, 66, 137, 147, 151, 154, 157, 167, 168, 187, 252
Army-Alpha test, 10, 12
Asch, S. E., 198
Asheim, Lester, 74, 76
Aspirations, levels of, 32-4; see also Motivation
Associations, 218-30, 237-41
Attendance studies, 82, 249-50, 267; see also Dropouts
Attitudes: change and rigidity, 19, 58-61, 142, 154, 167, 186, 212, 257ff, 263, 264; controversial, 50-1; defined, 49, 50, 53; dimensions of, 54-6; formation of, 18, 53, 172; in educational levels, 57-8, 92; nature of, 51-4
Auch, F. L., 10
Auer, Jeffry, 167
Audio-visual aids, 144, 152-62
Auditory acuity, 20, 21
"Auto-kinetic effect", 198
Avocations, 70-3

Bales, R. F., 196, 200
Baley, J. A., 73
Balser, B. H., 256
Banta, C. O., 250
Bauder, W. W., 219, 220, 221, 229
Beal, George M., 15, 112
Beals, R. A., 42
Beegle, J. A., 205
Behavior, 54-5, 142-3, 165, 166, 167, 170, 214, 245, 264; see also Groups
Bentel, D., 149

Berdie, Ralph, 64ff
Berelson, B., 95
Bias, 23, 51
Billings, E. G., 38
Birren, James E., 12
Bloom, B. S., 167
Bohlen, Joe M., 15
Brannon, Luther H., 131-2
Brenner, M., 193, 195
Bridges, J. W., 85
Briggs, Leslie, 36
Brim, Orville G., Jr., 254-6, 266
Brown, D. E., 155
Brunner, Edmund deS., 3, 25, 205, 216, 219, 231
Bryson, Lyman, 149
Buckman, R. O., 219, 220, 221, 222, 225, 227
Bunge, A. Frederick, 130
Bureau of the Census, 92
Burtt, H. E., 193
Business Week, 74
Buswell, G. T., 21

Campbell, D. T., 268
Canada, 43, 128, 137-8
Canadian Farm Radio Forum, 43, 137, 161-2, 174
Cancer education, 165-6, 260
Cantrill, H., 155
Carpenter, C. R., 160
Carter, L., 196, 200
Cartwright, Morse, 2
Cass, A. W., 122
Catholics, 110-1, 172
Cattell, R. B., 179, 200
Chamber of Commerce, 230
Change, 14-7, 166, 264-5, 268, 271; see also Attitudes: Change and Rigidity, Behavior; Opinions
Chapin, F. Stuart, 115
Chapin Social Participation Scale, 100, 115
Chapman, D. W., 32
Chave, E. J., 267
Chein, I., 259
Church groups, 99-100, 104, 106, 107, 123
Cincinnati, 262
Citron, A., 259, 265, 269
Civil defense, 100
Civilian Conservation Corps, 130
Clark, Burton, 120ff, 189, 216, 223, 229, 240
Clark, James, 149
Classification of interests, 66-7
Cleveland, 232
Cliques, see under Group
"Clock hour index," 267
"Cloze" procedure, 151
Clubs, see Community: Associations
Coffin, T. E., 158
Cologne, R., 233-4
Columbia University, 18
Committee on Evaluation of the Adult Education Association, 244
Communication, 223, 237, 238
Communism, 51
Community: action, 241-2; and adult education, 235-6, 238-42; associations in, 218-30, 237-41; councils, 231-5; defined, 214-5; development, 212, 239; organizations, 212-3; 217-8; primary groups, 204ff; studies in, 216ff; suburban, 108-10, 216

Conceptualization, 55-6, 67-8, 263-6
Conformity, 199, 201, 207
Conservation of Human Resources Project (Columbia University), 18
Cook, S., 270
Cooley, C. M., 202, 204
Cooperation, 228ff
Coordination, 212ff, 235-6, 238ff
Councils, see Adult Education Councils
Council of National Organizations, 224
Counseling, 40, 81-2, 129, 136-7, 145, 254
Craxton, F. E., 153
Credit programs, 126-7
Crile, L., 22, 145, 146, 159
Crossland, R. W., 43
Crutchfield, R., 29, 56
Cultural phenomena, 110, 169, 225, 227

Dale-Chall formula, 149
Deane, S. R., 44
Darter, V. W., 135
Davis, A., 204
Dennis, Wayne, 63, 77, 79
Denver, Adult Education Council of, 234
De Groat, Fannie M., 129
Department of Defense, 146
Dependent variable, 68, 271; see also Goals
Design, 130ff, 268-70
Deutsch, M., 270
Discussion: and opinions, 166-7, 194; defined, 164; leader, 171-3, 174ff, 184ff; research in, 170-1; theory of, 173-6; vs. lecture, 164-7, 168-9, 184ff; see also Groups
Doddy, H. H., 204, 209
Dollinger, V. M., 85
Doob, Leonard, 53
Drama, 156
Dropout rate, 140, 251-3
Dropouts, 140, 251-3
Duncan, J., 61, 133
Dunham, A. B., 212

Economics, see Social-Economic status
Education, general, 13, 15, 93, 145, 149; see also Schooling
Education, adult: agencies, 4-5, 45-6, 122-4, 130-41; associations in, 219ff; community, 216-8, 235-6, 238-42; coordination of, 212ff; councils, 232-5; enrollment, 2-4; goals, 245ff; history of, 1-2; in public schools, 120-2; national studies, 215; objectives, 122, 142, 273; see also Evaluation; Learning; Participation; Program
Educators, see Teachers
Eels, W. C., 153
Eisenberg, P., 155
Elliott, F. R., 158
Emotions, 69
Enoch Pratt Library (Baltimore, Md.), 123
Enrollment, 2-4, 39, see also Participation
Environment, 64, 74
Essert, Paul, 2, 247-8
Evaluation research: analysis, 270-2; attendance studies, 249-50; cancer education, 260-2; conceptualization, 263-6; defined, 244-5; design, 268-70; dropouts, 251-3; goals, 245-8, 250ff; instruments, 266-8; interpretation, 270-2; methods studies, 253-4; parent education, 254-6; participation, 250-1; procedures, 248-9; race relations, 256-60; techniques, 266-8; UN information, 262
Extension program, see University extension

Family life, 106-7, 135-6
Feder, D. D., 158
Fiedler, Fred E., 180, 184
"Field theory," 199
Films, 153-5, 158, 162, 263-4
Finances, 5
Flesch formula, 149
Flesch, R., 149
Flood, W. E., 43
Formal associations, 218ff
Fortune, 178
Foskett, J. M., 103, 106
Franklin, Benjamin, 2
Franklin, R. C., 257, 269
Freeman, S. D., 250
Fryer, Douglas, 65, 69, 82, 83, 85
Fund for Adult Education, 163, 233

Gallup, G., 10, 145
Gardner, B. B., 204
Gemeinschaft, 204
Geselschaft, 204
Gettel, G. F., 181-2, 223
Gibb, J. R., 196
Ginsberg, Eli, 12, 25
Goals, 32-4, 38, 45, 53, 188; as dependent variable, 264-6; of adult education, 245-8, 250ff, 266
Goldfarb, W., 21
Goldin, F. S., 156
Goldrich, D., 103
Goldstein, H., 158
Grattan, C. Hartley, 2
Gray, W., 73, 74, 148, 151
Great Books program, 44, 92, 94, 97, 126, 165, 177, 252
Greenwood, Walter, 34-6
Groups: and individuals, 193-7; cliques, 205, 206; community, 204, 217; defined, 192; dynamics, 197-203; future research, 208-10; informal, 218-9; inter-group phenomena, 203-8; leadership, 201, 203, 219; learning in, 22, 61, 143, 144; primary, 205-7; see also Discussion; Community Associations
Guilford, J. P., 66
Guttman Scale, 56

Habits, 158-9
Hale, C. B., 137
Hallenbeck, W. C., 49, 209
Harby, S. F., 130
Harding, J., 256, 259
Harrell, T. W., 155
Harrison, J. W., 126-7
Hart, C., 52, 55
Hartley, E. L., and R. E., 52, 55
Hartmann Social Attitudes Inventory, 171
Harvard Film Transfer Test, 152
Havighurst, R., 37
Hemphill, J. K., 200
Hendrickson, Andrew, 120
Hendry, Charles E., 178, 180
Hidden Persuaders, The (Packard), 27
Highlander, J. P., 156
Hobbies, 70-3
Hoffer, C., 124
Holden, J. B., 121
Holverson, Dorothy, 148, 151
Homans, G. C., 201, 207
Home-economics, 145
Horn-Solomon Scale, 260
Houle, Cyril, 11, 17, 58, 81, 97, 123, 137
Hovland, Carl I., 16, 58, 59, 154
Hudson, Robert, 80
Human relations, 257
Hunter, F. G., 181-2, 223
Husband, R. W., 157

Illiterates, 11-2, 20, 25, 92, 37
Income, 103
Independent variables, 67, 68; see also Program
"Index cues," 77
Informational levels, 55
Innovators, 15, 186
Instruments, 266-8
Intelligence, 10-1, 18, 20; see also Learning
Intelligence quotient, 71-2, 171
Intensity, 60
Interaction, group, 173, 174, 192ff
Interests: activities as indicators of, 63, 64; and attitudes, 53-4; and audio-visual aids, 156; and educational participation, 80-4, 92; and learning, 15, 85-8; and leisure, 70-3; and sex, 75; defined, 64-5, 66; reading, 73-9, stability of, 68-70; study of, 65-8
Interpretation, 270-2
Intervening variables, 270
Iowa State College, 157
It Happened in Taos, 7

Jaccard, C. K., 132
Jahoda, M., 270
James, B. J., 83
Jenkins, W. O., 180
Johnson, G. H., 37
Judgments, 198-9
Junto, The, 2

Kanner, J. H., 157
Kaplan, Abbott, 6, 171, 172, 194, 217, 246
Katz, O., 155, 205, 206
Kehman, H. C., 16
Kelley, H. H., 61, 193
Kempfer, H., 91, 128, 267
Key, William Henry, 108
Kidd, J. Roby, 128
Kiwanis, 230
Klapper, J. T., 158, 160, 162
Klineberg, Otto, 266
Knowles, Malcolm, 3
Kolb, J. H., 3, 204, 220
Krech, D., 29, 52, 56
Kreitlow, B., 61, 133
Kriesburg, M., 172
Kropp, R. P., 267-8
Kropp-Verner Scale, 267, 272
Kuhlen, R. G., 37

Labor unions, 123, 172, 185, 186, 230
Lazarsfeld, P. F., 28, 200, 205, 206
Lazarsfeld-Stanton Program Analyzer, 155
Leadership: and power structure, 181-3; community, 226, 227-8; defined, 178, 180; discussion, 171-3, 174ff; formal association, 241; group, 201, 203, 219; in public schools, 188-9; professional, 186-8; qualities of, 179-81; research in, 177-8, 189-90; 185-6; training, 184-5
Leagans, J. P., 82
League of Women Voters, 225
Learning: ability, 8, 9-10, 12-3, 20-1; and attitudes, 53; and interests, 67, 85-8; and schooling, 18-20; change caused by, 14-17, 166, 264; future research, 23-6; group vs. individual, 195; principles of, 22; processes, 13-15, 70, 143; socio-economic status, effects of, 17; tests, 11, 16; see also, Motivation; Discussion
Leary, B., 148, 151
Lecture, 156, 164-9, 184
Lennard, H., 207

Levine, Jerome, 51
Lewin, Kurt, 14, 17, 164-5, 199, 201, 202
Likert Scale, 56
Liveright, A.A., 190
Long Island (N.Y.), 130
Loomis, C. P., 205, 215, 230
Lorge, Irving, 11, 13, 18, 19, 24, 32, 58, 60, 151, 195
Los Angeles (Calif.), 120, 121, 127-8, 163, 170, 216, 229
Love, Robert, 38, 40, 45
Lunt, P. S., 204, 222
Lyle, Mary S., 135-6
Lynd, R. S. and Helen, 204

McClusky, H. Y., 124, 212
McGeoch, John A., 10
MacIver, R. M., 28, 36, 41
Maller, J. B., 30
Marble, Samuel, 3
Maryland, 120
Matthews, J. L., 132, 187
May, Elizabeth E., 132
Measurements, see Design; Instruments; Tests: Intelligence
Mental health, 255
Merton, Robert K., 183, 192, 206, 207, 271
Methods and techniques: audio-visual aids, 152-62; defined, 143-4; of evaluation studies, 266-8, 269; lecture vs. discussion, 164-7; readability, 148-52; role-playing, 146-7
Methods studies, 253-4
Migrants, 107-8
Miles, Walter R., and Catherine C., 10, 12
Miller, Harry L., 170
Millis, J. S., 157
Minnesota Multiphasic Personality Inventory, 256
Minnis, R. B., 234
Mobility, 206
Montross, H. W., 83
Morriss, Elizabeth, 148, 151
Morrow, E., 139
Motivation: and illiteracy, 11; and participation, 42-7; and work output, 30, 193; aspirations and goals, 32-4, 38, 104; change in, 14; defined, 29, 65; history of studies of, 27-31, 34-7; in educational program, 9-10, 38-40, 46-7, 92, 130; subjective, 40-6; to read, 78-9
Mumma, R., 120
Munroe, R., 73, 74
Murphy, Gardner, 28, 29, 51
Myers, G. C., 31
Myrdal, G., 93, 111

National Association for the Advancement of Colored People, 225
National Education Association, 215
National Health Survey, 20
National Infantile Paralysis Foundation, 101
National Institute of Health, 12
National Recreation Association, 72
Nedzel, L., 31, 39
Needs, 81-2
Negroes, 34, 98, 111, 258-9
Neighborhoods, 204, 205, 240
Newark (N.J.), Public Library, 123
New Brunswick (N.J.), 159
Newberry, J. S. Jr., 89, 104, 107, 183, 219ff, 226
New York (N.Y.), 120, 128
New York Adult Education Council, 5
Nicholson, D., 44

Occupations, 102-3
Ohio, 120, 137-8
Olds, E. B., 91, 94
Opinions, 14-7, 167-8, 184, 194
Organizations, 186, 217, 218; see also Associations
Orr, B., 37
O'Shea, Harriet, 64
Owens, William A., Jr., 12, 18

Parent education, 254-6
Parent-Teacher Associations, 177, 229, 230
Participation: and educational status, 92-3; and motivation, 42-7; and socio-economic status, 93-4; as evaluation research, 250-1; educational vs. general, 80-3; encouragement of, 89-90; future, 116-8; in discussions, 170-1, 173ff, 194; in groups, 208-9; in parent education, 254-6; in program planning, 130-4; participants, 22, 25, 95-8, 112-3, 130, 208, 271; research in, 90-2, 114-6; social, 98-114
Pennsylvania, 120
Persistence, 34-6, 65, 72
Personality, 36, 38, 57, 68
Philosophy, 5
Physical activities, 71
Power structure, 181-3
Program: as independent variable, 254, 263-4; credit and non-credit, 126-7; defined, 139; evaluation, 244ff; in adult education, 186-7, 208; planning, 128-41; socio-economic factors, 133-5
Protestants, 110-1
Przedpelski, B., 132-3
Public affairs education, 16, 19, 121, 127, 138, 173
Public schools: adult education in, 120-2, 127-9, 216; leadership in, 188-9

Race relations, evaluation of studies of, 256-60, 263-4, 265
Radburn (N.J.), 80
Radio, 153-4, 155-6, 158-62
Read, Charles R., 3
Readability Laboratory (Columbia University), 149
Readers' Advisory Service, 144
Reading, 73-9, 102, 159, 161; readability, 148-52
Recreation, 72-3, 74, 79; see also Hobbies
Reid, Jesse, 7
Religion, 5, 110-1; see also Church groups
Remmers, H.H., 267
Retention, 14, 22, 156; see also Learning
Richert, M., 133
Robinson, Karl F., 167
Rock, R. T., Jr., 157
Role-playing, 144, 146-7, 184
Rose, A., 256
Ross, Murray G., 178, 179, 180, 215
Rotary, 230
Rural areas, 3, 13, 17, 74, 83, 92ff, 97, 100, 103, 107ff, 114, 128, 131ff, 145-6, 150, 159, 162, 180, 184, 186, 204, 205, 219, 223, 230-1, 240
Russia, 51, 55

St. Louis, 233-4
Salience, 60
San Bernardino Valley College (Calif.), 139
Schooling, 18-20, 93, 97, 103
Schramm, Wilbur, 40, 77, 155

Sex: and associations, 230; and audiovisual aids, 156, 158; and group formation, 205; and interests, 75; and parent education, 254-6; and social participation, 106; and vocational goals, 38
Shangold, B., 128
Sherif, Muzafer, 29, 49, 198, 201
Shimberg, B., 157-8
Sillars, R., 46
Sills, David L., 101, 112-3
Silvey, R., 156
Simpson, R. H., 172
Smith, F. T., 258, 259, 270
Smith, H. Brewster, 52, 55
Social: economic status, 13, 15, 17, 93-4, 97, 133-5, 164, 254; interaction in discussion groups, 173, 174; needs, 36; participation, 98-114, 162; patterns, 80, 81, 220; role, 37, 40, 67, 69; status, 13, 15, 17, 38; see also Groups
Social personality inventory, 171
Social science training, 187-8
Sorenson, Herbert, 9
Spence, R. B., 122, 128
Status: educational, 13, 15, 93, 145, 149; socio-economic, 13, 15, 17, 93-4, 97
Steinzer, B., 200
Stice, G. F., 179
Stouffer, Samuel, 17, 180
Strauss, M. A., 268
Strong, Edward K., 68, 69ff
Strong's Vocational Interest Blank, 68, 70
Stryker, R. E., 153
Styler, W. E., 43
Suburban communities, 108-10, 216
Super, Donald, 70

Taylor, Carl C., 6, 231
Teachers, 4, 9, 65, 114, 143, 169, 188-9; see also Leadership
Techniques, see Methods and Techniques
Television, 153,4, 156-62
Test Cities projects, 233
Tests: intelligence, 10ff, 16, 18ff, problem solving, 23; time limit on, 10, 11, 30-1
Theory, 147-8
Thibaut, J. W., 193
Thomasville (Ga.), 224, 232
Thorndike, E. L., 8-9, 10, 68, 69-70, 71, 85, 87
Thurstone, L. L., 30, 35, 267
Time: as motivation, 31-2; awareness of, 38; "clock hour index," 267; limit on tests, 10, 11, 30-1; point of measurement of variables, 269; reaction, 21; transportation, 34
Tuckman, J., 58
Tyler, R., 75

United Fund, 231
United Nations, 262
UNESCO, 230
United States Department of Defense, 180
United States Office of Education, 92
University extension, 91-4, 97, 124, 131, 132, 135, 138, 144, 145, 157, 173, 177, 184, 187
Urban areas, 3, 74, 92, 93, 97, 102, 106ff, 114, 129, 223, 237

VanderMeer, S. W., 154
van Huhm, R., 153
Variables, see Dependent; Independent; Intervening
Verner, Coolie, 142ff, 267-8
Vernon, M. D., 153

Visual acuity, 20-1
Vocabulary, 12-3, 149-50, 151ff
Vocational education, 95-6, 127, 128, 132
Vocations, 68-70
Volkart, E. H., 61
Volkmann, J., 32

Waples, D., 41, 75-6
Warner, W. L., 204, 217, 222
Washburne, J. N., 152
Washington, State College of, 131
Wayland, S., 207
Weiss, Walter, 16
Welford, A. T., 12ff, 17

Weschler, D., 23
Westie, C. M., 200
Whyte, W. F., 204
Wilkening, Eugene A., 17, 134, 188
Williams, Robin M., 217, 256
Wilson, M. C., 93, 145, 188
Workshops, 257

Yugoslavia, 3, 127
YWCA, 197

Zander, Alvin, 65, 147, 169